Bureaucratic Failure
and Public Expenditure

This is a volume of
Quantitative Studies in Social Relations
Consulting Editor: Peter H. Rossi, University of Massachusetts, Amherst, Massachusetts
A complete list of titles in this series appears at the end of this volume.

Bureaucratic Failure and Public Expenditure

WILLIAM SPANGAR PEIRCE

Department of Economics
Case Western Reserve University
Cleveland, Ohio

ACADEMIC PRESS
A Subsidiary of Harcourt Brace Jovanovich, Publishers
New York   London   Toronto   Sydney   San Francisco

ACADEMIC PRESS, INC.
111 Fifth Avenue, New York, New York 10003

United Kingdom Edition published by
ACADEMIC PRESS, INC. (LONDON) LTD.
24/28 Oval Road, London NW1 7DX

Library of Congress Cataloging in Publication Data

Peirce, William Spangar.
  Bureaucratic failure and public expenditure.

  (Quantitative studies in social relations)
  Includes bibliographical references and index.
  1. Government spending policy--United States.
2. Expenditures, Public. 3. Bureaucracy--United States.
I. Title. II. Series.
HJ7539.P44   353.0072   81-10974
ISBN 0-12-550220-6   AACR2

PRINTED IN THE UNITED STATES OF AMERICA

81 82 83 84   9 8 7 6 5 4 3 2 1

For C. H. P. and M. K. P.
who wanted me to write a book that they could read

Contents

PART **II**

Cases of Bureaucratic Failure

PART **III**

Bureaucratic Failure and
the Agenda for Government

Preface

A typical political discussion includes a description of hideous social problems, the liberal's conclusion that the government should solve them, and the conservative's protest that "history shows us that government intervention will not help." As a person of liberal sentiments and conservative inclinations, I have often wondered what history *does* tell us about the capacity of government to improve our lives. The framework for the answer comes from microeconomic theory and especially the economic theory of public expenditure, which show how government action can improve the functioning of the market economy. But assuming that the government action will conform to the ideal intervention derived from the theory ignores much of the basis for the conservative's protest. For when the conservative appeals to history, he is really saying that Congress will not pass the ideal law or that the bureaucracy will not implement the law that is passed.

I found this topic of bureaucratic failure particularly intriguing: Once a law is passed, under what conditions will the bureaucracy fail to give the political leaders exactly what they ordered? I could find no extensive scholarly investigations of this topic, so I wrote this book to answer the question for myself.

I hope the audience includes a few others, as well. In particular, the case studies of failure and the discussion of problems of implementation should be useful for students of economics, political science, public administration, and organization theory. Some citizens who wonder why the performance of government rarely equals its promise may also be interested. Even some bureaucrats, to whom most elements of this book will seem familiar, may enjoy the explanation of why theirs is such a frustrating job.

This study deals explicitly with the federal government of the United States in the current era. Certain aspects of the theory could be applied to other large organizations or to other governments and times, but these are separate tasks.

The literature survey that forms the basis of Part I roams widely through economics, political science, sociology, public administration, and various related bodies of knowledge. Although much of this was unfamiliar terrain for an economist, the route was defined by the objective of identifying the conditions predisposing to failure. The 11 brief case studies that comprise Part II are based on reports by the United States General Accounting Office. Relying on this source permitted coverage of a broad selection of the nonmilitary activities of the government. Part III reexamines the hypotheses developed from the literature in the light of the cases and other studies of implementation. The final chapter consists of my ruminations on the implications of bureaucratic failure.

ACKNOWLEDGMENTS

Notes and references are the footprints that trace the scholar's path through the literature. In a journey as wide ranging as this one, however, the intellectual map one begins with is more significant than any specific reference along the way. My own approach to these questions owes a great deal to several teachers: E. C. Harwood and Robert T. Patterson at the American Institute for Economic Research, and Fritz Machlup and Richard Musgrave at Princeton. The most important influence, however, comes from my colleagues, especially Bela Gold and Gerhard Rosegger.

I would also like to acknowledge the cheerful assistance of Shirley Discenzo in preparing the final manuscript. Case Western Reserve University provided the sabbatical leave during which the research was begun. The heaviest opportunity costs, I hope, were borne by my wife and children.

PART I

When Does Bureaucracy Fail?

CHAPTER 1

The Problem and the Approach

FAILURE AS SEEN BY THE PUBLIC

Washingtonians discovered on December 31, 1974, that the National Park Service had decided, without any legislative instructions, to eliminate 600 of the 1000 parking spaces on the Mall within the next month.[1] Two of the four paved roads on the Mall were to be torn up and replaced with gravel bicycle paths, at a cost of $5 million, in preparation for the Bicentennial. In response to the complaint that most visitors to the Mall would probably prefer to park their cars so they could go inside the Smithsonian buildings, rather than bicycle on gravel, the Park Service replied that (a) the Mall was not intended as a parking lot; (b) the shortage of parking was so severe that loss of another 600 spaces would make no difference; (c) visitors did not park on the Mall because com-

---

[1] *The Washington Post*, 31 January 1975, p. C-1 reports most of the events. The issue was in the news during much of January and the following months.

muters took all the spaces despite the ban on parking before 10:00 A.M. and the 3-hr limit; and (d) the original plan of 1966 had called for ample parking at the Union Station Visitors' Center. The failure to complete the Visitors' Center on time and the substitution of parking at Robert F. Kennedy Stadium combined with shuttle bus service to the Mall by a private firm added to the furor, but it was the bureaucratic decision to eliminate parking that aroused the most intense opposition.

Although people expect bureaucracy to be high-handed, confused, and tied up in red tape, the failures of bureaucracy are rarely subjected to serious study. *Parkinson's Law* and *The Peter Principle* are too entertaining to be taken seriously; yet they are entertaining precisely because they subject to analysis and ridicule the very practices that confound and irritate us all.[2] Surely the experiences of millions cannot all be illusory: Bureaucracies do have their failings.

In the popular view the bureaucracy is usually a torpid creature, rarely rising to the heights of initiative displayed in the Mall plan. More consistent with the popular stereotype is the disposition of one of the better ideas of Cleveland's Mayor Perk: "I want to announce today the creation of a special freeway patrol unit on the shoreways and freeways. Motorists are forced to waste minutes in traffic tieups on the freeways because tow trucks cannot get the damaged vehicles quickly [press release, June 26, 1973]."[3]

Six months later a reporter discovered that the idea had traveled from the mayor's news secretary, Doris O'Donnell, to the safety director, James T. Carney, who had rejected it. Carney commented, "I don't think I ever told Doris the results because as I said, to me it was only a suggestion."

The same lapses in performance can follow important presidential orders. President Nixon ordered the destruction of U.S. stockpiles of biological and chemical warfare agents in 1970. Yet 5 years later both the CIA and the army still retained stocks of biological toxins.[4] Neither of these episodes is fully typical of the problems to be analyzed in this study because they represent failures that are political as much as bureaucratic. The distinction bears closer analysis.

---

[2]C. Northcote Parkinson, *Parkinson's Law and Other Studies in Administration* (Boston: Houghton Mifflin, 1957); Laurence J. Peter and Raymond Hull, *The Peter Principle* (New York: William Morrow, 1969). Both of these books present useful insights to problems faced by particular bureaucracies. They are not to be taken as universal, however, and bureaucracies would still often fail, even if the problems they describe were solved.

[3]Quoted in the article by Robert H. Holden (*Cleveland Plain Dealer*, 10 January 1974, p. 21-A).

[4]*Cleveland Plain Dealer*, 10 September 1975, and 16 September 1975; *New York Times*, 20 October 1975, p. 41.

DISTINGUISHING POLITICAL FROM
BUREAUCRATIC FAILURE

An activity undertaken by government generally requires both decisions by politicians and implementation by bureaucrats. The central theme of this study is that bureaucratic behavior is subject to regular and predictable limitations and imperfections. Political behavior has its own problems, which are mentioned peripherally in the following pages because political behavior and bureaucratic behavior are intertwined.

Bureaucrats are often blamed for problems that are created by politicians. The annual spring cursing of the Internal Revenue Service, for example, should be directed at the politicians who have written the tax laws. The agency merely designs forms to cope with legislated complexity and completes the unfinished legislation by writing regulations and decisions. Similarly, many conspicuous fiascoes, such as the attempt by the United States to reduce domestic crime by buying out the Turkish opium poppy crop, are planned at the highest political levels, not by the bureaucracy.[5] Even when the errors are made by top elected officials, however, the exculpation of the bureaucracy is not complete; for the staff of the top official constitutes a bureaucracy, and the poor performance of such organizations in keeping political leaders from making errors epitomizes the problem.

What seems like a failure to the observer, of course, may have been a success in the view of the politicians and bureaucrats. "You can't know something is ill-done unless you *assume* an aim other than the one achieved. . . ."[6] A politician is concerned with reelection as well as with national welfare, so his advocacy of, for example, controls on gasoline prices may be rational even if economists recommend free markets. Similarly, a regulation or procedure adopted by the bureaucracy that appears inefficient or counterproductive to the observer may be necessitated by the political context of the legislation, rather than the letter of the law. Programs justified as aiding disadvantaged localities, for example, are usually administered in such a way that small benefits are avail-

---

[5]The opium escapade still has its defenders. It did succeed in disrupting the world opium trade temporarily, but this had the result of encouraging the development of alternate supply routes and production, which exacerbated the problem once Turkey resumed production. In addition to this direct effect, one must wonder at the opportunity cost of the diversion of high level personnel (cabinet members) to this effort. For a popular account stressing the bungling, see Edward Jay Epstein, "The Incredible War Against the Poppies," *Esquire* (December 1974): 148 ff. See also the article by Victor Cohn, "Opium-Short U.S. Turns to Turkey," *Washington Post*, 5 March 1975.

[6]Arthur Allen Leff, "Economic Analysis of Law: Some Realism about Nominalism," *Virginia Law Review* 60, No. 3 (1974): 467.

able to a large number of geographically dispersed communities, regardless of objective measures of need. To accuse the bureaucrats of acting contrary to the wording of the law is pointless if they adopted the only policy that would result in continued funding.

Sometimes the perverse effects are not obvious when a law is passed because only after the regulations are written can the effects be predicted. And even when the law, itself, must be amended, the changes may originate in the bureaucracy. The direction in which these incremental changes in regulations and legislation push the programs is not random, but is a product of the forces acting on the bureaucracy. This will be examined later.

Poor administration of a law that seems reasonable may reflect either bureaucratic or political failure. Some bureaucrats are better managers than others. A public program can run into difficulties, just as a private firm can, if it is assigned a manager who lacks the necessary skills to carry it out. If those skills are widely available at the relevant rank in the bureaucracy, then the failure of the program can be attributed to bad management, and attention can be directed to the question of why such a poor manager was promoted to a job he could not handle. If the necessary managerial skills are very rare, it makes no sense to describe the failure as managerial; rather, it is a failure of program design. If administration requires talent that is not routinely available for less than $100,000 a year, it can ordinarily be expected to fail in a bureaucracy limited to salaries of half that amount.

Sometimes poor administration is the result of a political decision. Gardiner showed that police enforcement of gambling and prostitution laws depended very directly on the attitude of the mayor.[7] After a reform mayor took office, a police department that had formerly been quite lax in enforcement was able to drive most such vice from the city. Less dramatically, Ginzberg and Solow point out that if Congress is not really interested in a problem, but feels compelled to do something, it can establish a program without providing the agency sufficient funds to succeed.[8] In either event, what appears on the surface as a bureaucratic failure to carry out the provisions of the law results directly from a political decision.

Resources can be inadequate in less direct ways when the federal government relies on state and local governments or private firms to

---

[7]John A. Gardiner, *The Politics of Corruption: Organized Crime in an American City* (New York: Russell Sage Foundation, 1970), p. 69.

[8]Eli Ginzberg and Robert M. Solow, "Some Lessons of the 1960's," *The Public Interest,* Number 34 (Winter 1974): 216.

carry out its policies.[9] If the intermediaries lack the capacity to carry out the program, the federal bureaucracy will fail regardless of the resources available. Here, again, the attribution of blame is complex. If Congress devises a program that is supposed to be administered by local governments but that exceeds their capacities, it is a political failure. If the bureaucracy fails to carry out a program that requires local cooperation, however, one defense will surely be the utter impossibility of the task.

A more fundamental problem is that the objectives of a program (and hence the feasibility of accomplishing them) are not always obvious. If the objectives of the legislation are clearly stated in the law or hearings, analysis of the success of the agency is relatively straightforward. Sometimes the objectives are unclear or contradictory. Worse yet, a statement of very broad objectives may conceal basic political disagreement on particulars.

Such disagreements may exist within Congress or between Congress and the President. Arthur Maass stressed the frequent failure of the Army Corps of Engineers to follow executive policies.[10] Within the framework followed here, however, the Corps is successful when it produces the projects that Congress asks it to produce at the agreed cost. The variability of past usage suggests the importance of a fuller discussion of the meaning of bureaucratic failure.

SOME DEFINITIONS

The term *bureaucracy* has been used in so many different ways that it may have become worthless for scientific discourse.[11] In this work, bureaucracy means the assemblage of *bureaucrats*, who include all government employees *except* those who are elected and those whom the elected officials can legally remove from office in the normal course of events. Since this study focuses on the federal government of the United States, the possibility of rewriting the definition to extend it to nongovernmental areas has not been explored. This definition is less restrictive than some in that it includes *all* employees, not just senior officials. It refers to an objective characteristic and is neither a pejorative nor a compliment. It is not directly related to the sociological literature stemming from Max Weber. Although bureaucracy has sometimes been used

---

[9]*Ibid.*, p. 217.

[10]Arthur Maass, *Muddy Waters: The Army Engineers and the Nation's Rivers* (Cambridge: Harvard University Press, 1951).

[11]For a survey of the concept in sociology and related disciplines, see Martin Albrow, *Bureaucracy* (New York: Praeger, 1970).

to denote government by bureaus (a construction parallel with democracy), in this study the word bears no such connotation. Rather, the degree to which bureaucrats do act independently of elected officials and legislation is the question to be answered.

Defining failure requires the specification of a goal, the achievement of which would constitute success. This study follows the classical approach of treating explicitly legislated objectives as the goals. If the bureaucracy does not achieve the objectives set forth by Congress, a failure has occurred either in the design and financing of the program or in its implementation. The latter is a bureaucratic failure, unless it is clearly attributable to the intervention of politicians.

These definitions seem so commonplace that emphasis would be unnecessary were it not for a challenge that has arisen within organization theory to the classical view. Perrow distinguishes between an organization's official and its operative goals, where the former are spelled out in legislation, charters, and public statements, whereas the latter are "the ends sought through the actual operating policies of the organization."[12] A distinction of this type can be useful in analyzing organizations other than public bureaucracies, although it is difficult to avoid the teleological trap of interpreting "ends sought through the actual operating policies" as what the organization actually accomplishes. The effect of this is to define every organization as 100% effective in doing what it does. Thus, for example, the administration of Franklin D. Roosevelt could be considered to have had the operative goal of keeping the economy depressed from 1933 until World War II, whereas the administrations of Johnson and Nixon had the operative goal of losing the Vietnam War! Whatever the other virtues of such an approach, it is hardly useful in an analysis of failure.

When analyzing public bureaucracies, a more serious objection arises. As a matter of social philosophy it seems rather peculiar to accept the preferences of bureaucrats or the achievements of bureaucracies (and it is one of the central points of this study that the two will generally differ) as the appropriate goals for public policy. Yet the equivalent point of view has entered the literature in two forms: (a) that the bureaucracy is as representative a body as Congress or the President and therefore as much entitled to influence government action; or (b) that the political forces that are resolved in Congress also exert themselves on the bureaucracy, so it makes little difference where the policies are deter-

---

[12]Charles Perrow, "The Analysis of Goals in Complex Organizations," *American Sociological Review* 26 (December 1961): 854–866.

mined.[13] These issues will be considered in Chapter 3; the central question of this study can be rephrased to eliminate the value-laden reference to failure by asking: Under what conditions will the bureaucracy carry out the policies required by the legislation?

BUREAUCRATIC FAILURE IN THE LITERATURE OF SOCIOLOGY

Max Weber stressed the "formal rationality" of bureaucratic administration, and it was a short, but erroneous, step to equate that with "efficiency."[14] If bureaucracies are considered to be efficient by definition, however, discussion of particular organizations bogs down in the question of whether (or the degree to which) they are bureaucratic, rather than giving serious attention to the possibility of bureaucratic failure.

The tendency to assume that bureaucracies succeed is well illustrated in the literature surveyed by Bendix;[15] but the other theme in that literature is that, as monopolists of technical skills, bureaucrats might obtain a monopoly of power. The idea that the bureaucracy will do something different from what it is instructed to do pervades much of the sociological literature. But the underlying theme is that bureaucrats as a class or profession have some ideas and interests different from those of government or property owners and that they succeed in carrying out the objectives of their class, thus putting bureaucrats and managers increasingly in control of economy and society.[16] This raises the question analyzed by Mancur Olson of whether a group or class will, in fact, act in the interests of its members.[17]

[13]For the former see, e.g., Charles E. Jacob, *Policy and Bureaucracy* (Princeton: D. Van Nostrand, 1966) and Norton E. Long, *The Polity* (Chicago: Rand McNally, 1962). The latter position is expressed by some of the more extreme pressure group theorists.

[14]Michael J. Hill, *The Sociology of Public Administration* (London: World University, Weidenfeld and Nicolson, 1972), p. 15. I have relied heavily on this source and Albrow for guidance through the unfamiliar terrain of sociology.

[15]Reinhard Bendix, "Bureaucracy and the Problem of Power" *Public Administration Review* V (1945): 194–209; reprinted in Robert K. Merton *et al.*, *Reader in Bureaucracy* (Glencoe, Illinois: The Free Press, 1952), pp. 114–135.

[16]See, e.g., Hans H. Gerth and C. Wright Mills, "A Marx for Managers" in the Merton *Reader*. This theme is also found in such works as Adolf A. Berle, Jr. and Gardiner C. Means, *The Modern Corporation and Private Property* (New York: Macmillan, 1932); James Burnham, *The Managerial Revolution* (New York: John Day, 1941); and the writings of Veblen and Galbraith.

[17]Mancur Olson, *The Logic of Collective Action: Public Goods and the Theory of Groups* (Cambridge: Harvard University Press, 1965).

Although the sociological literature does not analyze the question in that form, some of the functionalist approaches raise similar questions. The focus on the unanticipated bad consequences of purposive action, or disfunctional aspects of bureaucratic procedures, provides some of the groundwork for the study of bureaucratic failure.[18] The two great difficulties with the functionalist literature are ambiguity about the appropriate goal and excessive generalization. At least three sets of goals can be specified when discussing government bureaucracies: the goals of individual bureaucrats, the survival (and strengthening) of the organization, and the goals specified by the legislature. Some commentators also try to discuss social goals or the public interest. Most of the functionalist literature seems to be directed at organizational survival, although Cohen's analysis from the baseline of legislative intent indicates that it need not be.[19] By accusing functionalists of excessive generalization the accuser opens himself to the same charge; nevertheless, there does seem to be a failure to differentiate among bureaucracies sufficiently on the basis of the expected output, the production process, or other relevant criteria.[20] The case studies that form the basis of sociologists' empirical investigations provide ample material for analyzing the types of decisions that must be made at different levels in the hierarchy. In their eagerness to move to higher levels of abstraction, however, sociologists have discarded this most significant raw material in favor of blanket generalizations that are either empty or misleading.

BUREAUCRATIC FAILURE IN THE LITERATURE OF POLITICAL SCIENCE

Political scientists did not traditionally devote much effort to studying implementation of policy until the present when the failure of so many of the Great Society programs became apparent.[21] Pressman and Wildavsky, Bardach, and Hargrove have combed the literature to uncover a few case studies.[22] Pressman and Wildavsky provided a survey of im-

[18]Peter M. Blau, *The Dynamics of Bureaucracy: A Study of Interpersonal Relations in Two Government Agencies* (Chicago: University of Chicago Press, 1955; rev. ed., 1966) is deservedly a classic.

[19]Harry Cohen, *The Demonics of Bureaucracy: Problems of Change in a Government Agency* (Ames, Iowa: The Iowa State University Press, 1965), p. 22.

[20]James L. Price, *Organizational Effectiveness: An Inventory of Propositions* (Homewood, Illinois: Richard D. Irwin, 1968) provides some egregious examples.

[21]The entire Winter 1974 issue of *The Public Interest* was devoted to this topic.

[22]Eugene Bardach, *The Implementation Game: What Happens after a Bill Becomes a Law* (Cambridge: M.I.T. Press, 1977); Erwin C. Hargrove, "The Study of Implementation"

plementation literature as an appendix to their case study of an Economic Development Administration project that failed. Bardach constructed a model of the implementation process and of the strategies available to opponents and proponents of implementation. Hargrove devised an agenda for further research, while focusing closely on the process of writing the regulations that are necessary to implement legislation.

The focus by these political scientists on the process of implementation is consistent with the emphasis in that field on the process of policy formation. It implies a lively concern with the personalities, proposals, counterproposals, compromises, and infighting involved both in policy formation and in implementation. Despite its congeniality to participants and observers of the art of government, however, the concern with process has inherent problems. The main drawback is that it tends to make each program unique. Retracing bureaucratic history memo by memo does not, by itself, develop a predictive theory. Furthermore, the immense amount of detailed knowledge necessary to reconstruct each case suggests that a massive undertaking will be necessary before the groundwork is established for a useful theory of the implementation process.

BUREAUCRATIC FAILURE IN
THE LITERATURE OF ECONOMICS

Recent years have seen an increasing amount of public concern for the failures of government programs. But this is seldom addressed in economics, except in those cases where government adopts a policy that will, if carried out, be counterproductive, for example, destabilizing fiscal policy or price controls that prevent the elimination of shortage. Economics has shown lack of concern for means by which legislative ends are achieved. This neglect is surprising in view of the important work being done on nonmarket decision making in general and bureaucracy in particular. The terminology is ambiguous, however, for analysis of the way the political process and the top levels of the bureaucracy make decisions need not involve analysis of the process of

(Washington, D.C.: The Urban Institute, March 12, 1975), Working Paper 0797-01; and Jeffrey L. Pressman and Aaron Wildavsky, *Implementation: How Great Expectations in Washington Are Dashed in Oakland; or, Why It's Amazing that Federal Programs Work at all; This Being a Saga of the Economic Development Administration as Told by Two Sympathetic Observers Who Seek to Build Morals on a Foundation of Ruined Hopes* (Berkeley: University of California Press, 1973).

implementation by bureaus. The two major works by economists dealing with the latter problem are Tullock's *The Politics of Bureaucracy* and
Downs' *Inside Bureaucracy*.[23] The former, in particular, includes a well
developed model of hierarchical control, which will be analyzed in detail
in Chapter 2. Downs' work provides a number of insights and conceptually testable propositions, but the overall theoretical structure is less
obvious and many of the propositions are too subtle to be useful in this
study. Niskanen's important work, *Bureaucracy and Representative Government*, is not useful for analyzing bureaucratic failure because the
bureaus in his formal model are assumed to produce efficiently.[24] The
problem Niskanen studies is the excessive output of bureaus under present institutional arrangements. The prescient work by Mises is an extended pamphlet, rather than an analytical study, and has had little
influence on the mainstream of economics.[25]

Unfortunately neither these nor other relevant bits of analysis of
property rights and information theory are well integrated into the public finance literature. While the normative theory of public expenditure
has been explored extensively during the past two decades, the positive
theory has received little attention. The normative theory asks the question: What activities *ought* the government undertake in a primarily
market economy? The answer is given in terms of characteristics of
particular goods that lead to the failure of private markets to supply an
appropriate amount. Such characteristics include jointness of supply
(once one person enjoys the good, it can be supplied to additional
people at little or no cost) and the infeasibility of excluding people who
do not choose to pay.[26]

It seems equally important, however, to ask the question: What activities *can* the government perform successfully? Although some of the

[23]Gordon Tullock, *The Politics of Bureaucracy* (Washington, D.C.: Public Affairs Press,
1965); Anthony Downs, *Inside Bureaucracy* (Boston: Little, Brown, 1967).

[24]William A. Niskanen, Jr., *Bureaucracy and Representative Government* (Chicago:
Aldine-Atherton, 1971).

[25]Ludwig von Mises, *Bureaucracy* (New Haven: Yale University Press, 1944).

[26]The classic articles include "A New Principle of Just Taxation," by Knut Wicksell,
reprinted in *Classics in the Theory of Public Finance*, ed., by Musgrave and Peacock (New
York: St. Martin's Press, 1967); "The Voluntary Exchange Theory of Public Economy," by
R. A. Musgrave, *Quarterly Journal of Economics* (1938); and "The Pure Theory of Public
Expenditure," by P. A. Samuelson, *Review of Economics and Statistics* (1954). Among the
numerous subsequent contributions "Public Goods and Public Policy," by J. G. Head,
Public Finance (1962) and *The Logic of Collective Action*, by Mancur Olson (Harvard, 1965) are
particularly useful. Dennis C. Mueller's "Public Choice: A Survey," *Journal of Economic
Literature* XIV, No. 2 (June 1976): 395–433, provides a good introduction to the field of
public choice, which deals with the positive question of what activities governments will
undertake, as well as the normative questions of public finance, but does not usually
concern itself with implementation.

early enumerations by economists of the appropriate functions of government were based on casual appraisals of the capacity of government, recent literature has been dominated by an abstract approach that ignores the means by which particular objectives are to be accomplished. This is consistent with the established tradition in microeconomics in which the economist simply assumes that the entrepreneur will strive to minimize costs for a given level of output and try to choose the output that maximizes profits.

Those assumptions are defensible for small firms, but not for bureaucracies. The owner of a small firm has a clear incentive to keep costs down in order to make current profits and increase the value of the firm when he sells it. In the large private firm, managers who gain very little from the firm's profits may choose to pursue sales revenue or managerial perquisites, rather than profits. Even such objectives, however, imply a substantial amount of pressure on the management to control costs. The discipline is complete in the case of sales-revenue maximization; the firm departs from optimality only in its excessive output.[27] This is equivalent to the assumption in Niskanen's formal model and implicit in much of the economic discussion of government expenditures.

Niskanen defends his assumption of cost minimization by pointing out that the head of a bureau must negotiate with the sponsor (Congress and the President) for the next budget. In order to gain a larger budget, the head of the bureau must promise a larger output. This is the pressure that squeezes out the excess costs. That is, the head of the agency does, ordinarily, have an incentive to deliver the greatest amount of service possible with the budget that he has, as well as to increase the budget. Wanting to minimize costs, however, is not the same as minimizing them. The extent of control by the head of the agency over his subordinates must be scrutinized.

The outlines of the basic problem are now obvious: Goods and services that are provided by government require political decisions and bureaucratic implementation. The political decision process is beset by a variety of imperfections. The head of the bureau wants to maximize his budget and provide as much output as possible within its confines. But, according to Tullock's model of behavior *within* the bureau, the control of the head of the bureau is severely limited. The problem is exacerbated by the fact that the typical bureaucrat, knowing that he will be paid for only a 40-hr week, may find the easy life a more attractive alternative than squeezing out excess costs. The problem of extending the incentive

[27]William J. Baumol, *Business Behavior, Value and Growth* (New York: Harcourt, Brace & World, rev. ed., 1967).

to cut costs down through the ranks of the hierarchy is much more serious in government than it is in business for reasons to be developed later.

The normative theory of public expenditure assumes that the goods and services delivered by government will correspond with the preferences of individuals. The points at which slippage can occur between preferences and delivered goods include (a) the process of electing representatives to a legislature; (b) the relationship between the votes of representatives and the preferences of constituents, given the multiplicity of issues between elections; (c) the problem of amalgamating diverse preferences through voting; and (d) the process of moving from the political decision (legislation) to the actual services delivered. The public-choice literature ventures into each of these areas, but that work is not well integrated into the mainstream of public finance. The sole concern of this study is the fourth stage—what happens between the legislated decision and the actual output of government. The relationship between consumer (voter) preferences and legislation will not be addressed.

The total *slippage* between individual preferences and the goods actually delivered by government will be called *government failure,* which can be divided into two components, *political failure* and *bureaucratic failure,* the latter being the topic of this study. The terminology was selected to emphasize the direct parallel with the concept of *market failure,* which is generally used in economics to indicate the circumstances in which the private market will not satisfy consumer preferences as fully as theoretically possible. Frequently economists jump directly from discovery of market failure to a call for government intervention, without any analysis of the possibility of government failure in devising and implementing the intervention.

Naturally, the better economists have recognized the problem. Buchanan, for example, commented: "To argue that an existing order is 'imperfect' in comparison with an alternative order of affairs that turns out, upon careful inspection, to be unattainable may not be different from arguing that the existing order is 'perfect.' "[28]

Similarly, Stigler's brilliant presidential address to the American Economic Association called on economists to find out what actually happens when government takes upon itself additional functions.[29]

---

[28]James M. Buchanan, "Politics, Policy, and the Pigovian Margins," in *Theory of Public Choice: Political Applications of Economics,* ed. Buchanan and Robert D. Tollison (Ann Arbor: The University of Michigan Press, 1972), p. 171.

[29]George J. Stigler, "The Economist and the State," *The American Economic Review,* LV, No. 1 (March 1965): 1–18.

Confronted by the obvious importance of government failure, economists have moved cautiously into terrain that one might expect to find occupied by political scientists, sociologists, and organization theorists. The results include a substantial amount of theoretical work on political failure, the beginnings of a theory of bureaucratic behavior, and some empirical studies, especially in the field of regulation. In addition, economists have contributed case studies of particular programs and agencies from which much useful information can be extracted. The serious case studies offer striking confirmation of the forms of bungling that characterize everyone's favorite stories of bureaucratic failure. Although this confirms the importance of the topic, the general familiarity of so many of the observations raises the possibility that a scholarly study will turn out to be merely a more ponderous version of *Parkinson's Law*.

OUTLINE OF THINGS TO COME

The next chapter of this book develops a hierarchical model of bureaucratic control and indicates some of its problems. The following two chapters discuss the reasons why outcomes are not quite so dismal, in general, as the hierarchical model would suggest. The first section of the book then concludes with a summary description of the types of bureaucratic failure. Throughout these chapters, hypotheses about causes of failure are noted explicitly in the text.

Part II consists of eleven cases of bureaucratic failure based primarily on General Accounting Office audits. Each case includes a brief comparison of legislated goals with bureaucratic performance. Part III relates the analysis of Part I and the findings of Part II to the standard economic theory of the role of government in a market economy. The final chapter includes some suggestions for living with failure.

Anyone who examines the U.S. federal government closely is struck by the vast knowledge and technical ability of individual employees, as well as the skills of individual managers, and the supporting framework of rules, procedures, and consulting help available in various government offices. Yet despite these elements and a great deal of good will and hard work, when all the pieces are added together the whole is less impressive than the sum of its parts.

This study is inspired by the adage that we can learn something from failure. Certain types of activities or certain features of activities can be predicted to lead to failure. If what I have to say in the remaining pages seems obvious, bear in mind that failures are still occurring, which suggests that their causes are less obvious before the fact than after.

The two underlying themes of this study are, first, that structural features make it possible to predict success or failure at the moment when the legislation is before Congress, and, second, that individual participants pursue their own interests as they see them. Specifying the structural features that should eventually make predictions possible is a large and difficult task that extends across the behavioral sciences and certainly cannot be completed here. But the central point is that failure is neither a completely random matter, nor something that can be avoided just by training better managers.

Failure, instead, results from the pursuit by individuals of their own goals (which may include benevolent ones) within the framework established by the legislative, economic, political, and organizational realities of the program. The solution is not to try to do away with self interest, but rather to accommodate the legislation to its realities. "Let us raise a standard to which the wise and virtuous can repair"—Ah, yes, but let us make sure that the corrupt and inefficient can carry it.

The term hypothesis is somewhat loosely used in connection with many of the propositions developed next. The goal has been to make statements that are conceptually testable; that is, that might be proved false by an appropriate empirical test. The lack of facilities and techniques for performing the tests in the foreseeable future has not, however, been used as a basis for rejecting any hypothesis from consideration. Many might be described as conceptually testable, but not soon or easily.

The hypotheses have varied and motley origins. Some have a rigorous logical grounding in the inapplicable theory of hierarchical control. Others are equally firmly grounded in particular cases or long experience. In effect, they are firm empirical generalizations crying out for full integration into a theory of bureaucratic behavior. Finally, some of the hypotheses are merely the casual observations of various analysts of bureaucracy; or, perhaps worse, are derivations from what passes for theory in some of the sloppier areas of social science. Since one man's rigor is another man's unrealistic assumption, however, all such propositions discovered have been collected so that the process of sorting and codifying can begin.

SOME WARNINGS ABOUT
TECHNIQUES AND SOURCES

Formal testing of hypotheses does not occur in this book. The cases developed in Part II are intended to illustrate the theory and hypotheses developed in Part I and to suggest, in a very rough way, the relative importance of various bits of analysis pieced together there. It is obviously impossible to test whether a particular condition leads to failure by examining a sample consisting entirely of failures. At this preliminary stage in the research, however, it seemed worthwhile to examine a relatively large group of programs that had encountered difficulties to see whether generalization is possible.

The decision to examine a number of cases simultaneously imposed certain constraints on the source of the cases. The literature contains a number of studies of particular agencies and programs, but most of these do not emphasize implementation per se. It did not seem possible to develop several original case studies of failure, despite the daily accumulation of leads. Analysis of failures requires access to data concerning operations that, although legally accessible to the serious researcher, are not widely advertised and are difficult and expensive to track down. Thus the decision was made to rely on General Accounting Office audits.

The GAO works for Congress, rather than the executive. Its auditors have full access to the records of the agencies, and its budget enables it to make field studies of the effectiveness of various programs. Investigations are made both on a routine basis and in response to congressional requests to investigate allegations of wrongdoing. The reports of the GAO are biased toward the discovery of egregious waste and corruption. The titles of reports tend to be somewhat melodramatic, particularly when the only problems discovered are routine managerial lapses in finding ways to cut costs. Overall, however, the reports provide extremely thorough and accurate analyses, and any biases are eagerly offset by the spokesmen for the agencies involved.

CHAPTER 2

Hierarchical Control

THE BASIC MODEL

The serried ranks and mechanical operations of the classical hierarchical model do not describe the real world of bureaucracy, but the classical model must, nevertheless, serve as the starting point of this chapter for two reasons. First, both the economic theory of public expenditure and its close cousin, democratic political philosophy, are based on the implicit assumption that the bureaucracy will carry out the directives of the legislature with the mechanical perfection of a frictionless machine. Second, the model is well worked out, simple to present, and part of the important task of introducing qualifications to the model has already been carried out.

The basic classical hierarchical model was neatly formalized in the work of Luther Gulick.[1] He prescribed an organization that is easily

---

[1]"Notes on the Theory of Organization," pp. 1–46 of *Papers on the Science of Administration,* ed. Luther Gulick and L. Urwick (New York: Columbia University, Institute of Public Administration, 1937). Gulick's model is consistent with the somewhat earlier one suggested by Jethro and promulgated by his son-in-law: "And Moses chose able men out of all Israel, and made them heads over the people, rulers of thousands, rulers of hundreds, rulers of fifties, and rulers of tens. And they judged the people at all seasons: the hard causes they brought unto Moses, but every small matter they judged themselves" (Exodus 18:25–26). A good summary of the classical principles of management is provided by Joseph L. Massie, "Management Theory," chapter 9 of *Handbook of Organizations,* ed. James G. March (Chicago: Rand McNally, 1965).

diagramed in an organization chart. The administrator would be charged with carrying out the tasks assigned hierarchically by the President in response to policy directives of Congress. Each administrator would be responsible to a single superior and, in turn, would have reporting to him (and to him alone) a limited number of subordinates. The basic structure could be replicated through as many levels as necessary to carry out the assigned task. The exact number of subordinates of each administrator at a particular level—the span of control—could vary in the general range of 3–12, depending on various characteristics of the executive and the task. The organization was to be designed according to function, location, or process to minimize the need for coordination outside the smallest subunit of organization. But where such coordination was essential, it would be permissible to build bridges, such as interdepartmental committees, between different individuals at the same level of the hierarchy to avoid the necessity of passing each problem up through the hierarchy to a common superior, who, in any event, would have to resolve any disputes. Nevertheless, the implication was clear that reliance on coordinating committees is a symptom of slovenly organization, as well as being "too dilatory, irresponsible and time-consuming for normal administration."[2] Once the organization was established, the administrator could devote himself to POSDCORB—planning, organizing, staffing, directing, coordinating, reporting, and budgeting. Successful performance of these functions would ensure the implementation of congressional policy.

This simplistic organization-chart view of public administration was challenged from the start.[3] Still, its essential and fallacious assumptions have underlain every attempt to reorganize the executive branch.[4] From Hoover to Ash and Carter, the reorganization plans proposed to move bureaus around so that coordination could occur hierarchically at lower levels. But the complex activities of a large organization can be parceled out to various offices in a number of ways. A particular task can be moved from the Department of Defense to the Department of Energy, or a separate office can be established for a geographic area or an administrative technique (e.g., computer programming). Reorganizations frequently shift activities among departments, but whereas the large changes may reflect political philosophy and the small changes may be

---

[2]Gulick, "Notes on the Theory of Organization," p. 36.

[3]See, for example, *Dynamic Administration: The Collected Papers of Mary Parker Follett,* ed. Henry C. Metcalf and L. Urwick (New York: Harper & Brothers, 1941).

[4]For a review of the political purposes that are served by reorganization, see Rufus E. Miles, Jr., "Considerations for a President Bent on Reorganization," *Public Administration Review* 37 (2) (March–April 1977): 155–162.

matters of administrative fashion, the effects on the efficiency of government are open to question.

For the classical system to work at all, the line of authority from the top executive to the lowest ranks in the hierarchy must be clear and unbroken, and there must be some means of comparing what the operatives are doing with what they are supposed to be doing.[5] Thus, there must be some mechanism by which the agency is required, in a representative democracy, to report back to the legislature.

Hypothesis 1: *Failure is more likely if the agency is not subject to the formal and actual requirements of accountability.*

In the United States most agencies and government corporations are subject to a General Accounting Office audit. Some activities pose special difficulties, however. Auditing the secret activities of the CIA, for example, is obviously a difficult task and the results frequently can not be published. Great Britain, in contrast with the United States, has not made the nationalized industries subject to audit, with some unfortunate experiences as a result.[6]

Chester I. Barnard, writing from his long experience in industry, focused on the individual employee rather than the organization chart or the top manager. He emphasized that authority rests upon the acceptance of a command by the individual recipient, which is likely only under certain conditions.[7] These can be reworked into the following four hypotheses:

Hypothesis 2: *Failure is more likely when the necessary commands are difficult to communicate.*

This suggests that programs requiring subtle or complex orders are difficult to implement.

Hypothesis 3: *Failure is more likely when the individual bureaucrat perceives his orders as being inconsistent with the interests of the public or the agency.*

In addition to the obvious classes of treasonable or grossly immoral orders that might well be rejected, this hypothesis implies that ideology (discussed in Chapter 4) may be important. It also raises a more complex issue: Some programs must be divided up in such ways that various

---

[5]Massie, "Management Theory," pp. 389–390, 396.

[6]E. L. Normanton, *Accountability and Audit of Governments: A Comparative Study* (New York: Praeger, 1966), pp. 412–413.

[7]Chester I. Barnard, *The Functions of the Executive* (Cambridge: Harvard University Press, 1968 [1st publ. 1938]) p. 165.

components may not be obviously consistent with the individual bureaucrat's conception of the public interest. Such programs will be difficult to implement.

Hypothesis 4: *Failure is more likely when the course of action to which the bureaucrat is led by his personal interests conflicts with the legislated objective.*

This, of course, is a very broad and general condition that constitutes the underlying theme of all economic analyses of bureaucratic behavior. In a sense, all of the other hypotheses can be viewed as attempts to identify the circumstances under which Hypothesis 4 will hold.

Hypothesis 5: *Failure is more likely when the task specified by the hierarchy is very difficult relative to the mental and physical capacities of those who must implement it.*

"Impossible" is the limiting case of "difficult." But even a task that is possible may be so irksome that it is set aside until more agreeable jobs are finished. Furthermore, the difficulty of a task must always be defined relative to the ability of the particular people who must carry it out.

CONTROL PROBLEMS

When Herbert Simon began his reevaluation of the received doctrines of administration from a behavioral view, he naturally built upon the work of Barnard. Simon noted that, outside the area of acceptance of authority, the employee will " 'forget' to carry out an order, will carry it out in such a way as actually to sabotage it, will refuse to obey, or will resign rather than carry it out."[8] As soon, therefore, as the focus shifted from the organization chart to the behavior of the individuals involved, the question of whether in fact the orders originating from the top of the hierarchy would be carried out became paramount. This is the basic problem of organizational control.

The topic was not entirely neglected in the classical literature, but the implication was clear that if the span of control were properly chosen the supervisor could ensure that all orders were carried out. Graicunas provided a celebrated, although slightly erroneous, mathematical demonstration that, if the supervisor actually has to supervise all possible combinations among all his employees, he will run out of time very quickly

---

[8]Herbert A. Simon, Donald W. Smithburg, and Victor A. Thompson, *Public Administration* (New York: Alfred A. Knopf, 1950), p. 184.

as the number of employees increases.[9] Whether or not every possible grouping of employees required supervision was not examined, but Graicunas's work provided some basis for Gulick's limitation of the span of control to approximately three to twelve subordinates.

Gulick also pointed out the conditions that made supervision more difficult: "Where the work is diversified, qualitative, and particularly when the workers are scattered, one man can supervise only a few. . . . [Furthermore,] a unit based upon a given specialization cannot be given technical direction by a layman."[10]

With some violence to Gulick, who envisaged limited spans of control and direction by qualified technicians, rather than failure, these insights can be translated into propositions relating to failure.

Hypothesis 6: *Failure is more likely when the organization performs many diverse tasks.*

Hypothesis 7: *Failure is more likely when the qualitative aspects of the work are very important.*

Hypothesis 8: *Failure is more likely the more the task varies over time.*

Hypothesis 9: *Failure is more likely when the work is performed at scattered locations.*

Hypothesis 10: *Failure is more likely when the workers are highly skilled specialists.*

Hypotheses 6, 7, 8, and 9 are intuitively obvious from the viewpoint of devising simple managerial procedures and minimizing the costs of control. They are summarized by Tullock in his Rule 1.[11] Hypothesis 10, however, is controversial; it is discussed in Chapter 4 at length.

The entire approach of detailed hierarchical control implicit in Gulick and reflected in the previous hypotheses has been subject to attack in more recent literature on organizations. The general point, which will be examined in greater detail in Chapter 4, is that detailed supervision of employees is based on the (incorrect) assumption that they do not want to contribute to production.[12] The comforting notion that we can liberate

[9]V. A. Graicunas, "Relationship in Organization," chapter ten in Gulick and Urwick eds., *Papers on the Science of Administration.* For the corrected mathematics see William H. Starbuck, "Organizational Growth and Development," chapter 11 in March, *Handbook of Organizations,* pp. 496–497.

[10]Gulick, "Notes on the Theory of Organization," pp. 8, 10.

[11]Gordon Tullock, *The Politics of Bureaucracy* (Washington: The Public Affairs Press, 1965), p. 179.

[12]For reviews of this basic idea, see Peter Michael Blau and W. Richard Scott, *Formal Organizations: A Comparative Approach* (San Francisco: Chandler, 1962), pp. 165 ff.; and

people to work is clouded by two qualifications: first, where output cannot be measured directly, it is easy to confuse the higher morale of unsupervised employees with greater quality and quantity of output; and, second, the substitution of internal for hierarchical control requires that the individual be able to perceive how his work contributes to the organization's overall task. This suggests two additional hypotheses:

Hypothesis 11: *Failure is more likely the more difficult it is to measure final output.*

Hypothesis 12: *Failure is more likely when individual employees must perform tasks that do not obviously contribute to what they perceive as worthwhile activities.*

Sheer size presents many problems. Organizations are set up when there is too much work for one man to do. The nominal head of the agency is not, therefore, in full control because no one can master all the details of the operations. Simon points out that the leaders of a complex organization are forced to rely either on their own prejudices or on their subordinates, because they do not have time to learn what is happening or to decide what should be done.[13] This leads quite directly to the hypothesis that:

Hypothesis 13: *Failure is more likely the greater the number of employees required for the assigned task.*

Within a firm or a particular government agency, it is conceivable that the economies associated with a larger scale of output may outweigh the loss of control associated with the larger number of employees. As the number of employees within an agency increases, however, their knowledge eventually overwhelms the capacity of the head of the agency. Similarly, as one moves toward the top levels of the hierarchy, the grasp of the details of particular agencies necessarily becomes smaller. In the context of the U.S. government, what is implied is a secular tendency toward increasing failure as the government has taken on more tasks. The President, Congress, and other political leaders confront more and more details, and naturally comprehend a smaller proportion of the whole. The important consideration for top leadership is not the size of the particular program, but rather the size of the govern-

---

Dorwin Cartwright, "Influence, Leadership, Control," chapter 1 in March, *Handbook of Organizations,* pp. 13–14.

[13]Simon *et al., Public Administration,* pp. 190, and 458; also, Herbert A. Simon, "Staff and Management Controls," *The Annals of The American Academy of Political and Social Science,* 292 (March 1954): 95.

ment as a whole.[14] Once it is recognized that hierarchical control has already broken down, it is not clear what the force of this hypothesis is. That is, it may apply with greater certainty to a conglomerate considering yet another merger than to the U.S. government, where various substitutes have already replaced hierarchy. Further analysis of this matter will be deferred until Chapter 20.

The converse of the span of control is the number of levels in the hierarchy, a variable that assumes great importance with the recognition that some slippage between the desires of the supervisor and what is done by the subordinates occurs at each level. If, for example, a task requires 100 operatives, it can be accomplished with 3 levels—one top executive and 10 foremen—if the span of control is 10 and no slippage occurs. If the span of control is only 5, however, the task requires 4 general supervisors under the top executive to supervise the 20 foremen. Thus any characteristics of the task, the operating rules of the organization, or the particular personnel that decrease the span of control will necessitate an increase in the number of hierarchical levels. If some loss of control (the failure of the subordinate to perform some functions desired by his supervisor as well as his performance of some functions that the supervisor does not desire) occurs at each level, the performance of the operatives departs further from the purposes of the top management as levels are added to the hierarchy. But there must be a tradeoff between the slippage at one level as the span of control increases and slippage between top and bottom as the number of levels increases. It is meaningful to think of an optimum organization, given the tasks and personalities involved, that minimizes the departure of operations from managerial intent. This would undoubtedly involve different spans of control at different levels in the hierarchy.

More important, the best organizational arrangement would certainly vary from case to case. This suggests that it is the type of decision that is best left to the properly trained and motivated manager, rather than specified as an inflexible rule. But this takes us full circle: How does one ensure that the motivations at the various levels in the hierarchy are directed toward organizational, rather than personal, ends? This problem bedevils every large organization, but is particularly acute in the federal government, where the public interest is not easily identified and has no readily identified spokesman and where decisions must be delegated through several levels of the hierarchy—even decisions on how best to structure the incentives for decision making.

---

[14]This is the essential logic developed by Michael Polanyi, *The Logic of Liberty: Reflections and Rejoinders* (Chicago: The University of Chicago Press, 1965, first published 1951).

Williamson, building upon a model sketched by Tullock, showed that the gradual accumulation of losses as information and instructions passed through the hierarchy is sufficient to limit the optimum size of the profit-maximizing firm, even in the absence of product-market or factor-market constraints.[15] Since Williamson was considering business, his model is too restrictive for analyzing government bureaucracies. Specifically, he assumes that expanding the size of the organization by adding another level to the hierarchy adds to total productive output. Although it is reasonable to assume that a profit-maximizing firm will not add employees unless they increase output, it is not obvious that a bureau will be so inhibited, especially when the effects external to the particular agency being expanded are taken into consideration. This matter will be considered further in Chapter 20.

It is necessary to examine more carefully the meaning of control loss in an effort to discover what circumstances will exacerbate the phenomenon. Tullock's model starts from his basic assumption that the intelligent and ambitious individual, when faced with a choice between furthering the purpose of the organization, as he sees it, and furthering his own goals, will often choose the latter.[16] Although some people will frequently choose to do what is in the public interest, rather than their own, such people will not advance as rapidly as the more ambitious and amoral—and hence will not be as important for the functioning of the organization. Since the ambitious bureaucrat is dependent on the good opinion of his superior for advancement, he will seek to provide the information that he judges the superior wants to receive. In the constant process of condensing and winnowing as information is transmitted up the hierarchy, therefore, it comes more and more to resemble the initial prejudices of the top officials, rather than the raw data observed in the field. In a particularly flagrant example, when President Kennedy cabled General Harkins in Saigon in September 1963 asking detailed questions on the progress of the war, he received answers composed by Maxwell Taylor in Washington.[17]

Although information flows down from the top, in Tullock's world actual policy is made at the lowest levels of the hierarchy because of the necessary vagueness of official policies. As these are expanded into pub-

[15]Oliver E. Williamson, "Hierarchical Control and Optimum Firm Size," *Journal of Political Economy*, 75, No. 2 (April 1967): 123–138.

[16]Tullock, *The Politics of Bureaucracy*, pp. 142–193, provides the basic model; Anthony Downs, *Inside Bureaucracy* (Boston: Little, Brown, 1967), pp. 112–157, supplements the insights of Tullock and works out numerous implications.

[17]David Halberstam's account of the origins of the U.S. involvement in Vietnam, *The Best and the Brightest* (New York: Random House, 1969), is replete with illustrations. This particular one is from p. 271.

lished regulations, formal operating procedures, and informal practice, the content gradually evolves until it corresponds with the preferences of operating people. The process is encouraged when policy is developed by a case-law approach as the bureaucrat finds himself forced to make decisions prior to the promulgation of policy from above. Since the superior officials are busy with other matters, the process proceeds until policy has been firmly established by the operating level.

Top officials can choose to exert their legitimate power in any particular area either to gather information from basic documents and observations or to develop specific policies and see that they are carried out. Such difficult and time-consuming interventions can be applied to only a few tasks, however.

Hypothesis 14: *Failure is more likely in programs that do not attract top-level attention.*

Counteracting this general point is the probability that the quality of information will be much lower in those areas where the prejudices of top officials are well known. Nevertheless, the insight that nearly any specific program can be made to work if it, and it alone, receives top priority is an implicit assumption in much of the maneuvering to obtain presidential attention for particular programs. It is probably the most meaningful way to interpret the assertion that age is related to failure.

Hypothesis 15: *Failure is more likely the older the agency.*

This is often challenged, for older agencies have overcome the confusion of routine housekeeping tasks, have well-developed communications systems, have been adaptable enough to survive, and so on. New agencies, however, have probably been set up reasonably well for the task they are to perform and are likely to receive high-level attention for a while. They may also include people who want the program to succeed.

INFORMATION

Since the head of the organization cannot know everything that is happening in the organization, he loses some degree of control. The subordinate is in a much better position to make many decisions than is his superior, but the decisions the subordinate makes will tend to advance his own interests. As Tullock stresses, "The resulting decision will be correct from the standpoint of the superior only if he has so organized his area of control that decisions which are best for his own interests are those that will also improve the position of the inferiors."[18] In a very broad sense, this is an information problem; that is, if the sovereign could grasp more and better information, the problem would not occur. In general, however, it cannot be solved by attempts to eliminate bias or reduce the noise in messages because it is inherent in the limited capacity of sovereigns, as well as supervisors at intermediate levels, to comprehend masses of information. Some forms of information are amenable to summarization in meaningful ways, whereas others are not. Various advances in bookkeeping and accounting have extended the size of firm that can be run effectively, but the qualitative nature of many of the outputs limits the effectiveness of such techniques in government.[19]

Hypothesis 16: *Failure is more likely the more difficult it is to obtain clear evidence that a particular policy decision is correct.*

The problem of assessing the correctness of a decision has a number of aspects, including the level within the organization at which the decision must be made. If the organization must deal with a large number of small unique cases, the decisions must be delegated to a low level of the hierarchy.

Hypothesis 17: *Failure is more likely in programs where a large number of dissimilar decisions must be made.*

Sometimes decisions that seem unique can be codified by intensive managerial effort into such categories that general rules apply. In his study of the Forest Service, Kaufman stressed the numerous procedures used intensively by that agency to retain control of the decisions made in a large variety of local situations by a large number of rangers.[20] Kaufman cites techniques for preforming decisions, including authorization, direction, and prohibition of specific actions in specific circumstances. These are set forth in great detail in the *Forest Service Manual*, supplements for various regions (and sometimes even particular forests), and technical handbooks. Fireplans and timber plans permit advance clearance of many of the unique decisions. Such preformed decisions, of course, are worth no more than the paper on which they are printed in the absence of a system to ensure compliance, which, according to Kaufman, is equally well developed.

---

[18]Tullock, *The Politics of Bureaucracy*, p. 73.

[19]Downs, *Inside Bureaucracy*, pp. 118–127, discusses techniques for reducing bias; Tullock, *The Politics of Bureaucracy*, pp. 178–220, analyzes various techniques for maintaining control.

[20]Herbert Kaufman, *The Forest Ranger, A Study in Administrative Behavior* (Baltimore: Johns Hopkins Press for Resources for the Future, 1960), chapter 4.

Although such control at the level of the bureau is essential, it is only part of the problem of assuring control by the "sovereign" over government activities. The elaborate system of administrative control is designed to achieve internal consistency in administration, but whether Congress and the President (or a referendum) would make the same decisions is an unanswerable question. Since most of the hierarchy have been promoted from the ranger level, the extent of their knowledge of conditions in the field is unusually great. What the Forest Service exemplifies, therefore, is a tight system of professional control, to be examined further in Chapter 4.

Rules, procedures, and other preformed decisions are useful only when the agency deals with conditions that are stable or change only slowly.

Hypothesis 18: *Failure is more likely when the agency must respond to rapid changes in external conditions.*

When conditions change rapidly, attempting to preform decisions results not in detailed control by the top administrator, but rather in a mass of irrelevant red tape which has to be selectively discarded by low-level officials for the organization to function at all. Such a situation puts the bureaucrat in the position of deciding among conflicting rules and, according to the Tullock model, choosing the one that advances his own career fastest.

Uniformity of conditions in different places can serve as a partial substitute for uniformity over time.[21]

Hypothesis 19: *Failure is more likely as the conditions facing the agency differ more from place to place.*

If the decisions to be made are the same in every local office, the top administration can devote much effort to keeping a uniform set of rules up to date. Even with such regional uniformity, however, it is still possible for rapid changes to overtake the capacity of the hierarchy to respond.

Hypothesis 20: *Failure is more likely when the agency must decide complex cases.*

Complexity will not be defined here. Many of its characteristics have already been touched on. The basic problem with applying rules to complex situations is that more than one rule can usually be construed as applying. This gives the bureaucrat the freedom to make his own

[21]Tullock, *The Politics of Bureaucracy,* p. 180.

choice in pursuit of his own goals. His alternative is to refer the matter to his superior at the cost of great delay and of overloading the channels of communication.

The overloading can cause leakage of authority, as will misunderstandings by subordinates, incompetence, unintentional errors, lack of time for subordinates to do all assigned tasks, and lack of time for top officials to follow up. Downs guesses that "Bureaus that have final outputs subject to close objective measurement may have leakage factors less than 10 percent. Those that have vaguely defined functions, outputs that are difficult to measure, or extremely dynamic environments may have leakage factors far larger than 10 percent."[22]

Hypothesis 21: *Failure is more likely the more vaguely the functions of the agency are defined.*

If even a small leakage occurs at each echelon, the cumulative effect is substantial if no correctives occur within the organization. Most federal programs have operatives at least seven steps removed from Congress, and some of those hierarchical steps are rather shaky ones.[23] If 10% of a message is lost in each transmission between levels of a hierarchy, then the part that survives two transmissions is $.9 \times .9 = .81$. More generally, the total loss in the hierarchy is $1 - t^{n-1}$, where t is the portion correctly transmitted and n is the number of levels in the hierarchy.[24] For $t = .9$ and $n = 7$ this expression indicates a total loss of 47% of the information.

Despite such a dramatic loss, this formula hardly does justice to Tullock's vision of bureaucracy; for the assumption of this simple model is that bits of information simply disappear. Tullock, however, was writing about a world in which information is distorted, not lost. If the message is biased in a consistent and predictable way, various counterbiasing techniques can unravel the code.[25] Whatever part of the distortion is not predictable is random, by definition. Random distortion is much more

[22]Downs, *Inside Bureaucracy*, p. 136.
[23]The U.S. State Department, always an extreme case, has a very tall, narrow hierarchical structure. An effort at administrative reform in 1965 included the removal of six levels separating the Deputy Under Secretary for Administration from the operating programs under his jurisdiction. The reform failed. See the detailed case study by Donald P. Warwick in collaboration with Marvin Meade and Theodore Reed, *A Theory of Public Bureaucracy: Politics, Personality, and Organization in the State Department* (Cambridge: Harvard University Press, 1975).
[24]Tullock, *The Politics of Bureaucracy*, pp. 137–141, describes the basic model. Downs, *Inside Bureaucracy*, pp. 116–118, works out some examples. Albert Breton also presents a control loss model of the same type in *The Economic Theory of Representative Government* (Chicago: Aldine, 1974), pp. 164–169. He attempts to introduce entropy as a separate factor, but an unfortunate typographical error mars the exposition.
[25]Downs, *Inside Bureaucracy*, pp. 118–127, describes the devices used to combat distortion.

serious than random loss, because the receiver cannot be sure which portion of the information to trust. The expression that Shannon provides for the loss of information in a channel subject to random errors is

$$\text{loss} = - [t \log_2 t + (1 - t) \log_2 (1 - t)],$$

where t is the probability of correct transmission of an individual bit of information.[26] If the probability of error is only 1%, the loss of information is 8%. If the probability of error is 10%, the loss of information is 47%. This is the loss between two levels of the hierarchy. If the loss were cumulative according to the standard control loss model, 98% of the information would be lost in a hierarchy of seven levels.

In some sense this proves too much because it suggests that hierarchical control of the bureaucracy is negligible. Yet the taxes are collected and Social Security checks are paid out. More generally, it is not clear what such numbers mean in connection with qualitative policy directives, but the implication is clear that hierarchies may devote significant resources to purposes other than those specified by the sovereign or, alternatively, that the sovereign will have to devote much effort to retaining control.

An administrator can use a variety of devices to improve the quality of the information he receives and to compensate for the biases. One of these is redundancy—using more than one source and channel of information to permit cross-checking. This technique becomes increasingly expensive of administrative time and other resources as the quantity of information increases.

Hypothesis 22: *Failure is more likely in programs that require the transmission of large amounts of information.*

Information can be transmitted more efficiently if it is coded, in the jargon of a profession for example. But the code and the habits of thought appropriate for one activity are not necessarily appropriate for another.[27]

Hypothesis 23: *Failure is more likely when a program is assigned to an agency that communicates in the jargon of an inappropriate profession.*

Similarly, variability in the type of information that must be transmitted makes standard codes difficult to employ.

---

[26]Claude E. Shannon and Warren Weaver, *The Mathematical Theory of Communication* (Urbana: The University of Illinois Press, 1959), pp. 35–36.

[27]Kenneth J. Arrow, *The Limits of Organization*, The Fels Lectures in Public Policy Analysis (New York: W. W. Norton, 1974), pp. 56–59.

Hypothesis 24: *Failure is more likely when an agency must communicate a variety of types of information to carry out its programs.*

When messages contain information with strong ideological or obvious policy implications the problems of bias and distortion are particularly difficult.[28]

Hypothesis 25: *Failure is more likely the more obvious the ideological and political implications of the messages transmitted.*

The Tullock model implies that the ambitious bureaucrat transmits to his superior the information that confirms the superior's prejudices. An approach concentrating on individual psychology—or the sociology of bureaucracy—by contrast, emphasizes the tendency of a person to see the world as he would like to see it, and to transmit data that confirm his view. Both approaches agree on the likelihood that communications will be slanted in such a way as to increase the importance and functions of the sender of the information. It is difficult for the recipient of information to guard against a Tullockian bias. Discounting for the obvious self interest of the zealot or salesman is a much easier and more stable process.

Some functions involve such complex processes of reconstruction of value-laden information from conflicting scraps that failures are inevitable. A striking example is intelligence; for, as Knorr points out, the data are so noisy that they cannot be analyzed in the absence of preconceptions (otherwise known as hypotheses).[29] The problems arise not from the use of hypotheses to serve as a framework and filter for noisy data, but rather from the poor quality of the hypotheses adopted and the failure to subject them to explicit criticism.

The subtlety of the messages that must be transmitted through the hierarchy is also a significant characteristic.

Hypothesis 26: *Failure is more likely the more subtle the information that must be transmitted.*

It is tempting to collapse subtlety and variability into simple matters of quantity. Once a message is in print it is meaningful to measure the bits of information or the channel capacity necessary to transmit the mes-

---

[28]D. T. Campbell, "Systematic Error on the Part of Human Links in Communication Systems," *Information & Control*, 1958 (1): 334–369. Bela Gold called attention to the tendency of specialists to delay offering their professional and technical judgments until they had determined the policy inclinations of superiors. See *Wartime Economic Planning in Agriculture: A Study in the Allocation of Resources* (New York: Columbia University Press, 1949), p. 536.

[29]Klaus Knorr, "Failures in National Intelligence Estimates," *World Politics* 16, No. 3 (April 1964): 455–467.

sage. *Subtlety,* however, refers to the problems involved in getting the information into words and the likelihood that the receiver will understand what the sender was trying to say. With enough time and channel capacity, one can transmit any number of telephone directories with as much accuracy as one is willing to pay for; but there is no guarantee that the State Department official in Washington will comprehend what the observer in some Asian village saw.

The discussion of various antidistortion and counterbiasing techniques generally presupposes that the superior who uses the technique is at least as intelligent as the subordinate who is trying to mislead him. Although Tullock argues that ability, on average, increases at successively higher levels in the bureaucracy, this need not be so at discontinuities; for example, where the highest-ranking civil servants deal with the lowest-ranking political appointees. Ely Devons in discussing his experiences with the British Ministry of Aircraft Production (MAP) during World War II, stated that the MAP used the number of man-hours required to produce each airplane as the method for weighting different types of aircraft and calculating production capacity. This was done despite general recognition within MAP of the limitations of this measure, because it was something the Cabinet could understand![30]

MEASUREMENT OF OUTPUT

Administrators commonly attempt to maintain control by budgeting inputs and measuring outputs without worrying much about the intervening steps. The private market works well on the same general principle: Each manager is concerned with the details of his own operation, but buyers of intermediate goods or final products generally need concern themselves only with the cost and quality of what they are buying, not with the details of how it is made. The crucial assumption, however, is that both the quantity and the quality of output can be measured adequately. Private firms often choose to make intermediate inputs in order to control quality if it is difficult to measure and significant for later stages of production. The problem is much more severe in connection with the outputs of government bureaucracies, many of which cannot be measured at all.

The significance of this point has not been missed. It is the essence of Hypothesis 11, and Tullock, as just described, uses the impossibility of

---

[30]Ely Devons, *Planning in Practice* (Cambridge, England: The University Press, 1950), pp. 120–123, 155 ff.

measuring the individual's output directly as the basic explanation for his main behavioral assumption: The individual strives to please his superior because the quantity and quality of his work cannot be measured well enough to serve as the basis for promotion. Similarly, Olson uses the impossibility of measuring output as the main explanation for the frequent assertion that governments are less efficient than other large organizations.[31] Many components of nongovernmental organizations are beset by difficulties in measuring output, but the overall inefficiency of such organizations is limited by actual or threatened bankruptcy. Conversely, governments can measure many intermediate outputs, but such measures are rarely used as the basis for rewarding employees for deep-seated reasons that are examined in Chapter 20.

Charles Schultze points out that the consequences of the failure to measure performance directly include (a) detailed regulation of procedures, inputs, and organization; and (b) defensive behavior to avoid any action that could be shown to be a mistake.[32] Once the red tape, associated with the detailed control of inputs and methods, has enveloped an organization, it may be difficult for the manager to impose yet another form of control by measuring output. Furthermore, he may not be able to use the output information for anything.

Imperfect measures of output can be disfunctional in achieving the legislated goals of the organization. Some of the strongest objections to the adoption of cost-benefit analysis and the program planning and budgeting system (PPBS) stressed the adage that "measured activities drive out unmeasured activities, and measured costs or benefits outweigh unmeasured costs or benefits."[33]

Hypothesis 27: *Failure is more likely when some aspects of the program are measured while important aspects are not.*

Blau refers to this as a variant of a standard sociological problem— "The distorting influence of the measuring instrument."[34] He recounts

---

[31]Mancur Olson, "Evaluating Performance in the Public Sector," pp. 355–384 in *The Measurement of Economic and Social Performance*, ed. Milton Moss (New York: Columbia University Press for the NBER, 1973).

[32]Charles L. Schultze, "The Role of Incentives, Penalties, and Rewards in Attaining Effective Policy," chapter 6 in *Public Expenditures and Policy Analysis*, eds. Robert H. Haveman and Julius Margolis (Chicago: Markham, 1970), p. 152.

[33]Not only do the unmeasurable variables fade in importance before the results that can be weighed and counted, but also the analyst may simplify by focusing on a few variables that are central to him, while ignoring effects that are of minor importance *to the analyst*. See Laurence H. Tribe, "Policy Science: Analysis or Ideology?" in *Benefit—Cost and Policy Analysis 1972* (Chicago: Aldine, 1973), p. 41, reprinted from *Philosophy and Public Affairs* 2, No. 1: 66–110.

[34]Peter M. Blau, *The Dynamics of Bureaucracy: A Study of Interpersonal Relations in Two Government Agencies* (Chicago: University of Chicago Press, 1955), p. 38.

how an early record system requiring the reporting of just the number of interviews led to maximization of interviews. This system was replaced by a more complex report of interviews, job referrals, placements, etc., which improved performance, but since the more time-consuming counseling interviews were not included in the report, they were rarely performed.

In addition to this very direct problem of misdirecting effort toward measured from unmeasured activities, Blau noted a number of other disfunctions of statistics.[35] Reliance on statistics alone tends to undermine the supervisor's authority. In Tullock's terms, of course, this is the advantage of a good objective work-rating scheme—it substitutes an exchange relationship for a political one. To take this position, however, is to assume that the objective measures come closer to rating progress toward the legislated goals than do the criteria on which supervisors base their ratings.

Statistics used to rate operatives are inherently suspect. Interviewers always manage to find ways to pad the numbers; for example, referring laid-off workers back to their old jobs at recall time. Since reasonably clever operatives always know more about the details of procedure than do even very able supervisors, it is almost certain that statistics will be partially falsified. If the purpose of the reporting system is to provide an objective system of rating the performance of individuals, it would be quite ironic to reward superior performance in fabricating records.

The collection of one set of statistics may sabotage efforts to collect a more important set. One crucial piece of information for the evaluation of the Employment Service is the duration of placements, but it has never been possible to interest the organization in collecting such data, perhaps because of the emphasis on number of placements and the reluctance to acknowledge that many are of short duration.

When Cohen examined the Employment Service some years after Blau's study, he found the situation worse, if anything, with much effort devoted to fabricating records to create a paper record of accomplishment, rather than serving clients.[36] For example, the procedure of counting as placements the referral of people back to the jobs to which they were being recalled anyway was contrary to policy when Blau made his study in 1949, but had become a formal program of the agency by the time of Cohen's employment there in 1956![37] The formal program was not discontinued until 1960, and it is easy to imagine that the practice

[35]Ibid., pp. 44 ff.
[36]Harry Cohen, *The Demonics of Bureaucracy: Problems of Change in a Government Agency* (Ames: Iowa State University Press, 1965), p. 131.
[37]Ibid., p. 95.

still survives. In Cohen's office these former-employer placements amounted to about half of the total.

Cohen also discussed the other great problem in the use of output measures in a bureaucracy: What purpose do they serve when promotions are based on other factors? Since firing was almost impossible under the Civil Service regulations, and promotions were based on written and oral examinations, it would seem that even the most sophisticated measures of output would have little effect on performance.[38]

Francis and Stone were more favorably impressed with the emphasis on placements than were Blau and Cohen.[39] They observed that the professional and managerial focus on placements was sufficiently strong that interviewers disregarded many of the rules and procedures in the operating manual that stood in the way of the legislated purpose of the agency. The office that Francis and Stone studied used another measure of output that was less closely related to service however—a document count, that is, the number of completed forms which comes close to matching the popular caricature of bureaucracy.[40]

Miriam Johnson's work is the most bitter criticism of the attempt to measure output in the Employment Service.[41] After describing an innovative attempt to assist the disadvantaged unemployed in learning to understand and approach the labor market, she describes how the experiment, just as it was becoming successful, was compelled to adopt standard forms and paper work. The result was not only to subtract from the time available for useful activities, but also to provide for the rating (which determined the budget) of the office in terms of placements and the other standard activities that did not match the categories found useful in the experiment. The experiment was killed by the statistical procedures, but this may have been intentional.

The problems encountered by the Employment Service in measuring output can be generalized. Unless the measurement captures all important aspects of the organization's purposes, it will misdirect effort. The design of good performance measures is an exceedingly tricky business requiring sensitivity to the legislated goals, the particular problems encountered in operations, and the impact of the activity on other agencies and people. Most measurements that can be made will be of intermediate goods. Thus it may be possible to increase the efficiency of

[38]Ibid., pp. 105–107.

[39]Roy G. Francis and Robert C. Stone, *Service and Procedure in Bureaucracy: A Case Study* (Minneapolis: The University of Minnesota Press, 1956), p. 85.

[40]Ibid., p. 135.

[41]Miriam Johnson, *Counter Point, The Changing Employment Service* (Salt Lake City: Olympus, 1973), esp. pp. 123–152.

given pieces of work—run motor pools more cheaply or type letters less expensively. Such routine managerial upgrading should remain secondary to the broader question of what the work is producing. The final output can rarely be measured adequately, but once some crude proxy is adopted as the basis for budgets and work rules, it will not easily be abandoned. Thus, for example, the placement rate is still a key statistic for the employment service.[42]

THE PREFERENCES AND ABILITIES OF BUREAUCRATS

Since hierarchical control breaks down and incentive systems are applied sporadically, the bureaucrat's behavior will often be determined by his own preferences. But people differ so much that efforts to predict behavior require some abstraction or simplification. Downs synthesized various speculations and conjectures to try to derive testable propositions.[43]

The five types of bureaucrats in Downs's world are climbers, conservers, zealots, advocates, and statesmen. They pursue some or all of the following goals in varying degrees: power, money income, prestige, convenience, security, personal loyalty, pride in proficient performance of work, desire to serve the public interest, and commitment to a specific program of action.

The *climber* is interested primarily in his own career, which he may advance through promotions within the bureau, expanding the importance and rewards of his existing job, or by taking a job outside the bureau. The *conserver* is also motivated by self-interest, but in his case he wants to hang on to the power, income, and prestige he has, and to enjoy them with the least possible effort. He is not ambitious for greater challenges with their corresponding rewards, as is the climber. Zealots, advocates, and statesmen, in contrast with climbers and conservers, are partly motivated by the public interest, as they see it. The *zealot* pushes for some very narrow policy for long periods of time. The *statesman* has much broader goals, which he holds equally firmly, but will compromise on the detailed means of their achievement. The *advocate* is not as firmly committed to a particular broad or narrow goal, but rather will fight aggressively for the course of action that best suits his organization.

Although the descriptions appear to have considerable richness and

---

[42]U.S. Department of Labor, Employment and Training Administration, *ETA Interchange* 2, No. 9 (September 1976): 1.

[43]Downs, *Inside Bureaucracy*, chapter 9.

realism, Wilson argued that Downs's model fails to provide definite testable empirical predictions. The various motives cannot be associated with particular behavior.[44] It is clear that some shortcuts are necessary, but all of them impose their costs.

Niskanen is not concerned with behavior within the agency.[45] The head of the agency tries to maximize his own utility, which depends on salary, perquisites of office, public reputation, power, patronage, output of the bureau, ease of making changes, and ease of managing. If all these variables were independent, predictions about behavior would be hard to make, but Niskanen argues (very convincingly in the case of *government* bureaucrats) that all but the last two are positively related to the total budget of the bureau, and ease of making changes and ease of managing are related to increases in the budget. Thus the bureaucrat becomes a budget maximizer, which leads to a theory that is simple enough for testing.

The two elements missing from Niskanen's model are the conserver—the lethargic, do-nothing bureaucrat of popular stories—and any mention of the public interest. Niskanen argues that the individual bureaucrat cannot pursue the public interest because of his limited information and the other constraints on his action.[46] Instead, he becomes an expert in a narrow field, and that usually leads him to advocate its expansion in the public interest. Also, those favoring particular policies are likely to join agencies that advance the policies. In any event, numerous commentators have noted the tendency for arguments to be phrased in terms of the public interest when the proximate effect would be an expansion of the pleader's agency.

The shortcut that Tullock adopts is different from Niskanen's, although in many situations it leads to the same prediction. Tullock's politician, when faced with a choice between his own goals and those of the organization, always chooses to pursue his own. This, in itself, is not specific, because individuals can have different goals. Tullock thus includes a subsidiary argument that the people who really count are the able and ambitious. The complex utility function of Downs is collapsed by Tullock into one dimension—personal advancement. Although Tullock begins by focusing on all those within the organization whose performance is not judged directly by results, he ends by restricting his analysis to a world of intrahierarchical climbers, to use Downs's term.[47]

---

[44]James Q. Wilson, *Political Organizations* (New York: Basic Books, 1973), p. 25.
[45]William A. Niskanen, Jr., *Bureaucracy and Representative Government* (Chicago: Aldine-Atherton, 1971), p. 38.
[46]Ibid., p. 39.
[47]Tullock, *The Politics of Bureaucracy*, pp. 20–21.

Tullock also argues that since the most able and least scrupulous people will most consistently choose correctly the action that leads to advancement, as one moves closer to the top levels of the hierarchy, the average level of ability will rise and the average degree of commitment to the organization's purposes and morality will decline. It is conceivable that Tullock's analysis has been colored by his personal experience in the State Department. Possibly this accounts for an overemphasis on the ability, ambition, and amorality of the average bureaucrat, as well as the failure of the whole enterprise. Whatever the reasons, his model is inconsistent with some of the popular wisdom, as well as the scholarly analysis, of bureaucracies. The *Peter Principle,* for example, holds that typically in hierarchies people are promoted on the basis of successful performance in the jobs they hold until they finally arrive at a position beyond their competence, there to remain fouling up the operations of the organization until retirement.[48] This view, of course, is as much an exaggeration as Tullock's opposite one, but both seem to touch upon familiar observations. Can they be reconciled? Is there any serious content?

One of the standard topics for disagreement in collective bargaining is the relative importance to be assigned to seniority and to merit in making promotions. Unions and the great mass of employees usually opt for the "objective" criterion of seniority, whereas management prefers to retain the flexibility of promotion by merit (although large organizations typically rely heavily on seniority, regardless of what the rules permit them to do).

Procedures within the federal bureaucracy include a variety of mixtures of seniority and merit, where merit includes such criteria as schooling and examinations, as well as a high rating by one's supervisor. Tullock based his mechanism on the latter criterion, which surely becomes increasingly important as one rises further in the hierarchy. At the lowest levels of the bureaucracy, all of the social and organizational pressures encourage reliance on seniority supplemented by (*a*) formal tests or other objective criteria (e.g., veterans' preferences); (*b*) the uncertain career implications of true incompetence; (*c*) some favoritism; and (*d*) ambition, which filters out those who want to rise from those who are content with their station. Point (*b*) permits the Peter Principle to apply; that is, true incompetence may earn a bad performance report and thus stop advancement within the hierarchy, but may it not equally as frequently result in lateral transfer to another hierarchy or promotion

---

[48]Laurence J. Peter and Raymond Hull, *The Peter Principle* (New York: William Morrow, 1969).

to an innocuous position in the same organization? Point (*c*) permits the Tullockian mechanism to work; the ambitious will seek to curry favor with their supervisors and the most able among the ambitious will be relatively successful, thus rising faster than the average. Tullock's bureaucrat is not influenced by prejudice about sex or skin color. He wants subordinates who efficiently fulfill his orders and succeeds in getting people who are proficient in conveying the impression that they do. Nevertheless, the evidence indicates that real-world bureaucrats do find some room to indulge their prejudices,[49] which is not consistent with the analyses of Tullock or Niskanen and will tend to offset the worst consequences of the Peter Principle, as will be developed in the following.

In view of the general breakdown of hierarchical control explicit in Tullock's model as well as in other serious studies of bureaucracy, it seems somewhat inconsistent to focus so much attention on the goals of the successful climbers. Most of the decisions and work of the bureaucracy will be left to those who are not so ambitious while the climbers devote their limited energies to pleasing their superiors, rather than to supervision.

With this as a background, it becomes important to consider the motivations of those who are not particularly ambitious to climb within the hierarchy. Some, of course, are simply indolent—the conservers who want to protect their positions, and will put in their routine 40-hr weeks in return for their pay. Those with a compulsion to rise above the herd (including academics who write books) exaggerate the ambitions of the majority of their fellow workers. Conservers, who probably constitute the mass of mankind, will carry out whatever instructions have to be carried out in the easiest possible way, without worrying particularly about the overall consequences for public welfare. By the same token, they need not make any great effort to please their superiors, since the position of a civil servant who follows the rules and does as he is instructed is quite secure.

Alternatively, some of the hierarchically unambitious may be strongly motivated ideologically or professionally. The effects of such internal

---

[49]Arthur J. Corazzini found significantly lower salaries for blacks and women compared with whites and men of apparently equivalent quality in the federal government. See "Equality of Employment Opportunity in the Federal White-Collar Civil Service," *Journal of Human Resources* VII, No. 4, (Fall 1972):424–445. These findings were corroborated by the larger study of Sharon P. Smith, *Equal Pay in the Public Sector: Fact or Fantasy* (Princeton: Industrial Relations Section, Princeton University, 1977), pp. 106–129. Smith found, however, that race and especially sex differentials were smaller in the public sector than in the private.

reward structures will be examined in Chapter 4. Such motivations serve in part as a substitute for hierarchical control.

Hypothesis 28: *Failure is more likely in an area that does not attract the professionally or ideologically motivated.*

The problem, of course, is how to attract competent people who do not have great ambition to advance within the organization. Professional or ideological motivations are possibilities, but there are others. Mac-Kenzie, in discussing the exceptional ability of employees of the British Exchequer and Audit Department, pointed out that it could hire lower middle-class boys of great ability, since this was one of the few offices giving power, prestige, and independence to a grammar school boy in Victorian England. Because class barriers foreclosed promotion, even the most able would remain on the job.[50]

Hypothesis 29: *Failure is more likely where the barriers to vertical mobility are weak.*

This happens to be one of the corollaries of the Peter Principle.[51] One of the costs of easy upward mobility is the general promotion of people until they reach their level of incompetence. If mobility is restricted, however, some highly competent people will be available at low levels in the hierarchy to accomplish useful work. Prejudice against women and blacks and examinations that are irrelevant to the job have imposed such barriers, but as they fall, social mobility is improved and the functioning of the bureaucracy deteriorates.

Since it is the predominance of climbers that creates the most intractable control problems, one would expect failure in areas that tend to attract climbers; for example, agencies or programs that are growing fast. It is difficult, of course, to distinguish between the failures that can be attributed to poor planning (often described as start-up problems) and those resulting from the attractiveness of rapidly growing agencies to the able and ambitious. In either case, however, it follows that failure is associated with rapid growth.

Hypothesis 30: *Failure is more likely where the growth of a program or agency is rapid.*

Slow growth, with its accompanying slow promotion, keeps most people below their level of incompetence and repels Tullock's eager schemers.

---

[50]W. J. M. MacKenzie in the "Forward" to Normanton, *Accountability and Audit of Governments,* pp. x–xi.
[51]Peter and Hull, *The Peter Principle,* pp. 75–77.

COORDINATION

A steel company, under pressure from the Environmental Protection Agency (EPA), enclosed its coke ovens in large sheds to control air pollution—and then was informed by the Occupational Safety and Health Administration (OSHA) that the concentration of fumes within the shed made that an unsafe workplace. Such anecdotal evidence of the lack of coordination between agencies is commonplace, as are contradictory statements on the same problem from different departments. On the basis of hierarchical theory, the truly surprising fact is that any coordination occurs in large organizations, not that it is occasionally subject to lapses.

The tidy picture from the organization chart should be expected to break down for a variety of reasons. If, for example, a cabinet secretary were to issue the same general order to two bureau heads, by the time the order was expanded into such a form that implementation was possible and instructions were written as the order passed through three or four levels of the hierarchy, the actual operating instructions of the two agencies would be quite different. It is not really a case of the general policy encompassing all specific cases, but rather that implementation requires the fleshing out of a vague idea with many specific decisions, which will be made differently by different people.

In this particular case, coordination need not be a problem. Two or more agencies can write implementing regulations jointly, but only if the participants know they are dealing with the same subject and only if the differences between the objectives of the agencies are not large. When OSHA and the EPA issue conflicting regulations, the problem is not lack of information but differing objectives. In the hierarchical model, this type of problem should be resolved by the common superior, but in this case the only common superior is the President (or Congress). It is hardly realistic to expect the President to know or care much about sheds over coke ovens and a myriad of similar issues.

Frequently, moreover, a lack of coordination reflects not outright confrontation, but just that "the left hand knoweth not what the right hand doeth." Agencies proceed with their ordinary tasks, as they have evolved over time, regardless of the changes that have created contradictory objectives in other parts of the government. Thus the Farmers Home Administration continued to subsidize mortgages for those who will devour a great deal of gasoline driving to work ("So if you're not willing to commute a half hour to work, we couldn't help you.")[52] at the

[52]Advertisement, Portland, Maine, *Press Herald*, 24 June 1975, p. 32.

moment when the Federal Energy Administration (FEA) was hoping to reduce energy consumption. Similarly, the decisions of electric utilities to meet air pollution regulations by converting from coal to oil or gas conflicted with the effort by the FEA to encourage the use of domestic coal rather than imported oil. This issue was prominent enough to attract presidential attention, but even that did not overcome the procedural obstacles to implementation.[53]

If two offices remain in contact during the whole process of implementation, the control losses that do occur along the way are at least consistent among the different parts of government involved. But the voluntary coordination of effort works only when no serious issues are involved.[54] If, for example, two agencies are assigned to perform equivalent inspection functions in the same industry and each is given a budget large enough to permit it to perform 5% of the job, the two agencies are likely to be able to reach a voluntary agreement on sharing the territory. When the stakes are larger and the decisions longer lasting—as in deciding who will have the primary authority in implementing a new program—the voluntary acquiescence of the losers seems unlikely. The decisions, therefore, must be made at a higher level by someone who knows far less about the actual procedures for carrying out the policy.

If such major disputes take place only when new programs are set up, the problem is manageable, but planning in general involves many of the same elements and long-term implications as the design of new programs. The knowledge and self-interest of the heads of separate agencies are pitted against the broader view, but ignorance of detail, of the higher official. The subplans of individual offices defy voluntary coordination because the stakes in terms of budget and power for the separate agencies are so high.

In addition to the lack of coordination that results from the conflict between separate agencies, there is also the technical question of the most efficient degree of centralization of decision making. Both centralization and decentralization impose as costs different forms of inconsistent action by the components of the organization. Needless to say, however, each bureaucrat will argue that the organization will perform best if most decisions are made at his level.[55]

---

[53]The Cleveland *Plain Dealer*, 28 May 1977, p. 5-A, includes a brief news item based on a staff memorandum of the House Commerce Subcommittee on Energy and Power, which reviewed the coal conversion program.

[54]Robert E. Goodin, "The Logic of Bureaucratic Back Scratching," *Public Choice* 21 (Spring 1975); 53–67, presents a good case study of cooperation among agencies. The crucial feature of this case seems to be the absence of anything worth fighting for.

[55]Devons, *Planning in Practice* p. 14, noted that, at each rank, individuals complained that action delegated to subordinates was uncoordinated, while simultaneously arguing that decisions made by their superiors ignored reality.

Traditional approaches to government organization have stressed solving the coordination problem by giving one agency a monopoly of related functions. More recently, however, Niskanen has argued that competition among bureaus in performing equivalent services has the great advantage of revealing to the review committee more information about the true costs of the activity.[56] Wagner points out that competition gives the sponsor more views about the future and about correct policy, permits dissidents to transfer to a more congenial environment, and keeps more alternatives open to the organization.[57] Thus the virtue of coordinating related activities should not be misconstrued as implying the necessity of monopolizing a certain type of function. Ideally, the manpower and housing policies of the Department of Defense would be consistent with those of the Department of Labor and HUD, respectively, but this is not equivalent to the argument that only one of the services should have strategic missiles.

The confusion between monopoly and coordination is one of the underlying issues in the contradictory positions taken by various writers on the appeal of interagency conflicts to the common superior. The received doctrine holds that the common superior *is* the formal coordinator of his underlings and naturally should be expected to mediate conflicts. It is suggested that proper organization results in the settlement of most disputes at a low level, but it is also pointed out that Franklin Roosevelt delighted in setting up overlapping agencies and grants of authority in order to ensure that controversial issues were brought to his attention. It has also been suggested that, FDR to the contrary, the President often does not want to intervene when cabinet members are in conflict over policy; he would prefer to remain aloof from petty matters, rather than dissipate his political strength and limited time and energy.[58] This same reluctance to take sides in open disputes between subordinates characterizes lower echelons of the hierarchy and results in a corresponding reluctance of subordinates to carry such disputes to the common superior. Lack of coordination, therefore, is likely to be concealed if possible, rather than confronted openly so a policy decision can be made. Competition for new or expanded functions brings the superior more information and the opportunity for choice; conflict among established agencies whose policies do not mesh brings only pain, and is, therefore, likely to be suppressed.

[56]Niskanen, *Bureaucracy and Representative Government*, pp. 155–168.

[57]Richard E. Wagner, *The Public Economy* (Chicago: Markham, 1973), p. 122.

[58]David B. Truman, *The Governmental Process* (New York: Alfred A. Knopf, 2nd ed., 1971), p. 408.

The traditional organization chart shows a pyramid with authority fanning out from one person at the top to numerous individuals in the field. As Kaufman points out, however, the pyramid might well be inverted from the viewpoint of the individual operative.[59] The forest ranger, for example, receives orders from an increasing number of line and staff people at each higher level of the organization above him. The line and staff dichotomy is meaningless to the subordinate who is confronted by a mass of contradictory orders. He may have to choose which rule applies when there are ambiguities, or to decide which to ignore when there are contradictions. (Part of the problem is that old rules stay in the handbook, even when contradictory ones are added.) The conflicting criteria for designing a road of the engineers, the watershed specialists, and the recreation specialists above him, in practice give the ranger some discretion to apply his own preferences and his knowledge of local conditions. Likewise, if he receives orders that he does not want to follow, the ambiguities and contradictions give him the opportunity to delay.

Hypothesis 31: *Failure is more likely the more ambiguous or contradictory the instructions issued to operatives.*

The position of the ranger is in some respects freer and in others more difficult as a result of the pyramid above him, but the results for the ultimate coherence of Forest Service policy are far superior to those that Gold found in his study of wartime agricultural planning. The various hierarchies within the Department of Agriculture—the Agricultural Adjustment Administration, the Extension Service, the Farm Security Administration, and the Farm Credit Administration—had their own agents in each of the agricultural counties of the United States. When World War II began, the rhetoric of Congress and the President switched from the restrictiveness born of the Great Depression to the goal of expanding output to help avert starvation in the countries ravaged by war. Although the rhetoric had adapted to the changed circumstances and targets had been set for modest increases in output, the coherent policies to achieve the targets were never developed and implemented.[60] The county-agent system, which apparently put agriculture far ahead of other sectors of the economy in capacity to mobilize resources, failed to make the transition to wartime tasks. One symptom of the failure to develop coherent wartime policies was the conflicting

[59]Herbert Kaufman, *The Forest Ranger*, p. 68; also *Administrative Feedback: Monitoring Subordinates' Behavior* (Washington: Brookings, 1973), p. 2.
[60]Bela Gold, *Wartime Economic Planning in Agriculture*, p. 284.

advice the county agents of the different agencies frequently gave to farmers. It is just such confusion that is avoided by the device of making the Forest Service ranger responsible for coordinating the conflicting instructions given him, or for calling irreconcilable demands to the attention of his superiors.

Hypothesis 32: *Failure is more likely when separate hierarchies deal directly with the public, rather than working through one representative.*

The necessity of forcing agreement on general policy in order to coordinate the activities of a large organization poses special difficulties when conditions are changing rapidly. Devons noted that the long lead-times required for details of implementation (e.g., designing and building manufacturing facilities) were inconsistent with the short-sighted view of the general policymakers.[61] The cabinet would not plan labor allocations more than 6 months ahead, but the Ministry of Aircraft Production had to consider capacity increases 2 years ahead. The resulting inconsistency between the detailed plans of the subcomponents and the general plan for the whole can result in either the waste of resources already committed by the subcomponents to their own plans or the de facto arrogation by the subcomponents of decisions that should be made by the general policymakers, with a resulting lack of coordination among subcomponent plans.

Hypothesis 33: *Failure is more likely when implementation requires planning far ahead.*

When decisions must be made quickly the practical extent of coordination may be limited to whatever can be done by the small number of top officials in daily contact. They, of course, cannot grasp all details, especially when many variables are changing simultaneously or when some data are distorted. After allowing for such problems, planning seems most nearly capable of producing coordination in a stationary state, but is quite unsuited to dealing with the fast-changing conditions of crises such as wars, when it is most likely to be called on.

Hypothesis 34: *Failure is more likely the more quickly decisions must be made.*

This raises the question of whether hierarchical coordination is possible at all. The experimental evidence suggests that hierarchies really are useful in coordinating the efforts of several people to solve a problem too

---

[61]Devons, *Planning in Practice*, pp. 131, 179–183.

large for one person.[62] When attention turns to the larger problems of society, the few serious efforts at analysis suggest that it is impossible.

Mises raised the question in connection with the possibility of socialist economic planning.[63] As Polanyi points out, the subsequent modicum of success of the Soviet economy does not refute Mises because, since the disastrous failure of central planning in 1919–1921, the Soviet system has relied heavily on individual decisions within a state-controlled framework.[64] Tullock, after developing his model of control loss in hierarchies, concludes that "The basic problem is that the degree of internal coordination which is necessary to accomplish a given task effectively may be greater than can be achieved by a hierarchic structure that is large enough to perform the task. If this is true, the task is organizationally impossible."[65]

Hypothesis 35: *Failure is more likely, the greater the degree of coordination necessary to accomplish a task.*

Enough evidence is available to suggest that Tullock's warning is not an empty one. The constant references to the coordination problem in subprograms where the observer can grasp the interrelationships among the activities suggests that the situation would appear far worse if we could consider the less obvious repercussions of particular actions. In any event, the hierarchical model suggests that much of the coordination that does occur is either informal or is based on (*a*) the professional and related internal forces (discussed in Chapter 4) and (*b*) bargaining among agencies (discussed in Chapter 3). These mechanisms, however, are far from perfect substitutes for hierarchical control.

STRUCTURE OF THE ORGANIZATION

Although the standard approach to organization calls for a structure that minimizes the need for coordination between subunits,[66] and economists may recommend minimizing spillovers of benefits or costs among agencies,[67] some analysts disagree. If the conflict is real, pushing

---

[62]Peter M. Blau and W. Richard Scott, *Formal Organizations: A Comparative Approach,* p. 125.

[63]The classic summary of the issues is the debate reprinted in Oskar Lange and Fred M. Taylor, *On the Economic Theory of Socialism* (New York: McGraw-Hill, 1964).

[64]Michael Polanyi, *The Logic of Liberty,* pp. 111–137.

[65]Tullock, *The Politics of Bureaucracy,* p. 125.

[66]Simon, Smithburg, and Thompson, *Public Administration,* pp. 164–166.

[67]Richard Zeckhauser and Elmer Schaefer, "Public Policy and Normative Economic Theory," chapter 2 of Raymond A. Bauer and Kenneth J. Gergen, eds., *The Study of Policy Formation* (New York: The Free Press, 1968), p. 74.

it into one box on the organization chart may just substitute in-tradepartmental for interdepartmental conflict. Furthermore, Meyer suggests that if components are regrouped to decrease coordination costs, management will find it necessary to increase its effort to obtain feedback in order to keep the more nearly self-contained units from being coopted by clients or suppliers.[68]

Hypothesis 36: *Failure is more likely the more nearly self-contained are the organizational subunits.*

The risk of cooptation is particularly great when the elements of the organization are grouped according to elements in the environment. Each subdivision of the organization will then deal primarily with one interest, which will influence the agency's behavior as discussed in Chapter 3.

The controversies in the literature about appropriate forms of organization are symptoms both of the lack of firm empirical knowledge of the relationship of organizational structure to performance and of the variety of disciplines from which forays have been made into this field. Unfortunately, the literature on structure is not developed enough to provide many hypotheses about conditions leading to failure, even though this is the aspect of government most often subject to tinkering in the interests of either efficiency or control.

Boyer has noted some political and structural factors that contribute to the "vertical independence" of the administrator from higher authority, which may be equated with failure of hierarchical control.[69] Hypotheses related to structure include the following:

Hypothesis 37: *Failure is more likely the greater the organizational complexity of the bureau.*

The executive in a large heterogeneous system becomes detached from issues of administrative policy.

Hypothesis 38: *Failure is more likely the greater the organizational autonomy stemming from technology.*

The problems of controlling technical people or functions dominated by an advanced technology (for example, electronic data processing) are discussed in Chapter 4.

Administrative structure should be adapted to the functions that the

---

[68]Marshall W. Meyer, *Bureaucratic Structure and Authority: Coordination and Control in 254 Government Agencies* (New York: Harper & Row, 1972), pp. 97–99.

[69]William W. Boyer, *Bureaucracy on Trial: Policy Making by Government Agencies* (New York: Bobbs-Merrill, 1964), pp. 47–48.

organization is to perform; but such adaptation may be difficult because of the inflexibility and political constraints in the public sector. Downs suggests that complex and detailed interdependencies require the tight coordination possible only with narrow spans of control and the corresponding tall hierarchy.[70] Since vertical coordination is time-consuming, however, such an organization is not as well suited to dealing with uncertainty as is a flat hierarchy, which leaves more discretion to individuals at each level. Thus uncertainty is best met by a flat hierarchy and complexity by a tall one, whereas a combination of the two poses special problems.

Hypothesis 39: *Failure is more likely when the environment combines uncertainty with complexity.*

Tasks differ in the number of decisions that must be made at various levels of the hierarchy. In a regulatory agency, decisions are made by a few people at the top; the staff is small, but should be organized to permit information and ideas to flow upward.[71] The Postal Service, in contrast, requires supervision of its thousands of operatives, rather than the flow of information or the making of large decisions. The most difficult problems are met when an organization has to transmit subtle information upward or varying orders downward, or when operatives must make a great many decisions. These are the conditions most conducive to a breakdown of hierarchical supervision. The output of the organization then becomes dependent on the judgment and structure of rewards of the operatives at the lowest level.

Hypothesis 40: *Failure is more likely when decisions must be made by operatives at the lower hierarchical levels.*

The difficulty of maintaining control in such a situation is aggravated when the contribution to output of each employee is difficult to measure. This basic control problem was not appreciated by many of the successful businessmen called upon to implement wartime controls. Novick explained their failure consciously to develop administrative competence at the War Production Board by the fact that administrative machinery is so well developed in established businesses that it is taken for granted.[72] This explanation is certainly plausible, but the alternative—that the problem is much more difficult in government,

---

[70]Downs, *Inside Bureaucracy*, p. 57.

[71]Charles S. Hyneman, *Bureaucracy in a Democracy* (New York: Harper and Brothers, 1950), pp. 499 ff.

[72]David Novick, Melvin Anshen, and W. C. Truppner, *Wartime Production Controls* (New York: Columbia University Press, 1949).

where results are hard to judge and employees can rarely be fired—may be equally valid.

Beveridge stressed the difference between modes of conduct in business and government. The former emphasizes speed, individual decision, and secrecy, whereas the latter stresses deliberation, accuracy, and openness to scrutiny, often with the referral of documents to an unnecessarily large number of people.[73] The characteristics of government—and Beveridge probably exaggerates the difference between large businesses and government—result from attempts to maintain parliamentary control under the difficult circumstances imposed by the nature of the tasks. The time-consuming nature of these control devices does, however, suggest a very real disadvantage for government bureaucracies in dealing with fast-changing and unique situations.

The tendency to consult other people about every decision can naturally be carried to further extremes as the organization increases in size. In addition to the losses of control cumulating through the various echelons, Brecht suggests that increased size of the agency makes access to its head more difficult, and this, combined with the growing number of conflicts among the growing number of officials (conflicts that must be mediated by the head), makes the enterprise increasingly inefficient.[74]

Hypothesis 41: *Failure is more likely the larger the size of the agency.*

This is an exceedingly difficult hypothesis to test, however, for tasks differ so much in ease of supervision that it would be ludicrous to suppose that the Postal Service is less efficient than the CIA just because it is larger. If unambiguous measures of efficiency were available for different times, it might be possible to relate changes in size to changes in efficiency for particular agencies. This, too, would present numerous problems, but the main difficulty is the lack of measures of efficiency. Studies of economies of scale in the provision of municipal or state services are relevant to this issue.[75]

Large size does have some advantages. In the smallest size range, the economies of scale that result from specialization and fuller use of indivisible inputs are important. Starbuck mentions such additional advantages as reduction in errors through larger sample size, greater resistance to change and therefore to outside pressure, greater spending on research and development and hence more stability and control over the

---

[73]William Henry Beveridge, *The Public Service in War & In Peace* (London: Constable, 1920), pp. 17–18.

[74]Arnold Brecht, "How Bureaucracies Develop and Function," *The Annals of the American Academy of Political and Social Science,* 292 (March 1954) issue on "Bureaucracy and Democratic Government": 7.

[75]Werner Z. Hirsch, *Urban Economic Analysis* (New York: McGraw-Hill, 1973), pp. 316–318.

environment.[76] Kaufman speculates that flexibility increases with size and centralization.[77] Similarly, since flexibility increases the chance of survival, old organizations are more flexible, on average, than new ones; therefore, the life expectancy of an organization increases with its age. Both Starbuck and Kaufman are concerned with the organization's survival and success in pursuing its own goals, rather than the objectives in the legislation. Hence some of their comments about the strength and stability of large organizations need not conflict with the judgment that larger organizations will fail to carry out legislative intent. Their conjectures, however, do disagree with those that associate large size with internal confusion.

Although Kaufman suggested that centralization is associated with flexibility, Schlesinger warned that it may lead to oversimplified analysis and neglect of messy qualifications and contingencies. While still an analyst of bureaucracy, before becoming a practitioner, he discussed the centralization of the Department of Defense brought about by strengthening the Office of Secretary of Defense (OSD):

> What does seem certain, however, is that the energy and imaginativeness of OSD personnel will decline. . . . The challenge of change attracts individuals of extraordinary merit. When creative fervor wanes, such individuals go elsewhere. As persons with lesser over-all ability inherit the system, lacking experience in its creation and in the reasons for change, the Nation may reap fewer of the benefits and begin to incur heavier costs . . . *de facto* decentralization, flowing from reduced ability at the center, may mitigate the effects. Nevertheless, a system placing a disproportionately high premium on the imaginativeness of a few critically placed men is peculiarly vulnerable to a decline of ability in men in key positions.[78]

By introducing the additional variable of the ability of the people at the center, Schlesinger has complicated the analysis somewhat and the testing substantially. Focus on centralization and the question of innovation does suggest one testable hypothesis:

Hypothesis 42: *Failure is more likely the further up in the hierarchy a program originates.*

The basic reasoning behind this was suggested by Hoffman.[79] The people with the operating experience are at low levels in the hierarchy.

---

[76]William H. Starbuck, "Organizational Growth and Development," chapter 11 of March, ed., *Handbook of Organizations.*

[77]Herbert Kaufman, *The Limits of Organizational Change* (University, Alabama: The University of Alabama Press, 1971), pp. 98–101.

[78]James R. Schlesinger, *Defense Planning and Budgeting: The Issue of Centralized Control* (Washington, D.C.: Industrial College of the Armed Forces, 1968), "National Security Management Monograph Series," p. 13.

[79]Fred S. Hoffman, "Public Expenditure Analysis and the Institutions of the Executive Branch," chapter 17 of Haveman and Margolis, p. 437.

As one moves toward the White House (and Congress), the breadth of view and willingness to propose large departures may increase, but the grasp of details decreases. The new programs initiated at the lowest levels will be less venturesome and more likely to work. If this is so, the flexibility of the centralized organization mentioned by Kaufman may be largely illusory, or depend on the extraordinarily able people who, as indicated by Schlesinger, achieve the centralization and then depart for more exciting ventures.

CONCLUSIONS

The extraordinary range of disagreement about the sources of failure collected so far, which will be expanded many fold in the succeeding chapters, suggests that the analysis has not advanced far beyond that of Jevons in 1867.[80] He raised the question of why government activities seem to range from the extremes of efficiency to the extremes of inefficiency. The answer he developed was that some activities, such as the Post Office, have such inherent economies of scale that even the mismanagement to be expected of government will not offset them. Government is incapable of administering capital efficiently or of accounting for its use correctly (a criticism which is still valid on both sides of the Atlantic) or of dealing with nonroutine circumstances.

The overall impression from reading the popular literature, the casual observations of intelligent people, and the attempts at models of hierarchical control is that government is impossible. Governments do exist, however, so it is important to try to resolve the contradiction. The first explanation is that in an economic sense much of government does not function. This is Tullock's dismal conclusion to which we return in Chapter 20.

The second explanation is that nonhierarchical controls of various sorts accomplish what the hierarchical controls are apparently unable to achieve. Many thoughtful observers have been forced to adopt this position. The alternative controls may keep the bureaucracy from running amuck, but they will not move it in the same direction as would perfect hierarchical control. The sources of control, and the probable directions of bias, are the main topics of the next two chapters.

---

[80]W. S. Jevons, "On the Analogy between the Post Office, Telegraphs, and Other Systems of Conveyance of the United Kingdom, As Regards Government Control" (1867), reprinted in *Methods of Social Reform* (New York: Augustus M. Kelley, 1965), pp. 277–292. This collection of essays was first published in London in 1883.

CHAPTER 3

Political Control of Bureaucracy

SOME CONCEPTUAL CONSIDERATIONS

The economic argument for varying the size of government is that the change will make the individual citizens happier. This innocent criterion rests on shaky ethical foundations and denies the possibility of national goals that transcend the preferences of individuals.[1] Nevertheless, its practical alternative as a criterion for government action is some form of minority rule.

The jump from individual preferences to government activities that will advance them is fraught with problems. First, in the absence of coercion, consumers will not reveal their preferences for goods. The market forces them to reveal their preferences for private goods because those who do not pay are excluded from consuming the good (the exclusion principle). The consumer reveals that watching a movie is not worth $2.50 to him when he refuses to pay that admission fee. Markets do not work well when either (*a*) excluding nonpayers is difficult or (*b*) the cost of serving an additional person is very low once the good is

---

[1]The ethical questions are explored by Sidney Alexander, "Human Values and Economists' Values," chapter 2 in *Human Values and Economic Policy*, ed. Sidney Hook (New York:New York University Press, 1967).

provided to anyone. Other cases will be considered in Part III, but the fundamental economic argument is that government enables consumers to satisfy their individual preferences more fully when markets fail to work perfectly.

Governments coerce their subjects to pay for public activities, so the relationship between the taxes one pays and one's estimate of the value of government activities is remote even in the legendary New England town meeting. It becomes increasingly tenuous in more complex forms of government.[2] In particular, delegating fiscal decisions to representatives who vote on many issues, some not even formulated at the time of the election, attenuates the connection between individual preferences and the size and composition of the budget.

Preferences of individuals differ markedly, moreover. In private markets the variation among families in, for example, the proportion of income spent on durable goods or recreation is substantial and the differences are larger if one looks at particular expenditures. In the private market each family allocates its own income; in the public sector, however, decisions made by government are imposed on all within the district. Thus some taxpayers protest their tax support of a CIA that they consider immoral, whereas others regret that they must support anything except the Defense Department and the FBI. Some relief from the compulsion inherent in public goods is afforded by differences between jurisdictions, but although new entrants to a metropolitan area may consider the quality of public services (chiefly schools) in choosing a home, few will cross state lines to suit their preferences for public services and fewer still will move to a different nation.

When tastes differ, it is also possible to encounter the "paradox of voting," under which no way of amalgamating the preferences of different individuals is fully consistent with common ideas about what seems reasonable.[3] In view of such problems, we know that laws written by a representative assembly may not reflect individual preferences, but what better choice do we have than to assume that they do?

[2]James Buchanan explored this relationship in *Public Finance in Democratic Process: Fiscal Institutions and Individual Choice* (Chapel Hill:The University of North Carolina Press, 1967).

[3]The ancient paradox is incorporated into Kenneth Arrow's classic work *Social Choice and Individual Values* (New York: Wiley, 1963 [1st ed., 1951]). Chewing over the theoretical issues raised by Arrow has kept myriads of dissertation writers out of mischief. That the problem is of little practical consequence is demonstrated by Gordon Tullock, "The General Irrelevance of the General Impossibility Theorem," *Quarterly Journal of Economics* 81 (2), (May, 1967): 256–270. Mancur Olson notes that the instability of choice expected as a result of the naive reading of the paradox is simply not a common form of behavior in democratic government, see "Evaluating Performance in the Public Sector," in *The Measurement of Economic and Social Performance* (New York:Columbia University Press for the NBER, 1973), p. 358.

Most economic analysis presupposes that the bureaucracy implements exactly the program specified in the law. This is equivalent to the classical approach in political science: Congress sets policy, which is then administered by the executive branch. Until recently, political science also has ignored implementation almost completely. Some of the broader streams in the political science literature are worth reviewing, however, both to highlight differences between the economists' and the political scientists' approaches and to see how the political setting modifies the hierarchical model.

Just as theoretical analyses and empirical observations have demonstrated that simple hierarchical control does not work, so also have modern political scientists rejected the notion of a strict dichotomy between politics and administration. Administration, too, is a political process, but this implies that the results of government action may differ from the legislation—just as the legislation may depart from the preferences of individual citizens.

The question of the degree of control by elected officials over bureaucracy has been phrased in both a positive way, "Can elected officials control the bureaucracy?" and in a normative way, "Should elected officials control the bureaucracy?" The focus in this book is on the positive question, but even to ask the normative question seems so bizarre to one steeped in the economic tradition of consumer sovereignty that it provokes close scrutiny. One argument holds that many decisions are too technical to be made by anyone except the experts in the bureaucracy. The attractiveness of delegating social decisions to value-free scientists has been waning as the public has learned that environmental decisions, for example, require choosing among deleterious side-effects affecting different people. When faced with such complex issues, it is not clear that the scientifically illiterate voters and their equally unprepared representatives can maintain control over the technicians and professionals. Nevertheless, acknowledging the practical problems is far removed from advocating that technicians make decisions involving the values and preferences of citizens.

The penchant for purely technical solutions seems, surprisingly, to retain a stronger grip in the social sciences. The professional-control literature, discussed in Chapter 4, is one example. A stronger illustration is afforded by Marris and Rein.[4] They argue that, since the bureaucracy in the United States has little independence in carrying out legislative orders (in contrast to the autonomy it enjoys in the United Kingdom), it

---

[4]Peter Marris and Martin Rein, *Dilemmas of Social Reform: Poverty and Community Action in the United States* (Chicago:Aldine, 2nd ed., 1973).

must continue to cultivate pressure groups in order to retain the political strength to placate Congress. Government agencies in the United States cannot, therefore, be effective agents for social change, whereas British agencies, unhampered by the need to obtain consensus, can be. This may be taken as a positive statement that the bureaucracy of the United States is better controlled than that of the United Kingdom, but the language connotes that political control interferes with the resolution of conflicts of interest.

This view contrasts with the glorification of pressure groups that has colored much of the literature of political science in the United States. Mancur Olson's fine review of pressure group theories need not be repeated here, but a few comments are necessary.[5] Those who see no special need for legislative control over bureaucracy include those who argue that government agencies are subject to substantially the same political forces, exercised by the pressure groups, as is the legislature. Whatever action is taken by the agency will, in this view, correspond with legislative intent. (It might conflict with the words of the legislation, but this would indicate that Congress had written down the wrong words or that the pressures had changed, and that the legislation should, therefore, be revised or ignored.)

If group interests determine political behavior, as Latham, Bentley, Truman and many others have argued, then the form of government and such details as the types of controls imposed upon the bureaucracy are irrelevant. The extreme form of this view leaves no room for further scientific analysis: Whatever is is right, so there is no point in further discussion! More moderate approaches recognize the great importance of pressure groups in the political process, but also accept the possibility that the institutional structure of government may influence government action. It is meaningful to ask how a particular change in bureaucratic structure or political controls might influence outcomes and also to use that information to evaluate various changes with reference to some ideal, such as majority rule. One of the key elements for answering both kinds of questions is provided by Olson's book, which corrects the fundamental error of the pressure group theories by indicating which interests are likely to be represented and which are likely to be ignored. This will be examined shortly.

A slight variation on this approach is to argue that bureaucracy, rather than responding to the same forces, is actually a more representative body than is Congress. Long, for example, asserts that "Important and

---

[5]Mancur Olson, *The Logic of Collective Action* (Cambridge:Harvard University Press, 1965), chapter 5.

vital interests in the United States are unrepresented, underrepresented, or malrepresented in Congress. These interests receive more effective and more responsible representation through administrative channels than through the legislature."[6]

The chain of argument that leads some to the necessity or desirability of having the political forces act directly on administration leads others to a different conclusion—that the bureaucrats themselves should be drawn from the various social classes in order to be truly representative.[7] Naturally, if the interest groups determine government actions as tightly as Bentley would have us believe, the social origins of bureaucrats are irrelevant for predicting government behavior. Bentley's bureaucrats are automatons just as the bureaucrats of public expenditure theory are, but they carry out the policies determined by group pressures, rather than the policies preferred by individual citizens. From a sociological perspective, however, the ideology of the individual bureaucrat is presumed to be an important influence on his official behavior—hence the studies of the class origins of bureaucrats and questioning of whether middle-class civil servants can implement socialist policies. The basic Marxist presumption that individuals act in the interests of their social class has been shown by Olson to imply a very peculiar form of irrationality; namely, that people will choose to disregard their own interests in order to work in the interests of a particular class, rather than society as a whole or some other group.[8] Unless one assumes that people have this form of irrationality, the literature on social origins is irrelevant to the problem of control of bureaucracy.

Finally, it is possible to argue that the bureaucracy should be directly responsible to the people. This notion has the ring of "New Left, 1970" about it. The problems of organizing any program or government in which individual bureaucrats interpret the will of the people directly

---

[6]Norton E. Long, *The Polity* (Chicago:Rand McNally, 1962), p. 68; see also Carl A. Auerbach, "Pluralism and the Administrative Process," pp. 1–13 of "The Government as Regulator," March 1972 issue of *The Annals* of The American Academy of Political and Social Science 400, ed. Marver H. Bernstein; and Joseph Pratt Harris, *Congressional Control of Administration* (Washington:Brookings, 1964). Also note the more traditional views in Charles S. Hyneman, *Bureaucracy in a Democracy* (New York:Harper, 1950); and Peter Woll, *American Bureaucracy* (New York:Norton, 1963), pp. 69–80. Herbert Kaufman discusses the shifting emphases among representativeness, neutral competence, and executive leadership in "Emerging Conflicts in the Doctrines of Public Administration," *American Political Science Review* 50, 1956, pp. 1057–1074.

[7]The foremost example of this view is John Donald Kingsley, *Representative Bureaucracy: An Interpretation of the British Civil Service* (Yellow Springs, Ohio:Antioch Press, 1944); but it is also expressed elsewhere, including John Merriman Gaus, *Reflections on Public Administration* (University, Alabama:University of Alabama Press, 1947), p. 131.

[8]Olson *The Logic of Collective Action*, pp. 102–110.

instead of listening to spokesmen for groups and carrying out the directives of legislatures seem insurmountable. This normative position in its stark form is not seriously advocated by scholars.

In the more elegant guise of the public interest, however, the same notion makes frequent appearances (in the writings on public administration of those who despair of the possibility of hierarchical control, for example). Hyneman is the quintessence of the classical approach in commenting that "the bureaucracy must be under the direction and control of elected officials. If the elected officials cannot direct and control the bureaucracy, who is there to see to it that the bureaucracy provides the kind and quality of government that the people want?"[9] Rather plaintively he then suggests: "Any large organization must operate in large part on faith. It is not possible to police all the individuals who hold important positions in the organization, coercing them to do what otherwise they might not do . . . men understand . . . and voluntarily do what others expect them to do."[10]

Thompson, although not joining Hyneman in the retreat to pious hopes, suggests that (*a*) hierarchical control is impossible (for the reasons already sketched); and (*b*) no one is interested in trying to attain it, given the narrow legislative constituencies and the limited energy of the President. His solution is to accept the existing situation in which the agencies create their own constituencies (interest groups), which have technical   competence   and   interest   in   the   subject   matter— "administrative constituencies which are both able to participate in policy-making, to evaluate the result, and to reward or punish the policy makers." The role of the central authority "is not control of policy but providing a legitimate means for interfering in policy whenever it seems politically desirable to do so."[11]

The normative and the positive elements are tightly tangled in the arguments of both the exponents of the classical control arguments and the pressure group analysts. The former are often in a quandary when the legislature passes laws that benefit only very narrow special interests. The latter have no basis for suggesting institutional changes unless they want to postulate such goals as democratic control or presidential power, which, are inconsistent with the most ruthlessly Bentlian extension of the pressure group arguments. The two approaches cannot really be reconciled. The one starts with the explicit value judgment of con-

[9]Hyneman, *Bureaucracy in a Democracy* p. 15.
[10]Ibid.
[11]Victor A. Thompson, "Bureaucracy in a Democratic Society," chapter 11 in *Public Administration and Democracy:Essays in Honor of Paul H. Appleby*, ed. Roscoe Coleman Martin (Syracuse, New York:Syracuse University Press, 1965), pp. 207–211.

sumer sovereignty, but encounters so many scientific problems (or ignores them) on its way to policy conclusions that the conclusions are thoroughly suspect. The other starts from the rudimentary positive analysis of pressure groups, but gathers in so many implicit value judgments that it, too, arrives at suspect (or no) policy recommendations. Perhaps it is best under these circumstances merely to state the assumptions, whether positive or normative, and to let the analysis proceed from them.

This was the approach that Maass took when he began his analysis of the Army Corps of Engineers.[12] Yet despite the effort to be realistic, the list of assumptions is as utopian as the most platitudinous public administration literature; for the agency, according to Maass, is to exercise discretion not only in how to do things, but also in what to do and who shall benefit. At the same time, the agency should answer to the President and his program, and through the President to the legislature. It should not, however, serve the President in his role as party politician, but only in his role as chief executive. Meanwhile the agency should build a constituency of pressure groups to which it should be somewhat responsive, but it should not try to answer directly to the general public.

Although the assumptions are too ambiguous to serve as criteria for success of the agency, they do clearly differ in emphasis from those of the hierarchical model. It is traditional to assume that bureaucrats are to be allowed technical discretion in meeting the legislated objectives most efficiently. The two difficulties with this are the impossibility of drawing a rigid distinction between technical and other questions (the choice of controlling floods through high dams or low dams is, in a sense, technical; yet it has numerous other ramifications), and the fact that the administrator has his own motives, which need not lead to the most efficient solution of even a purely technical question.

Although the responsibility of the bureaucrat to pressure groups is the main point of disagreement with the classical theory, another major issue for Maass was the strength of the President relative to Congress. The Corps of Engineers has traditionally ignored the President by appealing directly to Congress. In one sense, it is the ultimate in hierarchical control to attempt to subject all agencies to rigid coordination according to the President's policies. In another sense, however, it is somewhat ironic to try to deny to the legislature the possibility of direct control over the agency's activities once it is acknowledged that the direct line of control through the hierarchy does break down. In the case of the Army

[12]Arthur Maass, *Muddy Waters:The Army Engineers and the Nation's Rivers* (Cambridge:Harvard University Press, 1951).

Engineers, of course, the localized nature of the benefits combines with congressional representation by districts to create an unsatisfactory situation.

Maass strikes a much more balanced position than, for example, Long, who glorifies lack of presidential control as a sign that the pressure groups are doing their work.[13] The balance comes, however, at the expense of a certain flavor of contradiction: Can the agency really be responsive both to the strong President and to the pressure groups? In any event, to combine strong presidential control with the norm of greater responsiveness to private pressure groups than to the legislature seems somewhat eccentric, and it might be difficult to design institutions to achieve that if it were the agreed goal.

INTEREST GROUPS IN THE POLITICAL PROCESS

Theories of pressure groups in the political process, despite the years of reiteration and refinement, are not sufficiently well-developed to offer many interesting hypotheses about failure of government programs. The reasons for this gap in the literature include (*a*) the peculiar general neglect by scholars of the possibility that government programs may fail; (*b*) the temptation implicit in pressure-group theories to consider any outcome as the successful resolution of the particular set of pressure that is thereby revealed to have existed—an approach that precludes the possibility of observing failure; and (*c*) the difficulty of defining failure if one departs from the word of the law as the ultimate criterion.

Many studies have confirmed that interest groups influence all phases of the political process, including legislation, administrative development of implementing regulations, administrative development of standard procedures, administration, and evolution of legislation.[14] In an attempt to move beyond that basic insight Edelman offered the following general observations after studying a particular case:

[13]Long, *The Polity*, p. 56.

[14]Among the classics are E. Pendleton Herring, *Public Administration and the Public Interest* (New York:McGraw-Hill, 1936); David B. Truman, *The Governmental Process* (New York:Alfred A. Knopf, 1951); Marver H. Bernstein, *Regulating Business by Independent Commission* (Princeton:Princeton University Press, 1955); and Avery Leiserson, *Administrative Regulation:A Study in Representation of Interests* (Chicago:University of Chicago Press, 1942). A particularly good study of the alignment of firms and groups on one issue is provided by Raymond A. Bauer, Ithiel de Sola Pool, and Lewis Anthony Dexter, *American Business & Public Policy:The Politics of Foreign Trade* (Chicago:Aldine-Atherton, 2nd ed. with new prologue, 1972 [1st publ. 1963]). The later phases in the process are analyzed by Eugene Bardach, *The Implementation Game:What Happens after a Bill Becomes a Law* (Cambridge:MIT Press, 1977).

Proposition 1. The larger the number of interests which come to the attention of a single organizational unit, the less influential is any one of them likely to be.

Proposition 2. An interest able to affect other groups adversely through private action is at an advantage in its competition with rival interests in a governmental unit.

Proposition 3. Interests which are not part of the constituency or which make up a relatively small part of it are at a disadvantage.

Proposition 4. Governmental agencies represent to higher levels of the governmental hierarchy the "accommodated" interests of the groups that bring pressure upon them. Groups so represented enjoy an advantage over interests which must intercede directly on their own behalf with the higher levels of the governmental hierarchy.

Proposition 5. Fairly rigid separation of a subordinate agency from its superior agencies gives the interests represented by the subordinate agency a relatively stronger position.[15]

The propositions about agency behavior relative to the pressures suggest some hypotheses about agency behavior relative to legislative objectives, which are influenced by the same pressures differently weighted:

Hypothesis 43: *Failure is more likely the greater the discrepancy between the interests focused on the operative agency and those focused on the legislature.*

Sometimes the organizational form and procedures of a bureau will leave particular agencies within that bureau to deal with strong outside forces. This leads to a similar hypothesis:

Hypothesis 44: *Failure is more likely the more narrow are the interests expressed by the clients of an agency.*

Proposition 5 can be restated to afford an additional hypothesis, which is not nearly as trivial as it appears at first sight:

Hypothesis 45: *Failure is more likely the greater the independence of the subordinate agency from the larger organization.*

In the hierarchical model, independence of hierarchical control is practically synonymous with failure to follow orders. It is significant that the interest group approach leads to the same conclusion via a different route. The interests represented within an agency are always fewer than the interests that focus on an entire bureau or the legislature. Hence narrowing the focus to the agency level and leaving the agency independent leaves the narrow interests in control of agency policy.

---

[15]Murray Edelman, "Governmental Organization and Public Policy," *Public Administration Review* XII, no. 4 (Autumn 1952): 278–282.

Sometimes Congress retains control of the appointment of the head of the bureau and limits the authority of the department secretary over him. New administrative regulations, for example, may be issued by the bureau chief, rather than by the secretary. In such a situation the bureau is relatively independent of hierarchical control. Whether it departs from legislative intent depends on the vigilance of Congress in overseeing the bureau, and on the forces impinging on the committees charged with special concern for it.

An agency may also acquire independence by the alignment of pressure groups, but the theory is ambiguous and the predictions are contradictory. Bernstein argues that Congress is more likely to intervene when the interested groups agree, whereas the agency facing rival groups can balance one against the other.[16] This contradicts the observation that controversy gives the next higher level more power by raising issues to its attention.[17] The most plausible interpretation is that an agency can deviate from legislation more easily if it deviates in the direction favored by a united group of clients. Bernstein suggests that the agency least subject to legislative scrutiny is the one without an organized constituency, which generally means that it is operating in a noncontroversial area or that neither the costs nor the benefits of its actions are focused narrowly enough to concern anyone. At the other extreme, great administrative discretion to impose costs or confer benefits brings close legislative scrutiny.

This leaves open the question of whether Congress is more likely to legislate in an area where the interests are conflicting or where they are unified. In the latter case, the interest groups will hold the agency to the legislation, but the legislation might well depart from consumer preferences. Although politicians may prefer to ignore a controversial area, public outcry may force some legislative action. As the popular fervor wanes, the original sources of support for a program or agency may gradually be replaced by a distinctive agency clientele. As the interests of the clientele evolve, the agency may gradually shift its objectives so they are no longer consistent with legislative intent.[18]

Hypothesis 46: *Failure is more likely when the legislated goals do not conform to the interests of the clientele.*

---

[16]Marver H. Bernstein, *The Job of the Federal Executive* (Washington:Brookings, 1958), p. 103.

[17]William W. Boyer, *Bureaucracy on Trial:Policy Making by Government Agencies* (New York:Bobbs-Merrill, 1964), p. 47.

[18]Joseph L. Bower, "Descriptive Decision Theory from the 'Administrative' Viewpoint," chapter 3 of *The Study of Policy Formation*, ed. Raymond A. Bauer and Kenneth J. Gergen (New York:The Free Press of Macmillan Co., 1968), pp. 122 ff; Marris and Rein, *Dilemmas of Social Reform* pp. 258-259.

The legislation may evolve to remain consistent with the behavior of the agency, but only if the changes do not stir up forces such as public interest groups.

Sometimes a program attracts a clientele after it is already in operation. The implications of various legislative proposals may not be clear to affected groups, or the groups may not be formed until after the program is in operation, a phenomenon that is examined next. Wilson recounts the difficulties of lobbyists in persuading firms to take stands on legislation, because the issues seem remote compared with the pressure of daily business and individuals within the firm disagree about the correct position on legislation dealing with complex issues.[19] The exact impact of a bill is often difficult to predict, moreover, until the bureaucrats write the regulations. Once the program is in operation, however, the interests of various firms are focused on the specifics of its implementation. At this stage the pressures may induce the agency to depart from legislative intent or to try to amend the legislation in a direction not envisioned by its original sponsors.

Although Sharkansky contended that "A different approach to political accountability is direct client participation in agency decisions," many of the interest group theorists have expressed concern over the disparate influence of various groups, particularly at the implementation stage.[20] The concern has been especially strong in relation to the unorganized and often unrepresented consumer interest in regulatory proceedings. Leiserson, for example, recognized the danger to the unrepresented in his 1942 book, as did Truman in 1951. The former, however, could also state that "the general acclaim of the Interstate Commerce Commission as a model of administrative regulation both by students and by affected groups is generally attributed to its careful maintenance of the forms of judicial impartiality and restraint."[21] The ICC has few defenders among its students today, both because of the slowness of its procedures and its lack of concern for anyone but the regulated parties.[22] By the time that Bernstein wrote his study of regulation in 1955, he treated as commonplace the observation that regulatory commissions are captured by their clients. Indeed, his book is an attempt to document the occurrence and to explain the reasons, which include the absence of

[19]James Q. Wilson, *Political Organizations* (New York:Basic Books, 1973), p. 313.

[20]Ira Sharkansky, *Public Administration:Policy-Making in Government Agencies* (Chicago:Markham, 1970), p. 76.

[21]Leiserson, *Administrative Regulation*, p. 55.

[22]For studies of the results of ICC regulation, see e.g., James C. Nelson, *Railroad Transportation and Public Policy* (Washington:Brookings, 1959); Paul W. MacAvoy and John W. Snow, *Regulation of Entry and Pricing in Truck Transportation:Ford Administration Papers on Regulatory Reform* (Washington:American Enterprise Institute for Public Policy Research, 1977).

presidential involvement and the excessive devotion to adjudication of individual cases.[23]

Another explanation for regulatory failure is the mass of information that can easily overwhelm people who want to remain informed. The amount of effort a person or organization is willing to devote to a topic ordinarily depends on the benefits to be gained. As Leone points out, this applies to Congress as well as the public, with the result that most work is delegated to committees, most members are ignorant of most issues, and lobbyists can concentrate their efforts on a few key people.[24]

These remarks need not be restricted to regulation. When Congress is under pressure to solve a problem, it may find it simpler to pass a very general law that attracts little opposition, but leaves the serious political work of reconciling diverse interests to the agency. There the parties who are directly affected influence the outcome more strongly. Bardach also suggests that fear of losses is the strongest motive during the implementation process, perhaps because the losers are more readily identified than the gainers, which means that the most active parties will try to block implementation.[25]

Hypothesis 47: *Failure is more likely the more policy decisions are left to the agency.*

The legislation could be sufficiently open-ended so that failure could not be proved. Ordinarily, however, the legislative purposes are explicit even when they are contradictory.

In *The Logic of Collective Action*, Mancur Olson provides the theoretical explanation for the disproportionate influence of regulated firms and other directly affected parties long observed by interest-group theorists.[26] If individuals always acted in the interests of the groups of which they are members, consumers would repeal legislation benefiting producers. Olson explains their failure to do so by the basic economic postulate: A person will act in his own interest. In particular, he will add to his purchase of a good or service only as long as the benefit to him of an extra unit exceeds the cost to him of that unit. When the activity benefits all members of a group, each person weighs the total cost of the additional unit against the fraction of the benefit that accrues to him. If all individuals in a large group act rationally, no one contributes anything. Once a group is in existence and has some way to compel mem-

---

[23]Marver H. Bernstein *Regulating Business by Independent Commission*, pp. 3, 4, 73.

[24]Richard C. Leone, "Public Interest Advocacy and the Regulatory Process," in Bernstein, ed., "The Government as Regulator," p. 49.

[25]Bardach, *The Implementation Game*, p. 42.

[26]Olson, *The Logic of Collective Action*, chapters 5 and 6.

bership or to prevent nonmembers from obtaining significant benefits, it can levy dues or taxes to support the activity. Governments are in this position, as are certain other groups. Consumers are not.

Which groups are organized enough to exert any pressure? Olson concludes that the size of the group is the most important determinant of the adequacy of the collective good (such as lobbying activity) that the group obtains. The reasons are that the smaller the group (*a*) the larger the share of total benefits that each member obtains; (*b*) the greater the chance that each member will notice the behavior of others, and hence that implicit or explicit bargaining will evolve; and (*c*) the smaller the costs of organization that have to be borne. Thus small groups are more likely to organize and produce the optimum quantity of output than large ones; so interests that are common to only a few firms or individuals will be more fully represented than those common to large numbers of people. Professional organizations and trade associations can support lobbying activities because members of the profession or trade find the private benefits of membership, such as journals, employment exchanges, and conferences, worth the cost of the dues.[27] Similarly, labor unions are a political force, but they retain their membership through activities that serve the individual member, legal compulsion, or vigorous social pressure. Various organizations offer social activities, insurance policies, or information about consumer durable goods in order to attract members to support the lobbying activities that serve even those who pay no dues.

At the legislative stage the political pressures are systematically biased (from the viewpoint of the preferences of the citizens in general) in favor of occupational and industrial interests and the interests of other small groups. The bias is even stronger at the implementation stage. Some forms of activity at the legislative stage are general enough and inexpensive enough so that firms, public-interest groups, and even individuals can make contributions to the general debate. Individuals may participate either for personal gain or for idealistic reasons, but most people will not invest much money or effort unless they expect financial gain. Public-interest lobbying groups may be able to represent the interests of a large proportion of the population in some rough way for the handful of issues that attract major press coverage. Even in these particularly favorable instances, however, small groups still have the advantages of unambiguous goals, fewer compromises among different interests within the organization, and greater resources relative to the few issues of special concern.

---

[27]Ibid., chapter 6, but see the critique by Wilson, *Political Organizations*. p. 277.

Once the political process advances to the regulation writing stage, it becomes quieter (less interesting to the news media) and narrower. The innumerable questions involved in, for example, writing the implementing regulations for even such a well-publicized piece of legislation as the Federal Water Pollution Control Act Amendments of 1972 are highly technical and specific to particular industries and circumstances. It becomes, therefore an immense task to keep track of implementation in any general way; instead, the experts in particular segments concentrate their attention on them. Similarly, the Washington representatives for trade associations and other narrow interests concentrate their attention on particular parts of the regulations.

Hypothesis 48: *Failure is more likely the less widely diffused is technical expertise in the program area.*

If expertise in a regulated area is limited to the industry, the agency will have difficulty writing coherent implementing regulations without relying on the industry and risking a pro-industry bias. Even where a layman is able to grasp the technical knowledge, the costs of acquiring information and intervening in every decision increase rapidly as the general law branches into specific regulations. Similarly, for the public the payoff for any specific intervention—limited as it is to a narrow part of the problem—declines. Simultaneously, as the issues become more specific, the cost of intervention declines for special interests, whereas the potential benefit of specifically targeted regulations increases. Furthermore, the implications for the firm become obvious enough to motivate executives who ignored the abstractions of the law.

When regulations are applied to a specific firm, it and others bound by the precedent are the only ones concerned. At that level, the law is specific to one firm, but the decisions about numerous special cases eventually determine the policy. Information about the legislative stage is available in the better newspapers; information about the regulations requires either the effort of checking the Federal Register, paying someone to do the checking, or membership in an organization that supplies that information. The interpretations in specific instances, however, are beyond the resources of anyone but the specialist. The conclusion is quite straightforward: The political forces bearing on bureaucracy, far from duplicating the forces bearing on Congress as Bentley and Truman postulated, are systematically and inevitably much narrower and more specific. When Congress passes unfinished legislation that is to be completed by bureaucrats, therefore, the results will not correspond to the expectations of the broad coalition that worked for the legislation.

Olson's theory of group action has been criticized for its overemphasis

on economic motivations and neglect of the role of the political entre-
preneurs, who are capable of rallying latent groups for political purposes.[28] The concept of the entrepreneur helps to explain how large
groups come to be organized and the sources of popular support for
particular laws. Entrepreneurship, however, is of no importance in the
quiet phases during which legislation is implemented, so it may provide
another explanation for the divergence of results from legislated intent.
The legislation may respond to the publicity generated by the entrepreneur, but the implementation responds to more persistent forces.

The government agency, itself, often fosters the organization of an
interest group that can appeal to elected officials on behalf of the program of the agency. The effort of the Department of Agriculture to
establish strong farm organizations is a classic case.[29] More recently the
Office of Economic Opportunity tried to organize the poor. Even when
the agency does not intend it, however, information about the complex
regulations and ongoing interpretations and revisions is a new collective
good for the regulated parties. The predictable result is the formation of
some organization to keep track of agency activities, report to the members, and transmit the opinions of members to the agency. This is a
pressure group.

Once the interest group exists and has a working relationship with the
agency it can adopt the standard practices described by Boyer.[30] These
include (a) direct complaints about existing rules, which initiated more
than half of the rule-change proceedings in the case he studied; (b)
attempts to have the agency adopt the standards of conduct of the professional association as the rules and regulations for occupational licens-
ing by the state, preferably allowing the association (or union) to administer the testing; and (c) informal preliminary conferences between
the agency and the organization to identify burdensome provisions of
proposed policies, forecast problems of administration, and obtain the
consent of all parties. None of this is improper. In administering complex legislation it is folly to ignore the experts. When all the experts are
interested parties, however, the bias of the process is obvious.

Another bias stems from the fear of losses noted previously.

Hypothesis 49: *Failure is more likely in programs that threaten to impose
identifiable costs on organized groups.*

---

[28]Wilson, *Political Organizations,* pp. 195–211.
[29]Olson, *The Logic of Collective Action,* pp. 149–153; Truman, *The Governmental Process,*
pp. 55, 79, also cites examples of government activities that have facilitated the formation
of interest groups.
[30]Boyer, *Bureaucracy on Trial,* pp. 22–30.

The legislative process overemphasizes programs providing specific benefits to identifiable groups at the expense of widely diffused costs; and the losers can be appeased with special benefits. The combination of these forces at the legislative and implementation stages tends toward expansion of functions, budgets, and particular groups served at the expense of taxpayers and consumers as a whole.

POLITICAL MECHANISMS OF CONTROL

The vigilance of organized groups in protecting their own interests during the implementation stage subjects the bureaucracy to a measure of control, although the results are not identical with those that would result from a perfectly functioning hierarchical mechanism. Interest groups are only part of the political landscape, however; so it is necessary to examine other mechanisms for control.

One peculiarity of the U.S. political system is the contention between Congress and the President. This cannot be ignored in those aspects of government activity where the law provides only general guidelines, with the President nominally having broad authority to work out specific policies. Since Congress can conduct hearings and enact new legislation, disagreement between the President and Congress about policy poses special problems both for the bureaucrats involved and for the evaluators of their success in implementing policy.

Hypothesis 50: *Failure is more likely when the President and Congress disagree about policy.*

Of the cases analyzed in Part II, only in the compliance activities of the Federal Energy Administration was outright disagreement a significant factor. Although colorful and often complex, such cases are rare because of the limited range of problems to which the President can give his attention. The frequent disagreements during the legislative phase provide the fodder for popular political analysis. Such maneuvering can reflect genuine differences in objectives or judgment, but it often constitutes an attempt to assess the political forces, work out compromises, and obtain credit with the constituents. If the President is forced to accept a law over his veto, the issue must certainly be controversial enough so that congressional scrutiny would more than offset any lack of presidential diligence in administration. One might be more inclined to seek failure in areas where the President signs the bill without enthusiasm and proceeds to ignore the subsequent course of the program or where the President reluctantly acquiesces in certain provisions in order to enact desired portions of a bill.

If one were to try to draw a simple organization chart with Congress, as the board of directors, setting policy and the President serving as chief executive, the next steps below him would be as open to question as the top two. The cabinet members, themselves, are politicians by virtue of their office, regardless of background. The looseness of the President's control even at this level has been the subject of many an anecdote. Since the vast mass of decisions must be made without the President's knowledge and many of his orders will be ignored unless he is extremely careful in choosing what to order, the problems of exerting real control over even the apex of the hierarchy are immense.

It is at this point that the management consultants depart from the political scientists. If one accepts the premise that the bureaucracy is beyond hierarchical control, it makes sense to search for other methods that permit *some* form of control, rather than creating chaos by insisting on the impossible. One recommendation is that the President choose subordinates who agree with him. Hyneman suggests that they be "a part of the political leadership . . ." and that the bureau chiefs should be "men having a high loyalty to the party . . ."[31] With the looseness of party lines and ideology in the United States, however, this approach hardly seems to offer much coherence of policy.

Furthermore, when the President surrounds himself with political leaders, he is surrounding himself with able and ambitious climbers. If he chooses subordinates with ideological commitments or strong professional orientation, they, too, will be difficult to control.[32]

Whatever direct control the President actually retains over his immediate subordinates does not extend much beyond that. The jobs of secretaries and undersecretaries are difficult because the bureaus plus their constituent interests plus the interested congressional committees unite to oppose any effort by the department head to consolidate control in his own, or the President's, hands.[33] This inherent control problem is combined with the small amount of time remaining for supervision of subordinates after the necessary meetings with congressional committees, individual congressmen, interest groups, and heads of other agencies. Since the undersecretary, typically, is only resting in that position for 2 years as part of his flight upward in some other career,[34] he is rarely

---

[31]Hyneman, *Bureaucracy in a Democracy*, pp. 282–283.

[32]For an example, see Richard E. Neustadt's account of the disagreement between Truman and MacArthur in *Presidential Power:the Politics of Leadership* (New York:Wiley, 1960), pp. 44–46.

[33]Bernstein, *The Job of the Federal Executive*, p. 86.

[34]Assistant secretaries average 18 months to 2 years on the job, which takes at least 6 months to learn and may be vacant for many months between occupants, according to Rufus E. Miles, Jr., "Considerations for a President Bent on Reorganization," *Public Administration Review* 37, no. 2 (March–April 1977): 158.

able to discover what is happening, let alone influence the course of events.

Since the President can exert hierarchical control over only a few activities, the power has inevitably gravitated to Congress, but this means control of particular bureaus by particular committees. Some congressmen, through long tenure on a committee, have acquired great knowledge of particular functions; however, their knowledge may make them more persuasive supporters of the agency, not more trenchant critics.

In part because of its tendency to devolve into committee control, the very desirability of congressional control of administration has been called into question. Admirers of strict hierarchy, a strong President, parliamentary government, and pluralism have all criticized the practice. The former two positions have already been examined. Advocates of parliamentary forms must confront contradictions of their own. Howell suggests that British practice is to leave governing to the government, while Parliament confines itself to policy.[35] Morstein Marx suggests that the legislative leaders in a parliamentary government have greater knowledge of and concern with administration, which somehow makes them more willing to confine themselves to making general policy.[36] The problems faced by British cabinet officials in controlling the bureaucracy seem quite similar to those in the United States, however, if one is to judge by the memoirs of Richard Crossman.[37] Furthermore, Normanton comments on the obstacles to full accountability imposed by the Official Secrets Act, which severely restricts the indirect control initiated by the news media.[38]

At the opposite extreme from the glorification of the parliamentary form of the classical hierarchical model is the appeal to the desirability of multiple sources of power. In this view, the bureaucracy takes its place along with the other branches of government and various other forces, including pressure groups and the press, in performing the functions of government, including the setting of policy. As a positive description of what occurs the approach is easily defended, but it is also put forward as a norm. Riggs, for example, criticized "the unfounded assumption that

[35]David Howell, "Public Accountability:Trends and Parliamentary Implications," chapter 11, pp. 233–250 of Bruce L. R. Smith and D. C. Hague, *The Dilemma of Accountability in Modern Government:Independence versus Control* (London:MacMillan, 1971).
[36]Fritz Morstein Marx, *The Administrative State:An Introduction to Bureaucracy* (Chicago:University of Chicago Press, 1957), p. 15.
[37]Richard Crossman, *The Diaries of a Cabinet Minister; Volume I 1964–1966* (New York:Holt, Rinehart and Winston, 1975).
[38]E. L. Normanton, *Accountability and Audit of Governments:A Comparative Study* (New York:Praeger, 1966), p. 159.

elected assemblies ought to monopolize political power..."[39] He suggested that both policymaking and administration are performed better when a balance of power exists among bureaucracies, political parties, elected assemblies, courts, interest groups, the press, and professional associations. It is not clear how balance of power is to be defined, or what mechanisms or degree of control are appropriate. The most serious question, from a normative view, is the relationship between the behavior of the government described by Riggs and the preferences of the citizens.

The standard hierarchical principle calls for orders to contain the minimum detail necessary for the subordinate to carry out the objectives of the superior.[40] It seems doubtful that many orders are so carefully drawn, but the principle implies that Congress should not meddle with details of administration and that legislation should be carefully drafted to eliminate ambiguity. In practice, bills are often amended at the last moment without any concern for implementation, or complex House and Senate bills are combined into one compromise bill that in fact has not resolved the differences.

Hypothesis 51: *Failure is more likely the later in the legislative process the final bill originates.*

When a program is initiated under vague and contradictory instructions the details will be worked out between the committee and the bureau. This amounts to the determination of policy under precisely those circumstances where the bureau and the client groups have the greatest influence.

The classical notion of the separation of policy and administration is inadequate on both sides—not only do agencies establish policy, but Congress also concerns itself with administration. Arkes argued that such activity by Congress contributed significantly to the success of the Marshall Plan.[41] Congressional activity was particularly important in clarifying policy, holding the agency to the objectives even when techniques had to be changed, and providing coordination and other resources not available to a single agency. This episode, however, may be treated as an example of the basic lesson from the literature of hierarchical control: Congress and the President can make any one program work

[39]Fred Warren Riggs, *Administrative Reform and Political Responsiveness:A Theory of Dynamic Balancing* (Beverly Hills, California:Sage, 1970), pp. 577–578.

[40]Herbert A. Simon, "Decision-Making and Administrative Organization," pp. 185–194 of Robert K. Merton *et al.*, *Reader in Bureaucracy* (Glencoe, Illinois:Free Press, 1952).

[41]Hadley Arkes, *Bureaucracy, the Marshall Plan, and the National Interest* (Princeton:Princeton University Press, 1972), p. 12.

by devoting enough attention to it, but energy and time are too limited to make many programs work.

It has been argued that the highly technical nature of much administration makes an attempt at detailed regulation by the legislature harmful.[42] If the argument relates to oversight by a congressional committee of the activities of an agency, it seems irrelevant. The more technical the issues, the less will congressmen understand, and the more inclined will they be to let the bureaucrats determine policy. If, however, Congress attempts to freeze detailed regulations into legislation, they may quickly become obsolete. It becomes an empirical question whether legislation or administrative regulation is quicker to respond to changes in technology. Gaus, in a surfeit of technocratic optimism, finds "the role of the administrator is to achieve a reconciliation of the interests involved, and requires the winning of consent by the accumulation of exact and relevant knowledge."[43] Few analysts today expect technical skill to resolve conflicts of interest. Superficial consideration suggests that failure is more likely in highly technical areas because of the limited ability of Congress or the President to exert control, but further analysis of this is deferred to Chapter 4.

Certain types of expenditures are not subject to the routine controls of the annual budget.[44] Congress can repeal trust funds, repudiate debts and pensions, and halt ongoing projects midway, but most such matters should realistically be considered not subject to immediate control. Over a longer time period, Congress can take action to reduce the rate of growth of certain claims (e.g., social security), but the annual review can accomplish little and hence may be perfunctory. Furthermore, if the agency is not reviewed by the appropriations committee, it misses the broadest form of congressional overview. Agencies that generate more revenue than they spend, which includes the Federal Reserve System and various agencies that insure loans, are less subject to detailed control.

Hypothesis 52: *Failure is more likely the greater the independence of the agency from detailed annual budgetary review.*

One objection to detailed control by congressional committees is the difficulty of distinguishing an official act on behalf of Congress from a

---

[42]John M. Gaus, "The Responsibility of Public Administration," chapter 3 of *The Frontiers of Public Administration* by John M. Gaus, Leonard D. White, and Marshall E. Dimock (New York:Russell & Russell, 1967, [1st publ. 1936]).

[43]Ibid., p. 39.

[44]Murray Weidenbaum, *The Modern Public Sector:New Ways of Doing the Government's Business* (New York:Basic Books, 1969), pp. 172–177.

political act to benefit a congressman.[45] One can argue for control of administrators by the legislature, but no one argues that administrators should perform special favors for individual legislators (or Presidents). Legislative control is meaningless unless the individual legislator knows what is going on; his inquiries theoretically deserve deference and in practice generally receive it. Suppose, however, that he asks for the list of employees of the agency living in his district or inquires why a particular constituent was denied a contract? The particular ethical questions have been discussed at length elsewhere, but are there any general lessons more persuasive than a call for higher morality among administrators and legislators? Appleby suggests that culpable behavior is most likely to be found "in agencies not themselves exposed widely to the public . . ."[46]

Hypothesis 53: *Failure is more likely in an agency that does not attract much public attention.*

When newsmen are prowling around the agency, bureaucrats must be careful to avoid the improprieties that make good copy including partiality toward particular legislators or special interests. Although Riggs considers that excessive deference by bureaucrats to politicians indicates excessive weakness of the bureaucracy,[47] surely the inclination to conform to prevailing ethics is strengthened by publicity. Public exposure, however, depends partly on the newsworthiness of the particular agency and partly on the number of activities competing for the attention of newsmen. Behavior by low-level civil servants that would have attracted attention in the small-town Washington of 60 years ago would not be noticed in that busy and anonymous city today.

The other approach to the same question is to consider whether the agency has anything to give away. The conditions for favoritism toward legislators overlap the conditions leading to bribery and other forms of flagrant corruption. They are not identical, however, because politicians can deal in two different kinds of currency—ordinary money and votes. When the agency provides favors to identifiable firms or individuals, the conditions favoring illegal monetary payments are created.[48]

---

[45]Hyneman, *Bureaucracy in a Democracy*, pp. 158–175.

[46]Paul Henson Appleby, *Morality and Administration in Democratic Government* (Baton Rouge:Louisiana State University Press, 1952), pp. 111–112.

[47]Riggs, *Administrative Reform and Political Responsiveness*, p. 579.

[48]See the analysis by Robert O. Tillman, "Emergence of Black-Market Bureaucracy:Administration, Development, and Corruption in the New States," *Public Administration Review* 28, No. 5 (Sept.–Oct. 1968): 437–444.

Hypothesis 54: *Failure is more likely when the agency supplies a good to some members of the public for less than the market price.*

The official price may be set by the government anywhere between zero and the market price. If the government supplies the good to everyone at a low price, then neither favoritism nor bribery is likely in this country. In some others, however, bribes are routine for official papers of all sorts. If the good can be supplied to only some of the applicants, even the U.S. system is under pressure.[49] Rivalry for a good, such as a television channel, available to one private party from a number of applicants could result in either some form of bribery or some type of political pressure working through legislators or the executive branch. When the good is available to a lower level of government (e.g., a grant to build a transit system), the payment, if any, will take a political form. That is, the grant may be considered a favor from one politician to another for which some equivalent favor must be performed.

Government purchases of inputs above their market price similarly provide opportunities for individuals or firms to gain by supplying money or political favors to bureaucrats or politicians.

Hypothesis 55: *Failure is more likely when the government purchase price exceeds the market price.*

Patronage is not a serious problem if government pays less than private purchasers. (Even when a government salary seems low, however, it may exceed what an inferior political appointee could obtain in the best alternative open to him.) Whether a failure takes the form of a bribe or a political favor depends on the specific circumstances. The agency might be pressured by a congressman to award the contract to a plant in his home district—or the bureaucrat might be bribed by the plant owner. A variety of possible transactions could distribute the gains from the favor that the government grants. These could include such quasi-legal transfers as campaign contributions, lecture fees, legal fees, and consulting contracts, as well as bribes.

Any regulatory activity generates the possibility of bribes or political intervention.

Hypothesis 56: *Failure is more likely the more complex and ambiguous the*

---

[49]Partial funding of benefits is commonplace. One estimate of the additional spending necessary, above the amount appropriated for fiscal year 1974, in order to provide the services to which people are entitled by law was $250 billion for the Department of Health, Education, and Welfare, alone. See Laurence E. Lynn, Jr. and John M. Seidl, "Policy Analysis at HEW:The Story of the Mega-Proposal," *Policy Analysis* 1, No. 2 (Spring 1975): 248.

regulations and the higher the costs imposed on firms or individuals either by complying or by paying fines.

Complexity and ambiguity make it possible to conceal favoritism more easily. The costs imposed by regulation provide the incentive to bribe or to resort to political pressure.

Hypothesis 57: *Failure is more likely when a bureaucratic procedure delays private action.*

Whenever permits and clearances stand in the way of some private project,[50] the temptation to expedite matters by bribing a clerk or arranging for a congressman to inquire about an official clearance can become very strong. If routine requests are delayed many weeks by inertia, red tape, or excessive workload, or if partial funding permits the granting of only a fraction of the requests, then simply moving a routine request to the top of the heap becomes a valuable favor.

Hypothesis 58: *Failure is more likely when the law is secret.*

It may seem anachronistic to discuss secret law in a western democracy, but complexity and ambiguity, especially when combined with partial funding, lead to the same result. When the government has favors to distribute, or when it has limited resources to force compliance with laws and regulations, some device must be adopted to ration the distribution. In the simplest case, it is a direct bribe to the official who makes the distribution. In a slightly more complex situation, the favor may become part of the political currency—one favor will be exchanged for another, not to line an individual's pocket, but as part of the functioning of government. If, however, the agency is incorruptible in the usual ways, it may establish rules for determining which applicant will receive the service or grant. If the exact procedures—including all the internal rules and interpretations—are not published, the law is secret. Favoritism ranges from informing the favorite about the secret law to altering the procedures to benefit him. Will an urban renewal application be guided through the bureaucratic labyrinth better if the mayor supports the President's foreign policy? Such pressures are always present; secret law makes it easier to yield to them. Devons called attention to the problem in Great Britain, where the secrecy of internal procedures relating to financing of universities troubled him greatly.[51]

---

[50]Tillman, "Emergence of Black-Market Bureaucracy," p. 442.

[51]Ely Devons, *Papers on Planning and Economic Management*, ed. Sir Alec Cairncross (Manchester, England:Manchester University Press, 1970), p. 145.

The United States, with the Freedom of Information Act, has adopted a correct, but weak, mechanism to alleviate the huge problem.

Some other control devices can be mentioned briefly.[52] Control of one bureaucracy by another is a common device. The United States enjoys such control bureaucracies as the President's staff (including the Office of Management and Budget [OMB]), and the General Accounting Office (GAO), which reports to Congress. The Soviet Union has gone further in the use of this technique, which has always been common in Oriental empires, with the secret police under the Minister of the Interior and the party bureaucracy under the party leadership constituting a second and third hierarchy with agents everywhere and separate chains of command. Duplicate hierarchies are costly and also subject to control loss, although with different biases. Most significant, in an open society with uninhibited news media and freedom of speech the problem is not lack of information for the people at the top of the chain of command, but a lack of capacity to absorb information. Retaining the GAO and OMB as relatively small investigative and analytical agencies thus seems to make more sense in the United States than establishing vast checking hierarchies.

The appeals of individuals from arbitrary decisions are a traditional source of information about the functioning of bureaucracy.[53] The problems raised by aggrieved individuals have inspired proposals for such remedies as a more formal appeals process, including generalized administrative courts analogous to tax courts, and an ombudsman to help the citizen approach the bureaucracy. Although such proposals have some merit, the bureaucracy is already relatively well controlled in precisely those areas where the individual citizen feels the burden of failure directly. If an agency acts in an arbitrary and coercive way toward individuals, eventually someone will appeal through administrative channels, individual politicians, news media, or the courts. Well-recognized standards for due process in administrative proceedings have been developed and the regular court system—including the Supreme Court—are available to adjudicate cases not clearly covered by the precedents.[54] These appeals procedures are expensive, of course, so the supposition is

[52]These and other control mechanisms are discussed by Gordon Tullock, *The Politics of Bureaucracy* (Washington:Public Affairs Press, 1965); Arnold Brecht, "How Bureaucracies Develop and Function," *The Annals of the American Academy of Political and Social Science 292,* (March 1954), issue on "Bureaucracy and Representative Government": 1–10; Anthony Downs, *Inside Bureaucracy* (Boston:Little, Brown, 1966); and Karl August Wittfogel, *Oriental Despotism:A Comparative Study of Total Power* (New Haven:Yale University Press, 1957).

[53]John Merriman Gaus *Reflections on Public Administration,* pp. 93–123.

[54]For a convenient summary see Ernest Gellhorn, *Administrative Law and Process in a Nutshell* (St. Paul, Minnesota:West, 1972).

always strong that they work best where individual cases involve substantial amounts of money—and especially when the aggrieved party is a large firm.

In numerous instances of failure, however, the costs are not narrowly focused on an individual or small group who will find it worthwhile to protest or appeal.

Hypothesis 59: *Failure is more likely the more widely diffused are its costs.*

In the extreme case, the agency simply buys resources on the market and wastes them. The costs are borne by everyone in the economy, but no one would receive a large enough share of the savings to make it worthwhile to protest. The taxpayer who feels that his money is being wasted does not even have standing to present his case in court.[55]

The news media can be used as control devices. New stories may be instigated by dissatisfied individuals as an alternative to an internal appeals process. Since the top official has to answer questions when his department makes the headlines, public relations and control of the news are important tactics. Sometimes bureaucrats will try to involve the public directly in policymaking to gain some public relations advantage.[56] The probability of attracting attention depends on the public exposure and the vividness of the activities concerned. The Postal Service, for example, is an agency with which everyone has experience, but which is generally uninteresting. The CIA has the opposite characteristics, which probably makes the rapid diffusion of misinformation about its functions easier. Since the quality of vividness is hard to analyze, the generalizations will be offered that a bureau performing secret functions will depart furthest from legislated objectives, a bureau highly visible to much of the citizenry will perform best, and a bureau highly visible only to a special clientele will be captured by it.

Agencies differ not only in the visibility of their products, but also in whether or not consumption is compulsory.[57] Hirschman points out that "exit" and "voice" are alternative responses by customers to poor quality or high prices of goods.[58] The taxpayer cannot easily escape the high price of public services, but if he is willing to pay enough he can exit from some (e.g., public schools), the quality of which he finds in-

---

[55] *Ibid.*, pp. 248–255.

[56] Boyer, *Bureaucracy on Trial*, pp. 68–91.

[57] John G. Head, "Public Goods:The Polar Case," chapter 1 in Richard M. Bird and John G. Head, eds., *Modern Fiscal Issues:Essays in Honor of Carl S. Shoup* (Toronto:University of Toronto Press, 1972).

[58] Albert O. Hirschman, *Exit, Voice, and Loyalty:Responses to Decline in Firms, Organizations, and States* (Cambridge:Harvard University Press, 1970).

adequate, but not from others (e.g., foreign policy). He can supplement an inadequate police department with locks and watchmen, but he cannot exit from a corrupt one except by moving. The possibility of exit can drain off the articulate opposition of the wealthy elite from noncompulsory goods and services.

Hypothesis 60: *Failure is more likely the lower the cost of exit from a particular service.*

The well-to-do have alternatives to public libraries, schools, and recreation facilities, and thus do not protest the deterioration in service once it has become bad enough to drive them to the private substitutes. Middle-income families cannot afford as many private substitutes, but can afford to move from city to suburb for better service. Services are poor in the poor neighborhoods, not only because tax revenues are low, but also because the poor do not voice their discontent effectively. Although one can escape local services by moving to another jurisdiction, many federal services are effectively compulsory. Regulation is usually set up in such a way as to preclude exit. If attempts to exit fail, the regulated party will turn to voice, which includes all efforts to influence the regulatory agency. But responsiveness of an agency to the public is difficult to distinguish, in practice, from responsiveness to special groups most interested in the agency's activities. This fact lies at the heart of the entire control problem; it also affects the evolution of policy in ways to be outlined in the next section.

THE INFLUENCE OF BUREAUCRACY ON POLICY

Individuals plan for the distant future. Even teenagers, who are generally considered to be caught up in the present moment, will frequently plan an educational program that will launch them into careers 4 to 10 years hence. Adults often plan for retirement 20 years ahead. Individuals may even worry about the world their grandchildren will inherit in half a century, and join groups or movements to try to improve the far distant future.

When an individual works in a private firm, his time horizon is shortened. A chief executive may feel he has 5 years to show the directors substantial progress toward their goals, although a few decisions are made about raw materials as much as 20 years hence. When an individual is elected to high office he can no longer afford to think of the future. Even the wisest President needs results 3½ years after inauguration in order to be reelected. He will face a difficult time if he does not help his party through midterm elections less than 2 years hence. It has been remarked that long-term planning in government is thinking ahead as far as the next election. How could it be otherwise at the highest levels?

Turnover among the political appointees is so rapid that the time horizon is even shorter at the cabinet level. Downs states a "Law of Inescapable Discontinuity" that "High-level federal personnel change so fast that almost no major federal program is ever initially conceived of, drafted into legislation, shepherded through Congress, and then carried out by the same officials."[59] Whatever planning does occur under these conditions must constantly be redone as each new official strives to effect his own innovations.

At the lower levels of the hierarchy, however, planning can and does go on. The budget cycle, itself, forces agency heads to plan nearly 2 years ahead. Professionals within the agencies, moreover, are drawing up plans for structures, facilities, and programs several years in advance. The time horizon of the agencies at the lower levels, where the technicians dominate, may resemble that of ordinary firms. It does not begin to approach that of individuals, but is far less myopic than that of the highest levels of government. Naturally, such a difference in the framework for planning has some effect on policy. As decisions are made case-by-case and project-by-project at the lower levels of the hierarchy, the agency is gradually eased into various courses of action that can subsequently be identified as policy.

In new government agencies the top executive typically has the freedom to make many decisions that are policy by classical standards.[60] As the agency discovers the weak points in the original legislation, it can try to shape the law to correspond with what it is able to do. In the absence of some force from the top working to terminate useless programs and push others toward some public purpose, programs will drift in the direction of what is easy to do and what the client group wants. The committees concerned with the agency will feel similar client pressures and will also become aware of what the agency can succeed in doing. One result of incremental adjustments is, thus, to reduce the probability of failure by adjusting goals to match performance.[61]

[59]Anthony Downs, "The Successes and Failures of Federal Housing Policy," *The Public Interest* 34, (Winter 1974): 135.

[60]Robert L. Peabody and Francis E. Rourke, "Public Bureaucracies," chapter 19 in James G. March, *Handbook of Organizations* (Chicago:Rand McNally, 1965), p. 805.

[61]Bela Gold noted the tendency to adjust goals to performance in wartime agricultural planning, *Wartime Economic Planning in Agriculture:A Study in the Allocation of Resources* (New York:Columbia University Press, 1949), pp. 171-172.

Incrementalism in policy changes does have certain advantages, as stressed by Dahl and Lindblom.[62] These include (*a*) ease in predicting consequences, (*b*) ease in expressing preferences when the alternatives depart but little from current reality, (*c*) consistency with the adjustments among goals required by rationality, (*d*) ease in isolating the effect of specific changes, (*e*) ease in maintaining control by the superior, (*f*) reversibility, (*g*) survival of the organization by gradual adjustment while retaining standard codes, and (*h*) the resulting aid to the rationality of the electorate. These points are well taken, but they raise a more fundamental one: What is the relationship between the preferences of citizens and the incremental changes that originate in the interaction between the bureaucracy and Congress? Incremental changes are easier to administer and control within the agency, but one must still ask whose objectives will be achieved.

One result of incrementalism in general and agency initiation of policy in particular is the lack of support for new approaches. Minor changes of regulatory or tax law and minor amendments or expansions of policies can be worked out. Support for any radical changes in the law (e.g., eliminating the agency and its functions) has to come from outside the agency and the interests that have worked with it. Incrementalism generally involves increasing complexity, more special cases, delays for coordination and clearance, and the loss of policy orientation in a mass of detail. The emphasis on special cases and ad hoc solutions is hardly surprising, given the strong role that lawyers play in the process, the absence of anyone with a long-term interest beyond that of winning the particular case, and the initiation of most incremental changes at a low level in the hierarchy where forthright decisions to change policy are obviously inappropriate. In the absence of strong guiding policies, moreover, incremental changes are likely to pull different agencies in different directions, decreasing further the chances of achieving coordination.

Hypothesis 61: *Failure is more likely the greater the interdependence among the functions of separate agencies.*

CHARACTERISTICS OF LEGISLATION AND LEGISLATIVE CONTROL

It has been alleged that politicians knowingly pass ineffectual laws to placate the proponents of change without upsetting the opponents. Not only is the allegation cynical, it also imputes intelligence to the oppo-

---

[62]Robert A. Dahl and Charles E. Lindblom, *Politics, Economics, and Welfare:Planning and*

nents of change and stupidity to the proponents. In the process of compromise necessary to muster support for a bill in Congress, of course, what begins as a radical approach to a grandiose goal may be amended sufficiently so little but the goal remains. Bureaucrats cannot be blamed when Congress keeps the old preamble after eviscerating the substance of a bill.

A more serious problem is the passage of ambiguous and vague legislation that fails to specify policy. Ambiguity may reflect a rush to pass something before adjourning, reluctance to grapple with a difficult problem, a premature attempt to legislate in a difficult area, or all of these. As Herring has pointed out, even the best administrators will not succeed when the major political questions are unresolved.[63] Regulatory programs begin with the acute problem of having to cure the defects of the regulated sector that have been paraded before the public in an effort to gain support for passage of the legislation. Once the program is established, however, the crusaders disappear and the public loses interest. The inherent contradictions in the objectives of the legislation are exploited by the regulated sector to serve its own ends.[64]

Sloppy legislation can take a number of forms. It is often asserted that federal legislation, unlike that in some states and localities, is well drafted, meaning that bills are internally consistent with correct cross-references, grammatical correctness, and reasonable clarity, etc. Even this minimal standard is sometimes not met, especially when widely different House and Senate versions are combined under difficult political or time pressures.[65] A somewhat more demanding criterion is consistency between the new legislation and existing laws. More substantively, one can ask whether the objectives specified are mutually consistent and whether they can be achieved with the means provided by the legislation.

A task may be impossible because of either inadequate resources or the conceptual failure to specify the correct approach. That is, just as the professional review board might wonder whether the patient's death was due to the scarcity of leeches or to the fact that bloodletting was an inappropriate prescription for the particular illness, so a modern analyst of manpower retraining might ask whether it failed to reduce unemployment because the programs were inadequately funded or because they were not the correct way to cure the problem.

Politico–Economic Systems Resolved into Basic Social Processes (New York:Harper & Brothers, 1953), pp. 82–84.

[63]Herring, *Public Administration and the Public Interest*, p. 214.

[64]Truman, *The Governmental Process*, pp. 442–443.

[65]The Federal Water Pollution Control Act Amendments of 1972 afford a particularly egregious example.

Hypothesis 62: *Failure is more likely when the conceptual basis of the program is incorrect.*

Inadequate resources to accomplish the task would appear to be a less serious problem than poor initial design or inadequate conceptual basis. In the normal course of events, appropriations will be increased, especially for experimental programs that are successful in developing a strong clientele.

Hypothesis 63: *Failure is more likely when the agency lacks sufficient resources to carry out the task.*

Partial funding may mean that access to the publicly subsidized program must be rationed in some way and is therefore conducive to bribery, political influence, or arbitrary action. Furthermore, unless the appropriations language is very specific, the assignment of a large task with few resources gives administrative officials the power to decide what is most important or most interesting; that is, to set policy.[66] If the task is otherwise feasible, however, partial funding should ordinarily lead to provision of a small amount of the desired service, but not to failure, unless the task is indivisible: for example, building most of a bridge is a failure.

Another set of problems implicit in legislative control of bureaucracy is rooted in the geographic basis for representation in Congress. (This is not to be taken as an argument for moving to any other basis of representation; the prime alternatives are occupation and industry, which would be far worse.) Since agencies must retain support for their activities in Congress, they become extremely sensitive to activities that would change the geographic distribution of benefits. The location of field installations, in particular, is a matter that consumes much top-level attention, although it would appear to be a question of administrative efficiency rather than policy.[67] Similarly, one of the complicating factors in the inability of the U.S. government to come to grips with the food problem in World War II was the resistance of labor surplus areas to any reallocation of labor.[68] Since a great many public programs either impose heavy costs or confer large benefits on particular geographic areas, they become vital issues to certain legislators. Such legislative practices as logrolling make it difficult to adopt any change that imposes obvious costs on a district.

---

[66]Hyneman, *Bureaucracy in a Democracy*, pp. 126–127, 340.

[67]John D. Millett, *Organization for the Public Service* (Princeton: Van Nostrand, 1966), p. 52.

[68]Gold, *Wartime Economic Planning in Agriculture*, pp. 198–201.

Hypothesis 64: *Failure is more likely in programs that subject particular geographic areas to highly visible costs.*

BARGAINING AMONG AGENCIES

In the classical hierarchical theory, relationships between agencies are given little attention. But with the recognition that hierarchical control breaks down in large organizations, the direct contacts between agencies assume much greater importance. If coordination is to take place at all, it must be based on good working relationships between agencies (or individuals) since the formal methods are so time consuming and tenuous that, although they may serve to ratify agreements made at the lower levels, they certainly cannot overcome the resistance of people determined *not* to cooperate.

Dahl and Lindblom, in the first major analysis of direct relationships among agencies, suggest that bargaining is the result of relying on the bureaucracy to coordinate policies about which political leaders have not reached agreement. The results include an increase in the power of the bureaucracy, an increase in the influence of organized groups on policy, lack of coherent control over government by elected officials, and limits on the extent of rational social action. They note the similarity between government bureaucracy and international politics.[69]

Despite the disorderly nature of the process and the resulting imperfection of coordination, Lindblom remains optimistic about the overall results of bargaining. He hypothesizes that an official can increase his bargaining power by forming alliances, which means that the official must make his own goals consistent with those that are widely shared; that is, the public interest. Certainly during bargaining most organized interests are heard, the important facts are presented, the lower levels can have some impact on top-level decisions, and large problems are broken down into separate manageable decisions.[70]

These points are well taken, but the implications for government action are still serious. Coordination among the activities of various agencies will be haphazard. Pressure groups will have strong influence on the implementation of policy, as well as its formation, whereas poorly organized groups will be largely powerless. The action taken by the agency will be the result of negotiation, rather than the directives of

[69]Dahl and Lindblom, *Politics, Economics, and Welfare*, pp. 340–342, 344, 349–350.
[70]Charles E. Lindblom, *Bargaining:The Hidden Hand in Government* (Santa Monica, California:The Rand Corporation, 22 February 1955), RM–1434–RC, pp. 21, 26, 30.

elected officials. Furthermore, in the vertical bargaining process, agencies will probably be able to maintain enough organizational slack to carry out some activities of their own choosing, which is a separate aspect of control loss from failure to carry out legislated goals. An interest once given voice in the bargaining process through the creation of an agency will have the means to exert its power in a variety of bargaining situations, including the continued evolution of legislation and the direction in which implementation departs from legislation.

McKean stresses the role of bargaining as the "Unseen Hand in Government."[71] Unlike Adam Smith's invisible hand of the private economy, however, the unseen hand in government cannot be assumed to lead to socially beneficent outcomes. In particular, the imperfections that operate to prevent private markets from optimizing consumer welfare have their analogues in the public sector:

1. Monopoly by an agency leads, as Niskanen has spelled out, to excessive output, rather than restriction as it does in the private sector.
2. The free rider is a problem when there are spillovers in benefits from one jurisdiction to the next.
3. No mechanism to eliminate the obsolete agency works with the force and persistence of bankruptcy in the private sector.
4. Externalities are as unlikely to enter into the decision-making process of the agency as of the firm.
5. Minor imperfections include excessive expenditures on advertising and restrictions on the techniques permitted, including congressional determination not only of overall capital–labor ratios, but even of number of employees at various grades.

Hypothesis 65: *Failure is more likely in activities characterized by strong externalities.*

It would seem that bargaining by government agencies substitutes a highly imperfect market that works for an ideal mechanism (hierarchical coordination) that does not work. Bargaining in government has none of the self-correcting features that lead competitive markets to improve social welfare while the firms are merely trying to maximize their own profits.

Not surprisingly, economists studying imperfections in government have found monopoly by particular agencies to be among them. Thus Niskanen is concerned that monopoly restricts the amount of informa-

[71]Roland N. McKean, "The Unseen Hand in Government," *American Economic Review* 55 (June 1965). 496–506.

tion available to the sponsor, whereas McKean finds that the monopolist has an excessive advantage not only in bargaining with the sponsor on the quantity of output, but also in its relations with other agencies. Maass, a political scientist, does not share the enthusiasm for competition among agencies. In his study of the competition between the Army Corps of Engineers and the Bureau of Reclamation for the Kings River (California) project, he showed that competition led to delay, duplication of expensive planning efforts, and the expenditure of high-level (even presidential) time.[72] According to Maass, competition tends to take the form of price discrimination in favor of powerful interest groups and variations in product quality—neither of which is an aid to the sponsor in making a better decision, even if that is what he wants to do.

The bargaining approach to the analysis of bureaucracy yields some insights into bureaucratic feudalism, but does not yield many hypotheses and predictions about bureaucratic failure.[73] Much of the strength of an independent agency may be reflected in its obtaining the legislation that suits its purposes. It would then carry out that legislation without any lapses if the internal control of the head of the agency were perfect.

Davis used economic concepts to analyze relationships among agencies.[74] Exchange is, in some sense, a substitute for hierarchy, but Davis did not extend his analysis to consider the implications for the effectiveness with which public goods can be provided. In this regard, it is significant that only a limited portion of the services that agencies require of one another for effective performance of their legislated tasks are actually amenable to the exchange relationship. Sometimes, of course, agencies rent space or contract for services from other agencies, but this is not much different from hiring services from private suppliers. Of more interest are the occasions when agencies must rely on others for favors—casual requests for information, speedy processing of clearances, or expressions of support for a desired course of action. Here the analogy with the market system breaks down. For the bureaucratic world is still a very primitive barter economy where the participants must locate trading partners, bargain about the price, and arrange to deliver services valued at that same price by the trading partner. The

---

[72]Arthur A. Maass, "Duplication of Functions: A Case Study in Bureaucratic Conflict," Report Prepared for U.S. Commission on Organization of the Executive Branch of the Government (Hoover Commission), 1949, as reprinted in the Merton *Reader*, pp. 291–297.

[73]For a discussion of bureaucratic feudalism see Hans Joachim Morgenthau, *The Purpose of American Politics* (New York: Knopf, 1960), pp. 274–280.

[74]David Howard Davis, *How the Bureaucracy Makes Foreign Policy* (Lexington, Massachusetts: Heath, 1972).

efficiency that a common currency contributes to market transactions is missing from bureaucratic exchange. Furthermore, the typical relationship of one potential buyer negotiating with one potential seller (bilateral monopoly) is notorious even in private markets for the quantity of scarce resources, including especially the time and energy of top-level administrators, diverted into negotiations. It is no wonder that bureaucrats become weary of attempting to effectuate cooperation among agencies and lament the absence of good will. Private markets are blessed by being able to operate effectively with very little of either.

CONCLUSIONS

Consideration of the political aspects of controlling government bureaucracy leads to a slightly more optimistic conclusion than the pure hierarchical model. Since the bureaucracy is too big to be controlled in a unified way by a single intelligence, such control as does occur will be focused on particular activities, agencies, and issues by particular individuals and groups acting in their own interests.

Control by the legislature develops into control of particular agencies by particular subcommittees. Because the vast number of issues that comes before Congress far exceeds the comprehension of voters, the legislator is answerable for only that small proportion of his decisions that impose particular costs or benefits on his constituents. This imparts a bias against activities that impost heavy costs on particular congressional districts or on identifiable interest groups to benefit the general public, and, conversely, a bias in favor of activities that benefit particular districts or interest groups at the expense of the general public.

Control by public opinion, as bestirred by the news media, imparts a less predictable bias. The issues that attract public attention need not be as narrowly focused as those that elect legislators, but they must be newsworthy—a characteristic that is not easy to define. In general, however, it is easier to attract public attention with a survey of hideous problems than with the petty details of attempting to implement corrective legislation. As the public sector has grown, moreover, the proportion of total government activity that can attract widespread attention has diminished.

Individuals who incur heavy costs from particular bureaucratic decisions provide another form of control. Because such individuals have the incentive and well-developed methods to contest arbitrary action, bureaucrats will not often depart from the legislation in the direction of inflicting heavy costs on, or denying benefits to, particular people.

The implementation process is more likely to be biased in the opposite direction. Organized groups, which represent a very special subset of all the interests in society, are active in promoting their views at every stage of the political process from tentative discussions of policy to the details of implementation. At the implementation stage, because of the multiplicity of specific details, organized groups tend to have a disproportionate influence on decisions. As a general rule, therefore, the political control mechanisms give disproportionate weight to narrowly focused costs and benefits at the expense of broadly diffused benefits or costs. The incremental process by which changes are made contributes to the degree of distortion produced by the biases mentioned previously, as well as raising other problems. Since policy is rarely subject to a thorough and comprehensive review, it evolves in the direction of the small changes that occur step-by-step in response to the unremitting daily pressures of the organized interests that are most concerned. Some of the other problems that stem from, or are aggravated by, incrementalism include lack of coordination, increasing complexity and secrecy of law developed case by case, and the adjustment of legislation and goals to conform to performance. The lack of coordination among agencies is a particularly difficult matter because of the necessity for relying on bilateral negotiations in the absence of established prices for services or even of a common currency.

CHAPTER 4

Controls from Within the Bureaucrat

INTRODUCTION

Little was said in the preceding chapter about the individuals who make up the bureaucracy. The classical hierarchical approach took them as unthinking components of a great machine that carried out the policies devised by elected officials. Tullock replaced those cog wheels with ambitious men clawing their way up the hierarchy. Although Tullock's model may describe behavior at the higher levels of government, to which the able, ambitious, and unscrupulous rise most rapidly, the general breakdown of hierarchical control that Tullock's model predicts, and that political scientists have observed, suggests that individuals at the lower ranks of government are important determinants of what, if anything, the government does.

This chapter borders on some of the areas that are traditional in personnel management in all organizations. The delicate problem of encouraging initiative, morale, and creativity while maintaining managerial control is universal, but the political setting of government and the characteristics of the goods produced pose some peculiar problems. These do not necessarily show up at every level in the hierarchy. Routine managerial tools can improve the efficiency of writing checks, washing windows, or building roads.[1] The application of such tools, however, requires that incentives for efficiency and good management be built into the organization, and this brings us back to the question of the motives, incentives, and control of the decision makers at all levels of the organization.

The problem is not one of discovering techniques by which an omniscient and omnipotent "cost minimizer" can increase the efficiency of operations; nor is it one of describing how "super consultant" can devise incentives for the efficient performance of specified functions. The problem, rather, is to see that at every level of the hierarchy supervisors have an incentive to reward their subordinates for reducing costs. This has not been possible to solve in the federal government for a variety of reasons including (a) the impossibility of measuring many of the outputs of activities with the consequent stress on detailed control of inputs as a poor substitute; (b) the incentive that the individual bureaucrat has for increasing the budget and the number of subordinates under his control; and (c) the dominance of other objectives, which makes it unlikely that federal employees will consistently be rewarded for cutting costs.

Paring costs may be a relatively unimportant criterion by which to rate overall performance of the federal bureaucracy. Before asking whether an agency will produce at an acceptable cost, it is important to ask *what* the agency will produce. It is in this context that one must examine what the individual will choose to do in the absence of strong hierarchical controls or appropriately designed incentives.

Imagine an individual who has chosen to disregard the consequences of a decision for his own career. Suppose that he also does not feel constrained by his superior's orders or by the handbook of agency rules and procedures. Would such an individual be likely to go back to the legislation establishing his agency to ask, "What did Congress and the President really intend to have me do?" or would he instead act in the way that seemed best in the light of his education, deeper values, and knowledge of the situation? The internalized forms of control provide no guarantee that control loss will be corrected. They suggest only that the behavior of operatives will not depart randomly from legislation, but rather will be predictably biased, when there is slippage in the line of authority.

---

[1]For a good example of this type of work, see the reports by the U.S. Joint Financial Management Improvement Program of the Civil Service Commission (Bernard Rosen), the General Accounting Office (Thomas D. Morris), and Office of Management and Budget (Dwight Ink), *Measuring and Enhancing Productivity in the Federal Government* (June 1973) Phase III–Summary Report; and *Report on Federal Productivity* (June 1974) I, "Productivity Trends, FY 1967–1973"; II, "Productivity Case Studies."

The two most important themes in the literature on controls internal to bureaucrats center around profession and class. The notion of turning over control seems more popular among those who discuss the professional orientation of bureaucrats, but it has its defenders, too, among those who discuss class interests.

PROFESSIONAL CONTROL

Commonly, the delegation of policymaking is not a conscious decision, but rather a result of the inability of the elected officials to make the mass of policy decisions subsidiary to a program or project adopted. Sometimes the quality of decision making is worsened by the failure to recognize that decisions, in fact, are being made. As an illustration, suppose a department of highway engineers has for years been designing highways according to sound and accepted professional standards. Those standards may embody technical economic errors in the choice between capital costs and operating costs or ludicrous estimates of the value of commuting time, reflecting the obsolete textbook wisdom of 20 or more years past. More significantly, decisions on highway design are also important elements in the land use and environmental policies of the jurisdiction. As long as such policies are not on the political agenda, the engineers may make the decisions according to their own professional judgment. But the value of a straight road relative to a row of trees or an historic house, and the choice of a growth rate for the area should not be decided on technical grounds. When public opinion comes to emphasize esthetic and environmental issues enough to force a change, it becomes apparent that the agency was never under hierarchical control. It will prove difficult to enforce an order that the engineering department take the additional issues into consideration in their planning, in the absence of some professional incentives. The plans of the engineers can be made subject to land use and environmental policies of agencies established for those purposes, but the results will certainly include delay, disagreement, confusion, and bargaining, with the outcome being related both to legislative intent and to the preferences of the citizenry in only the most tenuous and indirect ways.

Hypothesis 66: *Failure is more likely when professional criteria conflict with legislative intent.*

This basic point is well recognized in the sociological literature.[2] Even

---

[2]See, e.g., Peter M. Blau and W. Richard Scott, *Formal Organizations:A Comparative*

when the legislature has not established specific objectives from which the professional criteria can depart, however, a different problem of equivalent origin may be encountered.

Hypothesis 67: *Failure is more likely when the conflicting standards of two or more professions must be harmonized.*

In the absence of hierarchical control the conflicting professional criteria produce long delays or conflicting activities by different agencies.

Since both profession and income are often assumed to influence behavior, it is interesting to note that the two are closely connected for an individual who perceives that advancement may necessitate changing employers while retaining the same occupation. The individual enhances his transfer wage (i.e., the best offer he can obtain from a different employer) by performing in such a way as to maintain the respect of others in his profession. This may mean writing reports of professional quality, designing dams that meet the standards of engineers, prosecuting cases skillfully by accepted standards of lawyers, and so on. Such professional standards can prevent flagrant deterioration of quality in fields where output is difficult for nonprofessionals to measure. The ambitious man is not forced to give his superior what he wants to hear because he can find another employer who will reward him for his professional integrity and ability.

The concept of professionalism as a control on the quality of effort does, therefore, coincide with the economic incentive to increase income under the condition that the skills involved in the job are transferable. This is an unusual definition of professionalism. It does not contain explicitly any of the standard criteria used by sociologists, such as a recognized body of knowledge and a common educational background. Implicit in the idea of transferability of skills, however, is some suggestion that the individuals share a set of experiences, but it can apply to a variety of blue-collar jobs, as well as to the learned occupations.

Hypothesis 68: *Failure is more likely when the skills of operatives are specific to one agency.*

When no other employer will reward the individual for the skills he has developed, his choices are restricted: He can change employers, but that means abandoning his human capital since his skills are specific to

---

Approach (San Francisco:Chandler, 1962), p. 73; and Dorwin Cartwright, "Influence, Leadership, Control," chapter 1 of James G. March, *Handbook of Organizations* (Chicago:Rand McNally, 1965), p. 2.

his present employer. He can relax in his present job, since the bureaucrat who avoids egregious misconduct is rarely subject to dismissal. Finally, he can strive to advance within his own bureau. The absence of opportunities outside the agency creates a situation in which an ambitious employee must strive to please his superior. As Buchanan notes, the relationship is identical with that between master and slave.[3] The implications for the individual are not quite as bleak as the word slavery implies, because the bureaucrat is enslaved only by his own ambition, but the implications for the functioning of bureaucracy are indeed grim.

When skills are transferable the superior can obtain objective information about the value of the subordinate's work from other professionals and the subordinate can advance himself by changing to a different employer. The outside labor market, however, does not reward the ambitious man for doing his assigned job well, it rewards him according to the special criteria of that profession, which will generally coincide only in part with the job assignment. The ambitious economist working in a government agency would not want to have his name attached to analysis that the profession would regard as inferior, but he advances professionally by writing abstract articles, rather than solving the problems he was hired to solve. In other cases the career bias may be so severe as to incapacitate the agency; for example, the staff of a regulatory commission may discover that advancement means obtaining jobs with the regulated firms. In the absence of outright bribery, this precludes incompetent work since firms seek real ability. It also precludes animosity toward the industry and may preclude any regulation aside from the imposition of a cartel-like discipline on the industry.

Transferability of skills causes problems when public and private wage structures are not equivalent. (Equivalence does not mean "equality of money wages" if fringe benefits or enjoyment of the work differ.) Downs stated that high personnel turnover leads to frequent and large performance gaps, that specialists using skills in demand in other organizations are likely to have a high turnover rate, and hence that performance gaps are *more* likely when skills are generally useful than when they are specific to the agency.[4] This disagreement with Hypothesis 68 can be resolved by considering wages and quality of employees. For an occupation such as attorney, where the quality range is immense, the very compressed federal salary structure serves as a filter to select relatively low-quality people and drive out the most able.

[3]James M. Buchanan, "Foreward" to *The Politics of Bureaucracy*, by Gordon Tullock (Washington:Public Affairs Press, 1965), p. 5.
[4]Anthony Downs, *Inside Bureaucracy* (Boston:Little, Brown, 1967), pp. 190, 208–209.

That is, if the entering salary for new law school graduates is competitive, then the government will attract law school graduates of various abilities. The most able will move toward the high pay of the private sector unless they enjoy government. If they are able and ambitious, they will be Tullock's climbers, who create the most serious problems for control. If they are not able (or are simply indolent), they will find the regular salaries of the civil service better than what they might obtain chasing ambulances. The ranks will become clogged with the incompetent, the lazy, and the preoccupied. Although it is possible to attribute the agency's failures to the stream of bright young people who pass through, it seems more reasonable to blame those who remain because they are paid more than their worth. The bright people who pass through will perform according to the standards of the profession, rather than attempting to please their superiors.

This problem is widespread because the Civil Service salary schedule is not related to the observed experience–income profile for any profession.[5] Thus any comparison of federal salaries for a particular occupation with nongovernmental salaries is certain to show a number of stages at which either the best people will find it profitable to leave government or the worst people will find that they have to stay in government. Such selection of the incompetent both weakens the technical proficiency of the bureaucracy and weakens its ties to the profession, thereby setting in motion Tullock's climbers and filling the ranks with the other caricature of the bureaucrat—Downs's conserver, who is deathly afraid of any change in the routine.

Setting government salaries high to keep the ablest worsens the problem of control because it weakens professional motivations. In order to better himself the individual is forced to climb within the agency. Thus we are back in Tullock's world of ambitious men in the most extreme form, since the high salaries will attract very able climbers.

Money is not the only reason for doing a job well. A person might want to retain the approval of colleagues or friends, even if he plans to keep his job. Similarly, the instinct of workmanship or other internal motives for doing the job "right" may be worth something. Still, one must ask how the individual will behave when forced to choose between

---

[5]For the theoretical analysis of the relationship between experience and income, see Jacob Mincer, "On-the-Job Training:Costs, Returns, and Some Implications," *The Journal of Political Economy,* Supplement:October 1962, LXX (No. 5, Part 2):50–73. For a description of salaries in the U.S. federal government, see U.S. General Accounting Office, "Federal White-Collar Pay Systems Need Fundamental Changes," Report FPCD–76–9, 30 October 1975.

doing the job right and pleasing his superior and thereby obtaining a promotion.

The nonpecuniary motives may be of greater significance at less dramatic moments. Both the individual who would rather go fishing than go to the office and the individual who would rather be promoted than do what is right may well prefer to do a job right rather than do nothing or do a job poorly. Even when supervisors know or understand little of what their subordinates are doing, the workmanlike pride in accomplishment may be enough to keep the wheels of government turning.

One limitation of relying on professional or related individual appraisals of what is right is that the individual operative may not understand what behavior is correct.

Hypothesis 69: *Failure is more likely when the task is so complex that the operative does not understand his role in it.*

If hierarchical control were perfect or if employees were interested only in their own careers within the bureaucracy, whether or not individual employees understood what they were doing would be irrelevant. They could follow rules and orders in the first case, or give the superior what they thought he wanted in the second. The idea that individuals within the organization can correct for control loss, if they understand what is going on and are properly motivated, has been a standard theme in the literature at least since Barnard.[6]

The employees of the Employment Service studied by Blau understood that the basic purpose of the agency was to find good jobs for people who wanted to work. Often they disregarded regulations that interfered with that objective.[7] Similarly, Francis and Stone, studying the Employment Service in a different state, found that interviewers first decided whether a client deserved unemployment compensation, and then used the rules to achieve the correct outcome. They concluded that a professional desire to provide service kept the agency from bogging down in procedures.[8]

In the enforcement agency that Blau studied, by contrast, the agents

[6]Chester I. Barnard, *The Functions of the Executive* (Cambridge:Harvard University Press, 1938); see also Bernard L. Gladieux, "Top Management in the War Agencies," chapter 2 in *What We Learned in Public Administration during the War* (Washington:U.S. Department of Agriculture Graduate School, 1949), p. 20.

[7]Peter M. Blau, *The Dynamics of Bureaucracy:A Study of Interpersonal Relations in Two Government Agencies* (Chicago:University of Chicago Press, revised edition 1966 [1st publ. 1955]), p. 23.

[8]Roy G. Francis and Robert C. Stone, *Service and Procedure in Bureaucracy:A Case Study* (Minneapolis:The University of Minnesota Press, 1956), pp. 127, 153–154.

had to refer to a manual of 1000 pages plus volumes of administrative explications and court opinions. The objective of providing service is relatively simple to understand, but the enforcement agents had to go by the rules regardless of how they felt about social effects, which would have been hard to assess in any event.

Relying on the employee's own myopic viewpoint as a professional or as a loyal member of the organization can create an acute problem when what looks correct at the lowest levels of the hierarchy is in fact inconsistent with overall policy. This reasoning has led to the suggestion that the amount of red tape is inversely related to the appearance of rationality in the procedures.[9] In other words, employees must be very tightly controlled if the manager wants them to do something that seems unreasonable.

Another problem that arises from professional control is the limited ability of the top of the hierarchy to bring about changes at the bottom. This can be considered a symptom of the underlying lack of hierarchical control, but in an organization that has been able to function tolerably well by relying on professional control, the top administration may very well have deluded itself into thinking that it had the power to make changes.

Hypothesis 70: *Failure is more likely when an organization relying on professional control tries to institute changes not in accord with professional criteria.*

Change is possible under such circumstances and may even be greeted enthusiastically by professionals if it is a reasonable response to perceived problems, or if it conforms with professional fashions. Neither Gross nor Blau found any strong resistance to change in general, at least among the abler bureaucrats, but undoubtedly a change seen as pernicious, or as imposing a heavy cost on the bureaucrats, would be resisted.[10]

If an organization is to rely on professional control, it is important to select the right type of professional. It will do best if it can attract able people who enjoy the work so much that they would be willing to do it for less than they are currently paid and do not want to be promoted out of it.

---

[9]Frederic S. Burin, "Bureaucracy and National Socialism:A Reconsideration of Weberian Theory," written for *Reader in Bureaucracy*, ed. Robert K. Merton, Ailsa P. Gray, Barbara Hockey, and Hanan C. Selvin (Glencoe, Illinois:The Free Press, 1952), p. 43.

[10]Neal Gross, Joseph B. Giacquinta, and Marilyn Bernstein, *Implementing Organizational Innovations:A Sociological Analysis of Planned Educational Change* (New York:Basic Books, 1971).

Hypothesis 71: *Failure is more likely in programs or agencies that attract ambitious people.*

This hypothesis follows directly from Tullock's model, but it is strengthened by an analysis of professional controls. The example provided by the U.S. Forest Service is particularly noteworthy because the organization, according to Kaufman, manages to retain very good control over the activities of its rangers, despite the difficulties inherent in their scattered assignments in remote and varied locations. The Forest Service uses a variety of techniques to achieve this control, but the one of interest here is the careful selection of people.[11] The recruiting literature stresses the low pay, slow advancement, and hardships of outdoor work at all seasons. The message is clearly not "Join the Forest Service and Rule the World," but rather "This Is a Way to Stay in the Woods without Cutting Pulp." Since enough promotions would eventually move the employee into a city office, promotions are not very attractive for the people who are brought in by the recruiting literature. Other agencies with field offices can also find superior personnel who do not want promotions that entail moving into large cities.

The recognition that professional control provides some substitute for hierarchical control has led to suggestions that professional identification be increased. The preceding argument implies that such efforts are useless for improving control unless they succeed in increasing the transferability of skills among employers. It is barely possible that creating the paraphernalia of a profession—journals, conferences, codes of ethics, educational or other entrance requirements, etc.—could increase awareness of the transferability of skills and hence be productive.

REPRESENTATIVE BUREAUCRACY AND THE PUBLIC INTEREST

Advocacy of representative bureaucracy represents a radical step beyond recognition of the difficulty of achieving hierarchical control.[12] The basic arguments of this school can be summarized as follows:

1. Since problems are largely technical, Congress lacks the expertise to do any more than set broad policies.

[11]Herbert Kaufman, *The Forest Ranger, A Study in Administrative Behavior* (Baltimore:Johns Hopkins Press for Resources for the Future, 1960), chapter 6.

[12]An explicit statement of this view is John Donald Kingsley, *Representative Bureaucracy:An Interpretation of the British Civil Service* (Yellow Springs, Ohio:The Antioch Press, 1944).

2. Control over administration is exercised not by Congress but by individual congressmen, who derive their power from committee assignments, seniority, or influential constituents.
3. The bureaucracy is more representative than is Congress.[13]

The mechanism by which bureaucracies represent the public is poorly specified in the literature. Since references are often made to studies of the class origins of bureaucrats, however, part of the representative function must be presumed to be derived from the bureaucrat's acting as a spokesman for the class into which he was born. Other versions of the argument (except those that blend into the pressure group theories reviewed in Chapter 3) are even more mystical, with comments such as "administration always reflects the total social complex and cannot be expected to rise much above or fall much below the average for the rest of society."[14] The bureaucracy, presumably, mirrors the true character of the public.

The idea of decentralizing bureaucracy so that it might become more responsive to the grass roots was part of the dogma underlying the Tennessee Valley Authority. Selznick's description of this attempt at nonhierarchical democracy confirms the pressure-group analysis[15] Freeing TVA from detailed congressional control did not make it more responsive to the people at large. Instead TVA adjusted its objectives to retain the support of strong local groups, such as the land-grant colleges.

When the administrator does not yield to pressure groups but encounters ambiguities in the law, he can examine the statutes more closely for clues to legislative intent or he can make his own decision consistent with current ideas of social justice.[16] As Schubert has shown in his careful review, the meaning of public interest is elusive, so the administrator is left with various admonitions from the literature of public administration that Schubert summarizes as: "'Be Clever!' 'Be Wise!' 'Be Good!' 'Be Zealous!' and, perhaps, 'Be God!'"[17]

[13]See the unsympathetic critique by Charles E. Gilbert and Max M. Kampelman, "Legislative Control of the Bureaucracy," *The Annals* of the American Academy of Political and Social Science 292 (March 1954):76–87.

[14]Marshall E. Dimock and Gladys O. Dimock, *Public Administration* (New York:Rinehart, 1953), p. 512.

[15]Philip Selznick, *TVA and the Grass Roots:A Study in the Sociology of Formal Organization* (Berkeley:University of California Press, 1949).

[16]Alan Keith-Lucas, *Decisions about People in Need:A Study of Administrative Responsiveness in Public Assistance* (Chapel Hill:University of North Carolina Press, 1957), p. 61.

[17]Glendon A. Schubert, Jr., "'The Public Interest' in Administrative Decision-Making:Theorem, Theosophy, or Theory?" *The American Political Science Review* LI, No. 2 (June 1957): 346–368.

THE BUREAUCRAT AS AGENT OF HIS CLASS

To a Marxist the notion that bureaucrats could represent the people would appear absurd. According to Marxist doctrine, the bureaucracy will be controlled by the bourgeoisie in capitalistic society and will, therefore, serve the interests of that class.[18] This point of view has a good deal in common with the other two that Hill summarizes: that the civil service will carry out the orders of the political leaders (the liberal tradition), or that bureaucracies have power, but can be made subject to the power elite (the pessimistic view of C. Wright Mills). All these approaches view the bureaucracy as a machine that does as it is ordered, but differ regarding the party that is presumed to have the key to the control panel.

Since following the orders of anyone is essentially a matter of hierarchical control, which has already been disposed of, the remaining argument is whether the bureaucrat serves the interest of his own class. The basic problem with this approach is that no one has been able to suggest what incentive the individual would ever have for trying to discover the interests of his class and then trying to advance them.[19] Attachment to a profession offers the possibility of material rewards for conformity to its standards, but behavior on behalf of one's class is not rewarded in any material way. People may pursue nonmonetary objectives, but it would seem more plausible to suppose that a person who is not greedy would be humanitarian, in a broad sense, or at least nationalistic, rather than loyal to his class. The bureaucrat from a tenant background may work more eagerly to impose taxes on land rents than his landlord colleague, but the number of issues on which class interests seem clear is small indeed. Even within its own peculiar framework, the argument that bureaucrats always act in the interest of their class fails; for if they did, the problem of bureaucratic failure would not exist in bourgeois societies.

IDEOLOGY AND INCENTIVES

In Tullock's world, ideology and values have little impact on the outcome, because the scrupulous man is passed by the unscrupulous and,

---

[18]For a review of the sociological literature see Michael J. Hill, *The Sociology of Public Administration* (London:World University, Weidenfeld and Nicolson, 1972).

[19]See the review and analysis by Mancur Olson, "Orthodox Theories of State and Class," chapter 4 of *The Logic of Collective Action:Public Goods and the Theory of Groups* (Cambridge:Harvard University Press, 1965).

therefore, does not rise in the hierarchy enough to influence the activities of the agency. Once allowance has been made for the factors that soften the harsh world of universal climbing—as discussed in the section on professional controls—deeply held values may have some role to play, but they lack the force of the professional codes that are backed by both emotion and money.

The importance of ideology for the effective functioning of organizations has been stressed by numerous commentators. Price, for example, from his survey of the literature finds that organizations having an ideology are more effective, and that effectiveness is related to the importance and internal consistency of the ideology, as well as the extent to which actual behavior conforms to it.[20]

More generally, Hayek observed that, "Coercion can probably only be kept to a minimum in a society where conventions and tradition have made the behavior of man to a large extent predictable."[21] If this is so, then not only effectiveness but freedom depend on that core of traditions, values, and expressed goals common to a particular group.

Variations of these ideas are common in the literature dealing with business and public administration.[22] Dahl and Lindblom mentioned the particular importance of internalized rewards and penalties in activities "requiring enthusiasm, loyalty, discretion, decentralization, and careful judgment."[23] Internal controls are not merely discussed by scholars, they are routinely used in many organizations. In some they develop naturally from the process of recruiting people of common background, training, and outlook.[24] Special education and indoctrination have also been important for a variety of professions ranging from the ancient Chinese Mandarin administrators to modern economists and forest rangers.

Agreement, thus, prevails on the usefulness of individual controls of various sorts if the organization is to remain effective and coordinated despite the many forces leading to independent action by its various

[20]James L. Price, *Organizational Effectiveness:An Inventory of Propositions* (Homewood, Illinois:Richard D. Irwin, 1968). These are Price's Propositions 4.2, 4.3, 4.4, and 4.5.

[21]Friederich A. Hayek, *Individualism and the Economic Order* (Chicago:Henry Regnery, 1972 [1st ed. 1948]), p. 24.

[22]Consider, for example, Barnard's stress on the knowledgeable and motivated employee as an offset to hierarchical control loss; and the discussion of "administrative man" by Herbert A. Simon, Donald W. Smithburg, and Victor A. Thompson, *Public Administration* (New York:Alfred A. Knopf, 1950), p. 82.

[23]Robert A. Dahl and Charles E. Lindblom, *Politics, Economics, and Welfare:Planning and Politico-Economic Systems Resolved into Basic Social Processes* (New York:Harper, 1953), p. 115.

[24]H. E. Dale, *The Higher Civil Service of Great Britain* (Oxford:Oxford University Press, 1941).

components. In particular, if members of the organization have a common ideology, which expresses the purposes of the organization, they may be able to refer back to that in order to keep their own individual behavior in line with purposes. This general concept, however, is beset by difficulties. The first is the general question of why it might be expected to work.

A common ideology might increase effectiveness by decreasing the burden on hierarchical coordination. If different people see things in the same way through a common background, have been trained to react in the same way, and share a common ideology specifying the long range goals, then detailed supervision is not necessary. Each superior can give general guidance to a large number of subordinates. In such a flat hierarchy, the problems of coordination and of control loss through successive stages of a hierarchy are much less.[25] The coordination that must be formally arranged is much simpler because people share the same attitudes, implicit assumptions, and goals.

Control loss, in the sense of messages garbled in transmission, can be offset at each stage as the employee compares his instructions with the ideology. This explains how ideology can simplify the problem of transmitting information and eliminate some of the confusion and conflict that arise from ignorance of what other parts of the organization are doing. It does not, however, solve the problems that arise because of differences between the objectives of individuals and the goals of the organization. It is possible that the unifying ideology can simplify administration enough so that the latter problem is alleviated, but some careful structuring of incentives for correct behavior is still essential.

It is also possible that the causality is reversed. Common objectives develop most readily, according to Downs, when the organization carries out a narrow range of simple, indivisible, and clearly defined functions under stable environmental conditions in one place in an external power setting characterized by strong consensus about the functions.[26] These conditions are also conducive to effectiveness.

Ideology can attract exceptionally able personnel to an agency either because its expressed goals are currently popular or because of more deep-seated ideological sympathies. If ideology attracts enough labor at the standard wage, the agency can be selective in its hiring.

Hypothesis 72: *Failure is more likely in agencies that do not have enough labor slack to be selective in their hiring.*

---

[25]Downs, *Inside Bureaucracy* p. 57.
[26]*Ibid.*, p. 152.

Thus the ideologically attractive agency has the same sort of advantage as an agency that permits travel to resort areas or offers exceptionally pleasant working conditions. Whether the labor slack that is afforded by such nonmonetary amenities will be used to increase the effectiveness of the agency depends on the ability and objectives of the administrators.

As noted earlier, a disparity between the actual wage and the wage at which the employee will quit the job can arise at any step in the hierarchy. If part of the initial attraction of the job is ideological, the agency may have a somewhat different pattern of turnover by grade level than would an agency that provides "just a paycheck." It is not possible to say anything more specific about this, however, because to do so would require assumptions about the trade-off between psychic and monetary income at different stages in the career of the individual, and about whether the agency keeps its ideological promises.

Ideology attracts people who want to carry out the agency's purposes. Obviously, the agency is better off with people who strongly approve of its purposes than with people who disapprove, for the former will have opportunities to advance those purposes and the latter can easily sabotage them, even though both may choose to advance their own careers when it comes to a clear choice between ideology and ambition.

A danger arises, however, when an agency's ideology, rather than appealing to a relatively small and specialized group (as does that of the Forest Service) is so politically fashionable that it attracts the ambitious seeking positions of high visibility from which to advance their careers. This is one of the problems encountered by agencies that are crucial parts of the program publicized by a President (e.g., the Office of Economic Opportunity in the Johnson administration or the Department of Energy in Carter's). This provides another reason (in addition to ignorance of operational realities) why programs initiated at the top of the hierarchy are more likely to fail.

Another problem is that although the ideology alleviates the internal control problems of the agency, it does not necessarily keep the bureaucracy under the control of the public. The agency may be easier to bring under control, once it attracts high-level attention, if it does not have a well-developed ideology. This possibility inspires the frequent assertions that new tasks should be assigned to new agencies, because old agencies will just do more of whatever they have been doing. When the employee's identification is with his co-workers, rather than with specific goals, the group can be set to work on new tasks, or the goals can be modified from above, which is difficult when the identification is professional or ideological.[27] If the identification is restricted to a particular office, it is hard to achieve control from the departmental level. Reorganizations, under these conditions, are mere rearrangements of self-contained units on an organization chart, which scarcely change the behavior of those units.[28]

The ideology or statement of goals may not describe the behavior that is actually rewarded. Warner and Havens suggest that when that is so, the sanctions provide a better predictor of behavior than the goals and, further, that the disagreement itself creates conflicts.[29] Not only do the climbers achieve their own goals at the expense of those stated for the organization, but they demoralize the ideologically motivated by demonstrating that rewards are given for self-serving behavior. Yet the divergence between stated goals and rewarded behavior is very likely to occur because intangible goals have a great attraction, whereas performance is likely to be rated according to something that can be measured.

The other great drawback of ideology is that although it may help to control the behavior of agency personnel, it may also blind them to the realities of the outside world. Banfield provides a fine example of this in his study of the failure of the Casa Grande farm community during the Depression.[30] The bureaucrats assumed that the settlers wanted financial success and would accept any reasonable condition that assured it. The settlers, however, were engaged in the emotional interactions and power struggles of a small community. The bureaucrats attempted to solve every problem by encouraging democratic cooperation, in accordance with the agency ideology, rather than attempting to diagnose the actual problem in the field. The individual bureaucrats appeared to be acting as the head of the agency himself might have acted; that is, the control loss within the agency was overcome, but the activities were futile because they failed to deal with reality.

THE HUMAN SIDE OF BUREAUCRACY

Differences in terminology and in emphasis notwithstanding, the various disciplines that study formal organizations have arrived at the same

---

[27]Simon, Smithburg, and Thompson, *Public Administration*, p. 98.
[28]*Ibid.*, p. 110.
[29]W. Keith Warner and A. Eugene Havens, "Goal Displacement and the Intangibility of Organizational Goals," *Administrative Science Quarterly* 12 (1968):550.
[30]Edward C. Banfield, *Government Project* (Glencoe, Illinois:The Free Press, 1951), esp. pp. 231 ff.

conclusions regarding the condition that leads to bureaucratic failure: Individuals are rewarded for behavior that does not advance the goals of the organization.

This suggests that one should examine the structure of rewards within the organization. The first rule in devising an effective organization—just as in training children or other small animals—is to ensure that behavior that does not advance the goals is never rewarded whereas behavior that does advance the goals sometimes is. In order to take this first step, however, it is necessary that something be known about the preferences of the subject, and that someone have the knowledge and motivation to devise the correct structure of rewards. At this point the analogy with animal training breaks down, for the bureaucrat does not jump to the whip of a benevolent master. The problem of devising incentives is so important and pervasive that it will be examined at length in Chapter 20.

Because the incentive structure cannot possibly be adjusted perfectly, forecasts based on the assumption that "men are motivated by greed" will differ from forecasts based on the assumption that "men want to achieve the goals of the organizations of which they are a part." Each of these is a great oversimplification. Organizations do benefit from various internal controls that are suggested by such terms as *morale* and *professional standards*. In their absence, the workplace takes on the sullen, resentful atmosphere of a slave labor camp. But although the assumption that greed is the sole motive is unnecessarily pessimistic, does the analyst (as distinct from the manager) make a serious mistake by adopting it?

The main message of Douglas McGregor's work is that the manager can extract more and better work from his employees if he can integrate the goals of the individual and the goals of the organization in such a way that the individual will advance the organization's interests as he pursues his own.[31] McGregor expands the concept of greed by drawing on modern speculations regarding motivation, which suggest that relatively rich people may crave self-esteem and status more than money and may even derive pleasure from their work. He restricts his analysis, however, to the relatively simple case of the manager who knows what he wants done and must motivate his subordinates to do it. The manager can do that better if he changes his techniques to conform to a correct view of human behavior. Some of these managerial changes can be instituted at low levels in the hierarchy; they are matters of managerial style that could be taught as part of the routine process of managerial

[31]Douglas McGregor, *The Human Side of Enterprise* (New York:McGraw-Hill, 1960).

improvement within the civil service. It must be noted, however, that such theories are not well developed and tested, and their range of applicability may be limited to certain types of employees performing particular types of tasks.[32] But the more fundamental problem is that the bureaucrat who institutes such managerial improvements does so to advance his own goals, not those of the public.

Another serious problem is that the bureaucratic form of organization, itself, may be incompatible with the functions to be performed—a possibility that returns us to Tullock's proposition that some tasks are organizationally impossible. Governments have a range of organizational forms on which they can draw, of course, but whether a task is assigned to a bureau or a commission or a college the problems of ensuring compliance with legislative intent must somehow be solved. When output is hard to measure directly, the bureaucratic approach is to measure and control inputs more strictly. Such pettiness may drive out the best professionals or it may interfere so much with their freedom of operation that they accomplish nothing.

A vast number of conjectures relating sociological and political variables to the characteristics of agencies and their functions can be developed.[33] This may be a fruitful direction to follow in the very long run, but the large number of poorly specified variables has defeated efforts at rigorous testing, meaningful generalization, and forecasting. Thompson and Tuden use a more manageable classification scheme to attribute failure to the inappropriateness of the decision unit for the task at hand.[34] Bureaucracy, for example, is appropriate for computing the correct answer when agreement prevails both in beliefs about causation and

[32]See the comments by James Q. Wilson, *Political Organizations* (New York:Basic Books, 1973), p. 242; and David Silverman, *The Theory of Organizations:A Sociological Framework* (New York:Basic Books, 1971), p. 84.

[33]Examples include Slesinger's modification (Model 22) of the Janowitz–Wright paradigm giving nine types of public bureaucracy arrayed according to instrumental-goal orientation and policy–goal orientation, Jonathan A. Slesinger, "A Model for the Comparative Study of Public Bureaucracies," *Papers in Public Administration*, No. 23 (Ann Arbor:University of Michigan, Bureau of Government, Institute of Public Administration, 1957); Adrian Webb relates managerial style to the structure of the organization, which includes the proportion of the client's day taken up by the agency, the type of function it performs, its orientation toward clients, and the identity of the beneficiaries, "Social Service Administration:A Typology for Research," *Public Administration* (Journal of the Royal Institute of Public Administration, London) 49 (Autumn 1971):321–339; Amitai Etzioni expects organizations to be more effective when the kind of power, kind of involvement, and type of goal are all congruent, *A Comparative Analysis of Complex Organizations:On Power, Involvement, and Their Correlates* (New York:The Free Press of Glencoe division of Crowell-Collier, 1961).

[34]James D. Thompson and Arthur Tuden, "Strategies in Decision-Making," chapter 19 of Fremont J. Lyden, George A. Shipman, and Morton Kroll, eds., *Policies, Decisions, and Organization* (New York:Appleton-Century-Crofts, 1969), pp. 310–330.

in preferred outcome. On the other hand, the collegial form with majority judgment is more appropriate when beliefs about causation disagree
and bargaining by representatives is appropriate when preferred outcomes differ. If an organization set up to deal with one class of problems
is faced with deciding another type, it may not be able to make the
transition. Similarly, as knowledge advances or recedes, problems with
which an organization was dealing successfully may shift to a type it
cannot handle.

Hypothesis 73: *Failure is more likely when the decision unit is of a form
inappropriate to the problem.*

The relationship between bureaucrats and the bureaucracy has also
attracted the attention of analysts. Merton has tried to show how organizations change personality, whereas Crozier has stressed the problems created for the organization by the efforts of individuals to protect
their personalities.[35] Formally, one can identify different personalities
with different preference functions. This does not pose any analytical
difficulty as long as what seems good to one person also seems good to
another. One man may value a congenial work group heavily, whereas
another is primarily concerned with money income, but as long as each
feels that an improvement in either aspect of his work (all else remaining
unchanged) improves his lot, then the analysis is straightforward. If,
however, one prefers an increase in risk and the other finds the reduction in predictability and security distasteful, then the analysis becomes
more complex. It can be guessed that the stability of old bureaucracies
will attract those who value security, but whether the employees will
then develop an even stronger preference for strict adherence to rules
and cautious approach to change is still an open question. Observation
is complicated by the fact that individuals choose organizations that suit
them and then proceed to change in different ways as they grow older.

The analysis by Argyris of the malfunctioning of the State Department
is based firmly on the assumption that the individual pursues his own
interests.[36] Argyris analyzed the specific behavior that the living system
of the Foreign Service rewards, which, he contends, "predisposes it to
managerial ineffectiveness." The norms that have developed "inhibit
open confrontation of difficult issues and penalize people who take

[35]Robert K. Merton, "Bureaucratic Structure and Personality," pp. 361–371 in Merton,
Reader in Bureaucracy; M. Crozier, *The Bureaucratic Phenomenon* (Chicago:The University of
Chicago Press, 1964).

[36]Chris Argyris, "Some Causes of Organizational Ineffectiveness within the Department
of State," U.S. Department of State, Center for International Systems Research, *Occasional
Papers*, 2, 1966.

risks . . ."[37] The problems of the Foreign Service illustrate the fact that, in the absence of good objective measures of individual (or small group) output, ambitious individuals find they are rewarded by conforming to the norms that have developed in the organization. Since rewards are based on conformity, the available scraps of information about the effectiveness of employees are ignored, especially when the norms are inconsistent with effectiveness. In part, at least, the behavioral style rewarded in the Foreign Service has developed to protect the individual from unfair punishment in an organization where policy is ambiguous and subject to unpredictable reversals from the top, or from the political leadership outside.[38] A different set of norms would be difficult to develop, given the rationality of the existing ones in serving the ends of the individuals in the organization. Ironically, the reforms proposed by Argyris failed abjectly because the changes he prescribed for the living system ignored his own cogent analysis of the ways in which it served the individuals within the organization.[39]

The literature on innovation offers two additional hypotheses.[40] First, any organizational change is difficult to implement from the top, except pure expansion or addition of functions.

Hypothesis 74: *Failure is more likely when an organization must change in order to implement a new program.*

This does not mean that individuals resist change. Successful change, however, requires careful planning and coordination, which are clearly the weakest functions of the bureaucratic form of organization. Innovations requiring much coordination, are particularly likely to fail.

Hypothesis 75: *Failure is more likely when an innovation requires changes in professional role performance.*

Since coordination breaks down during the process of innovation, the individual is left without meaningful external control. If professional standards can guide him, he may accomplish something useful. If the innovation requires changes in his professional role as well, however, he has lost this mooring, too.[41]

This raises again the question of why coordination and planning are

[37]*Ibid.,* p. 2.
[38]*Ibid.,* p. 17.
[39]For an account of the failure, see Donald P. Warwick, *A Theory of Public Bureaucracy:Politics, Personality, and Organization in the State Department* (Cambridge:Harvard University Press, 1975), especially the "Appendix, Biography of a Research Project," pp. 219–237.
[40]See especially Gross *et al., Implementing Organizational Innovations.*
[41]*Ibid.,* p. 206.

so difficult in the bureaucracy. The answer must be found in the extraordinary demands that such activities put on individual bureaucrats, combined with the difficulty in arranging an intensive individual commitment except at the very seat of political power. If a program requires 80-hr weeks of effort by one person for its initiation, that is not the equivalent of having two people each work 40-hr weeks. Coordination has to occur inside one head. The infinitely more complex and time-consuming coordinating task of the bureaucracy is undertaken by people who are not driven to the feats of endurance and personal effort that the threat of bankruptcy extracts from the small businessman. Under the sheltered conditions of civil service life, change is not particularly threatening, but it is not very promising either.

CONCLUSIONS

The most notable aspect of the various approaches to the study of organizations surveyed here is the wide range of agreement about human behavior and the sources of organizational failure. The only aberrant theme is the emphasis by Marx and some more recent writers on social class and other group affiliations as strong influences on individual behavior; this must be considered as an analytical dead end, albeit one of great historical importance. The recent behavioral approaches stress the complexity of human motivation and the inadequacy of money income as a motive. In this, they offer a different emphasis from the standard economic approach, which tends to stress money income and hope of promotion to better jobs as the most important goals of the individuals who are most influential in the organization.

Nevertheless, the central message is the same. The individuals within the organization will pursue their own goals, which are not necessarily consistent with those of the organization. The classical approach to reducing the discrepancy is detailed managerial control of the behavior of subordinates. More recently, theorists have suggested that the manager should strive to arrange matters so that the individual obtains his greatest rewards by pursuing the objectives of the organization. If that can be arranged, the subordinate can be allowed more independence to make fuller use of his abilities to the benefit of himself and the organization.

The two crucial assumptions implicit in this literature are, first, that some means can be devised for checking the subordinate's progress toward the organization's goals and, second, that the superior knows the organization's goals and is motivated to work toward them himself.

The first of these conditions is often not met in government and the second condition is almost never encountered in the federal government of the United States. Thus, although the problem of bureaucratic control is identical with the standard problem of managerial control, the means for its solution are not.

The remoteness of the government bureaucrat from accountability for serving the public interest is inherent in the long chains of command, difficulty of measuring output, and uncertainty regarding the meaning of the public interest. Yet this is only one of the features that distinguishes public bureaucracy from the private sector. Indeed, many large private firms have sections that are characterized by these difficulties in some degree, but the public bureaucracy is afflicted by some unique problems. When output cannot be measured, one reaction of management is to control the use of inputs with a detailed structure of rules. Such red tape in the private sector is designed to prevent theft and to control the most flagrant manifestations of indolence. In the public sector, the red tape must also serve the functions of preventing misuse of the bureaucracy for political ends, protecting the rights of individual citizens, controlling favoritism in administration, and adjudicating conflicts among agencies. The net result of this inevitable dependence on a structure of detailed rules is to make the control problem qualitatively different and far more complex in the public sector. It is not surprising that managerial reforms, even when they work in the private sector, do not have much impact on government bureaucracies.

CHAPTER 5

Types of Bureaucratic Failure

Bureaucracies can fail in a variety of different ways, just as they can fail for a variety of reasons. This chapter focuses on the different types of failure, and thus represents a reorganization and review of material that has appeared, at least tangentially, in the earlier chapters.

CORRUPTION

Corruption is a traditional complaint about bureaucracy. The word can imply moral rot unattended by illegality, as well as the commission of outright crimes by individual bureaucrats. Both moral and legal standards of righteous behavior change over time, but moral standards also vary from person to person at a moment of time, which makes the identification of moral lapses subjective. The career orientation of most federal bureaucrats in this century has reduced illegal behavior to a relatively unimportant problem. It is worth listing because of the intrinsic newsworthiness of the episodes discovered, because it can be a symptom of the same conditions that cause some of the other types of failure, because conditions favor its reemergence as a major problem, and because it is currently serious for some other governments.

The most important forms of corruption are (a) the theft of money and materials; (b) the theft of time; (c) acceptance of bribes; and (d) using the bureaucracy to further the interests of the party or person in power to an extent not sanctioned by the law. The most flagrant manifestations of all of these are readily detected and identified, and are, therefore, rare in well-ordered governments. Complex government functions, however, provide ample opportunity for behavior that probably would not result in a conviction by the courts, but that, nevertheless, seems illegal or unethical to outside observers.

Petty appropriation of materials for personal use occurs in all organizations, but routine control techniques are designed to keep this within bounds. Use of paid time to plan or execute personal business, or simply working at a leisurely pace, may be more serious problems where output cannot be measured and civil-service regulations make firing difficult.[1] Often, however, public agencies, like private firms, have slack periods. It may be difficult to tell whether the bureaucrat is indolent or whether the organization has no way to use his time. More complex, still, is the problem of the professionally motivated employee who uses the agency's time to further his career. Whether his professional activities improve his performance at the agency is difficult to determine. If the agency responds by detailed regulation of activities and petty restriction of reimbursement for professional travel and expenses, it will have difficulty in hiring professionals.

Acceptance of bribes is obviously a crime, but the infinite variety of forms in which personal influence and favors can be used makes the issue complex. Some uses of consulting services and honoraria seem to be attempts to buy favors, but other interactions between private parties and government officials are necessary. As the functions of government become more complex, these issues become more pervasive. At the same time, however, they are newsworthy enough to be subject to considerable external control. They are also matters on which individual standards of ethics exert some beneficial influence, because the individual is confronted by the question "Are you willing to sell your integrity for this price?" rather than the more difficult choice between what is right and what leads to promotion.

---

[1]Victor A. Thompson discusses administrative self-indulgence in "Bureaucracy in a Democratic Society," chapter 11 of *Public Administration and Democracy:Essays in Honor of Paul H. Appleby* (Syracuse, New York:Syracuse University Press, 1965), p. 214. At the time of this writing (March 1978) the newspapers and magazines are filled with accounts of the difficulty of firing incompetent or unproductive civil servants. See, for example, *Time*, 6 March 1978: 13–15, and the reports of President Carter's proposals for reform of the Civil Service system carried in the morning newspapers on 3 March 1978.

The use of the bureaucracy to further the interests of the party or person in power poses the most difficult questions. Many of these have been raised in the debate since Watergate, and there is no need to duplicate that discussion here. Some activities are clearly illegal and laws can be tightened to deal with other clearly unethical actions. Still, the boundary is fuzzy between the President's program for the country (which will, if it is correctly chosen and well implemented, gain him votes as an expression of confidence in his leadership) and blatant efforts to buy votes for the party in power.[2] The criterion of requiring legislative sanction for legitimate public programs would seem a reasonable one in a representative democracy, but in fact the President has enough power under existing legislation to establish some programs that are as legitimate as many of the other activities of government.

"New Towns in-Town" is an example of a program without specific legislative authorization, but which seems generally to have been an appropriate and legal use of resources.[3] Use of political pressure to influence the award of contracts, or similar favors, to key districts or individuals is generally considered an abuse when it is carried to an extreme, but since some such behavior is an inherent part of the political process it is difficult to draw a definite boundary between corrupt and acceptable behavior.[4] It would be tempting to try to differentiate corruption from other failures by defining corruption as a situation in which the bureaucrat personally profits from crime. If, however, he plays favorites in response to the unspoken wishes of his superior in the expectation of more rapid promotion, the reward for improper behavior comes in a perfectly legal and open form and the behavior, itself, cannot easily be identified.

The most serious problems of corruption arise at the points where the bureaucracy interacts with the economic sector of society. Traditional problems have included the acceptance of bribes by bureaucrats in exchange for the following: (a) lenient application of regulations that are supposed to be imposed on all firms in a specific category; (b) lax appli-

[2]Charles S. Hyneman, *Bureaucracy in a Democracy* (New York:Harper, 1950), p. 27.

[3]Martha A. Derthick provides an account of the origins, implementation, and failure of the program in *New Towns-In-Town, Why a Federal Program Failed* (Washington:The Urban Institute, 1972).

[4]Although precise lines are hard to draw, the public reaction suggests that the Nixon administration went beyond what is acceptable when H. R. Haldeman had Frederic V. Malek draw up an explicit plan for shifting federal expenditures and ending certain federal investigations of wrongdoing in order to aid President Nixon's reelection. See *The New York Times*, 16 January 1974, "Nixon Aide Admits Grants Were Used to Win Votes in '72," p. 1, for a brief report. It is difficult to argue that any specific part of the plan was inconsistent with past practices of numerous administrations, but the whole package had an excessively calculated quality that seemed offensive to many.

cation of quality standards to purchased work or materials; (c) award of contracts to a firm other than the one offering the best terms to the public; and (d) routine processing of private applications and permits that do not in themselves involve wrongdoing. Item (d) is usually just petty extortion that transfers some money from members of the public doing business with the government to particular bureaucrats. Except for the inefficiency, inequity, and general reduction in the moral tone of society, it does not cost anything. Item (c), similarly, is a transfer from the public as a whole to a particular firm. Items (a) and (b) involve the possibility of costs to the public far exceeding the savings to particular firms; for example, the poorly processed meat that poisons people or the weapons that misfire in battle.

When people say that the federal government of the United States is relatively free of corruption, they are usually referring to the infrequency of *overt* bribes. As the activities of the government have reached further into our complex society, however, problems of conflict of interest not involving specific bribes have multiplied. They may be as blatant as ownership by an employee of a regulatory commission of stock in a company that his agency regulates. Yet anyone who acquires expertise in an industry by regulating it may learn about sound investment opportunities in that industry. In the absence of a code of ethics that may seem unreasonably strict, he can easily drift into a situation that involves the potential for conflict of interest. As companies and regulatory agencies broaden the scope of their activities, the chances for such conflicts grow.[5]

The conflicts of interest that arise from the actual or potential movements of individuals between jobs inside and outside the government are far more serious than the impersonal conflicts arising from the bureaucrat's investment portfolio. The financial connections remaining from private employment (e.g., stock options, stock holdings, and pension plans) have been subject to considerable comment because they constitute an obvious problem every time a new President appoints his cabinet. The average man probably does not have enough financial assets to affect his integrity. The potential employment opportunities in the organizations with which the bureaucrat deals officially, however, may provide a stronger inducement for incorrect behavior. Moreover, the prospect of a job offer leaves no trace in the files.

---

[5]The Oversight and Investigations Subcommittee of the House Commerce Committee found financial conflicts of interest in 243 of the 630 files it examined of employees of the Federal Communications Commission, the Environmental Protection Agency, and the Food and Drug Administration. Many of these conflicts are not illegal. The investigation was reported in a *New York Times* release carried in *The Cleveland Plain Dealer* 19 February 1978, section one, p. 25.

Complex shadings of personal interest and behavior that dances on the borders of the ethical and legal are introduced by the heavy reliance on outside contractors to plan and organize government activity.[6] Individuals shuttle among government agencies, universities, and consulting organizations writing requests for proposals and then the proposals that meet the specifications they or their cronies have set. The review panel of outside experts that judges the proposals consists of the same cast of characters. Even if a particular episode, taken by itself, involves different sets of people at the various stages, the long-term community of interest among them may convert what looks like a competitive process of contract awards into a modern version of the ancient spoils system. A particularly flagrant and simple example of this is summarized in Chapter 16.

ALLOCATIVE FAILURE

The allocative question has dominated the theoretical literature on public spending: Does society allocate too large or too small an amount of resources to public goods? The right amount is defined as the amount that maximizes the welfare of consumers. Yet it is not possible to determine how much people want to buy unless you know the cost per unit. The assumption that public goods will be produced at the minimum possible cost for the chosen level of output overlooks a host of complications, including some related to the particular mix of goods provided by the government. Even the forms of corruption that merely transfer resources from the taxpayers in general to particular criminals, without directly introducing any inefficiency in the use of resources, may influence the allocation decision by (a) raising the price of particular services to the taxpayers, and (b) creating a small group of people with a very strong interest in seeing that the particular service from which they benefit corruptly is maintained and extended.

TECHNICAL INEFFICIENCY

Technical inefficiency includes such problems as (a) using the wrong interest rate to discount future costs and benefits; (b) using an expensive combination of inputs; (c) using an excessive quantity of inputs; (d)

---

[6]Daniel Guttman and Barry Willner provide a compendium of horror stories in *The Shadow Government:The Government's Multi-Billion-Dollar Giveaway of its Decision-Making Powers to Private Management Consultants, "Experts," and Think Tanks* (New York:Pantheon Division of Random House, 1976), a project of the Center for Study of Responsive Law.

managing poorly, with problems such as turmoil, indecision, confusion, and obvious waste; (e) innovating too quickly or too slowly; and (f) spending too much on advertising, product differentiation, or other pathological forms of competition. Inappropriate investment decisions have received a great deal of attention from economists at least since Jevons.[7] Similarly, the choice of the least expensive combination of inputs is standard grist for the economist's mill, so particular institutional constraints that prevent cost minimization have been subject to some analysis.[8] For example, traditionally the General Services Administration has assigned space, for which no rent was charged, to government agencies; the new approach is to charge rent and to allow the head of an agency to decide how much space to use. Similarly, managers could be granted more flexibility in the choice of numbers of personnel at different grade levels within a limited total budget, but this is still subject to tight control by Congress. Of course, any move to give the manager more discretion in the expectation that he will decrease costs (or increase output) rests on the assumption that the manager has an incentive to minimize costs (or maximize output).

If the manager uses more inputs than are necessary to accomplish the task, whether they are combined in the most efficient ratio is irrelevant. Niskanen suggests that sometimes the budget is so large that if it were spent efficiently the legislature would be more than satiated. An additional road or public housing development, for example, in many urban areas would be worth less than nothing to the politicians because of the controversies over the exact location. In such a situation, the agency will spend all its funds on the limited activities open to it.

This is distinct from the problems of poor management, which are particularly likely to show up at the inception of a program. Some managers are worse than others; some can benefit from formal training. These routine matters in the struggle against waste are not of concern here except where the bureaucratic setting is particularly conducive to poor management. Economists usually do not tell managers how to minimize costs because the owner of the firm has an incentive to do it and the manager knows more about the actual details of operating any firm than the economists. When the institutional arrangements are such

---

[7]W. S. Jevons, *Methods of Social Reform* (New York:Augustus M. Kelly, 1965 [collected essays first published in London, 1883]). See the analysis of the choice of the appropriate discount rate by William J. Baumol, "On the Discount Rate for Public Projects," chapter 6 of *Public Expenditure and Policy Analysis*, ed. Robert H. Haveman and Julius Margolis (Chicago:Rand McNally, 2nd ed., 1977).

[8]E.g., William A. Niskanen, Jr., *Bureaucracy and Representative Government* (Chicago:Aldine-Atherton, 1971).

that the incentives for technical efficiency are eliminated, however, these internal managerial questions enter the realm of the economist. If the manager has some goal other than technical efficiency, it is still generally assumed that he will pursue his goals effectively, without confusion and waste. Thus the hired manager of a large company may maximize his salary and perquisites at the expense of the owners' profits, or the managers of a regulated utility may use excessive amounts of capital because of quirks in the regulatory process. Still, the organizations should run smoothly and with apparent efficiency except for the specific departures from the theoretical optimum.

Although managerial incentives to avoid obvious fiascoes are also strong in government, several characteristics of government make abject failure more likely. In the first place, the government does not have any force for weeding out unfit administrators that is as strong as bankruptcy.[9] Furthermore, the rigid federal salary structure does not allow the individual to be compensated according to his merit. As the best managers are hired away, the remaining people are, on average, overpaid for their abilities, although salaries are comparable for equivalent job descriptions in the public and private sectors.[10]

Although public managers will on average be of lower quality than private, they also have a more difficult job. The political setting imposes a vast number of constraints upon the administrator, while at the same time the Civil Service Regulations decrease the degree of commitment that he can expect from his subordinates. Moreover, the task of coordinating the activities of several agencies must be effected by bargaining and bartering of favors.

The public sector creates conditions that are particularly conducive to poor administration because of the inability of politicians to decide on coherent long-range plans. The effects on the bureaucracy include vacillation, the reluctance of the superiors at each level to take any firm positions that would permit their subordinates to get on with their work, constant efforts of everyone to protect himself against being caught on the wrong side of policies that have not yet been decided, and the

---

[9]The "Sunset Law" would not change this. Sunset Laws call for programs to expire after a certain number of years unless specifically renewed by Congress. The assumption is that programs fail because of poor legislation, rather than ineffective administration. Although this may be generally correct, it still leaves the problem of weeding out those managers who are ineffective. For a compendium of papers and testimony about sunset laws, see Sunset Act of 1977, U.S. Senate, Committee on Governmental Affairs, Subcommittee on Intergovernmental Relations, 95th Congress, first session, 29 March 1977, esp. the statements by Robert D. Behn, Robert P. Biller, Garry D. Brewer, and Henry James Decker.

[10]Sharon P. Smith, *Equal Pay in the Public Sector:Fact or Fantasy* (Princeton:Industrial Relations Section of Princeton University, 1977).

periodic crises in which activities and expenditures that have long been delayed must suddenly be completed in an impossibly short time.

The political setting also influences the adoption of innovations. Although it is not clear that bureaucrats innovate too slowly, it does seem that the choice of innovations is influenced more by political fashion or the desire to augment services than by potential for saving resources.[11]

Excessive expenditures on advertising and other pathological forms of competition, including excessive product differentiation, have been standard topics in the discussion of various private markets that depart from perfect competition. The subject is rarely discussed in connection with the public sector, except in the Galbraithian assertion that *private* wants are synthesized by excessive advertising and, by implication, *public* wants are not.[12] The latter contention has probably lost many of its defenders in this era of increased cynicism about the motives of politicians and allegations of news management. Anyone who reads the newspaper or the list of new publications of the Government Printing Office can see that agencies do use an appreciable amount of resources for public relations or advertising—whatever name is given to the activity.[13] It would appear from the study by Maass that they also engage in nonprice competition under duopolistic conditions.[14] Finally, the frantic efforts by government agencies to define a new mission when the original objective is abandoned or met are similar to the efforts of private firms to create new markets.

[11]Irwin Feller and Donald C. Menzel with Lee Ann Kozak, *Diffusion of Innovations in Municipal Governments* (University Park, Pennsylvania:The Pennsylvania State University Institute for Research on Human Resources, Center for the Study of Science Policy, 1976); and Irwin Feller, "Managerial Response to Technological Innovation in Public Sector Organizations," *Management Science* 26, No. 10 (Oct. 1980):1021–1030.

[12]John Kenneth Galbraith, *The Affluent Society* (Boston:Houghton Mifflin, 1958), esp. chapter 11.

[13]An article by Karen Elliott House, *Wall Street Journal*, 9 March 1976, p. 1, mentioned that the Federal Energy Administration had 112 publicists among its staff of 3400 employees. Although the job of the publicists was partly to sell national policy (energy conservation), they also tried to convince Congress and the public of the importance of the agency. The agency had other advertising expenses, as well, including a billing for $602,000 for an energy conservation campaign in 1973–1975. (See the *Wall Street Journal*, 12 September 1977, p. 21, for a report about certain disputed charges.) In addition, it has been suggested that one of the main purposes of the studies by outside consultants commissioned by the agency was to make the continuation of the agency seem essential. Obviously, the line between promoting national policy and promoting the agency is as hard to draw as is the distinction between *informational* and *excessive* advertising in the private sector.

[14]Arthur A. Maass, "Duplication of Functions:A Case Study in Bureaucratic Conflict," Report Prepared for U.S. Commission on Organization of the Executive Branch of Government (Hoover Commission), 1949, reprinted in Robert K. Merton *et al.*, *Reader in Bureaucracy* (Glencoe, Illinois:The Free Press, 1952).

FAILURE TO ACHIEVE ANYTHING

Closely related to the concept of inefficiency in the sense of excessive use of inputs relative to outputs are the extreme cases where there is no output. These include (a) the abject public failures that make the headlines; (b) quiet ineffectuality; and (c) errors in the analysis or the information provided to higher levels of the government. Abject public failure is not common except where the agency is attempting to provide a good that can be sold on the market. When people refuse to consume a heavily subsidized good, they reveal that it is not worth the resources put into it. It may be worth less than nothing; for example, a housing project that is so poorly designed that it destroys the neighborhood, as well as remaining unfilled.[15] Unless the output is for sale, such extreme failure is hard to document. The agency that labored for 16 years to produce the industrial mobilization plan for World War II that was never used may have produced a good plan, but no one will ever be certain.[16] Similarly, an agency that is charged with coordinating something or facilitating the adoption of the latest managerial panacea will rarely make the headlines if its output is zero or negative. The provision of erroneous analysis and incorrect information to policymakers is sometimes publicized after major crises, for example, Pearl Harbor or the Cuban missiles. Such egregious errors in visible functions are a relatively small part of the whole problem, however. The prevalence of erroneous forecasts is rooted in the fact that the bureaucrat is rewarded for offering advice that seems sound to his superior, rather than being substantively correct. The problem is far more severe in the public than in the private sector because the long continuation of a zero or negative output is almost impossible except in government (and, perhaps, in some nonprofit organizations including universities). The elimination of the discipline of the marketplace makes the continuation of such failures possible. Moreover, people are promoted on the basis of skill at bureaucratic maneuvering, so success, in the bureaucratic setting, is not related to the use of resources to solve the problems of the world outside the bureaucracy.

---

[15]Pruitt-Igoe in St. Louis is the standard example of the bad housing project, but similar cases can be found in other countries. See E. L. Normanton, *Accountability and Audit of Governments. A Comparative Study* (New York:Praeger, 1966), pp. 160 ff.

[16]The unused plan is mentioned by David Novick, Melvin Anshen, and W. C. Truppner, *Wartime Production Controls* (New York:Columbia University Press, 1949).

SUBSERVIENCE TO CLIENT OR
OTHER INTEREST GROUPS

The observation that regulatory agencies tend to be "captured" by the firms they regulate has been made so often that it is a cliché. There is a similar tendency for a service agency to become subservient to its clientele.

LACK OF COORDINATION OF
RELATED ACTIVITIES

Failure to coordinate related activities is one of the traditional complaints about bureaucracy. Strict hierarchical coordination becomes progressively more difficult as the size or complexity of the organization increases. The problem of coordinating federal, state, and local activities is particularly intractable. Not only is there no formal hierarchical control mechanism, but in addition the flows of information are often poor in both directions. Furthermore, differences in local conditions make general federal rules seem ludicrous, which only strengthens the zeal of local governments for preserving their independence. The local or state government may also be the focal point for the uncoordinated policies of different federal agencies, which further decreases the likelihood of arriving at a consistent policy.

CONFLICT BETWEEN THE OBJECTIVES OF
DIFFERENT AGENCIES

Lack of coordination suggests that agencies are groping and stumbling in the same direction less effectively than they would if they could be forced to work jointly. Sometimes, however, the basic objectives of two agencies differ so sharply that improving the communications would worsen the conflict between them. If, for example, the Occupational Safety and Health Administration wants to protect hospital employees from contamination by requiring plastic liners in hospital wastebaskets, whereas the Department of Health and Human Services prohibits plastic liners in order to reduce fire hazard, the problem is not poor communication, but differing objectives. Under such conditions, coordination requires more than bureaucratic skill and the good will of participants.

SUBSERVIENCE TO INDIVIDUAL POLITICIANS OR PARTIES

Although the bureaucracy is supposed to answer to the elected representatives of the people collectively, it is not supposed to provide favors for individuals. The principle is clear, but the application is exceedingly fuzzy, especially since (a) the agency is mainly in contact with the handful of senior legislators on the particular subcommittees that oversee its activities and (b) individual citizens will frequently ask their representatives to provide access to the bureaucracy for routine services. It is a matter of courtesy to move the constituent's request to the top of the in-basket when a legislator inquires, but if the in-basket is heaped so full that only those inquiries moved to the top receive any action, then the result comes closer to a patronage or spoils system than to a civil service. The likelihood of such behavior depends not only on the ethics of bureaucrats and legislators, but also on the types of activities that the agency engages in.

PURSUIT OF POLICIES DIFFERENT FROM THOSE SPECIFIED IN THE LEGISLATION

The most flagrant instances of bureaucratic failure occur when the agency undertakes activities that differ from those that the political leadership has specified. This can include (a) failure to change the agency's activities to correspond with a change in the legislated directives or executive orders; (b) initiation of unauthorized projects; and (c) selecting activities to meet the bureaucrat's preferences from an excessive number of authorized activities. Organizations with enough slack can initiate projects before they are authorized. Good management requires some preliminary investigation by the bureaucracy in view of the inability of the politicians to plan ahead. If a project begins to have some impact on the citizenry before it has been approved by the elected officials, however, control over bureaucracy has failed. The converse case is the bureaucrat who has been assigned too many tasks to complete and therefore chooses to ignore the ones that do not suit him. If outputs and work loads are hard to measure, the argument that resources are inadequate can always serve both as an excuse for failing to follow orders and as a means of obtaining a higher appropriation.

FAVORITISM IN DISTRIBUTION OF SANCTIONS

The borderlines among favoritism in the distribution of rewards and penalties, bribery, the political spoils system, and oppression of political enemies are sometimes vague, and there is little point in devoting much effort to sharpening the distinctions. When regulations are very complex or programs are partially funded, bureaucrats acquire some power to decide who will be steered carefully through the procedures necessary to obtain favors and who will be left to flounder. Similarly, the complexity of regulations regarding myriads of matters including health, safety, taxes, and the environment implies that enforcement must be selective. No government has a large enough army of inspectors to go through all the records of all the firms, which is fortunate because a thorough audit is expensive even when no errors are found. The power to investigate is the power to bankrupt. Since the bureaucracy does have the power to inflict heavy costs or confer significant benefits on particular individuals, it clearly does have the power to display favoritism based on bribes, political contributions, expression of radical opinions, race, or other characteristics.[17] Similarly, favors can be distributed in such a way as to buy off those who potentially constitute an articulate opposition. The legislature, also, can use such a tactic by setting aside a certain proportion of total funding of a program for research grants, thus ensuring enthusiasm for the legislation from most academic experts.[18]

INORDINATELY SLOW PROGRESS TOWARD THE CORRECT GOAL

Foot-dragging in implementation is the time-honored technique for bureaucratic sabotage of unwanted programs. It is a symptom of the poor control exerted by the hierarchy that the bureaucrats must be convinced that a program is in their own interests before they will move to implement it promptly. At each stage in the process of implementation, delay can readily be created by those opposed to a program. The possibilities for delay are vastly expanded when a program requires clearance and cooperation from more than one agency.

---

[17]The "Enemies" list of the Nixon administration is the most publicized example.
[18]This may explain the delay in academic criticism of the Manpower Development and Training Act long after its ineffectuality was obvious.

DISPLACEMENT OF GOALS

The sociological literature discusses the process by which the legislated goals of the agency are displaced by others such as survival, power, expansion, an easy life, strict adherence to rules and procedures, pursuit of the activities at which the agency is successful, or the professional goals of the bureaucrats. The shift toward strict adherence to rules is a standard topic in the literature. In the absence of a good way to measure output, it is not possible to design a correct structure of incentives. Hence the superior promulgates rules that give ludicrous results in certain circumstances. An imperfect measurement of output is not much help, because that measure then becomes the goal, displacing the formal goals of the organization.

When an agency is successful at some small part of its assigned tasks, it may tend to shift its efforts further in that direction. If the shift in goals toward what is actually accomplished takes place through the process of incremental changes in the legislation, the result cannot be considered a failure to meet the goals specified by Congress. As time passes and the laws are modified, the behavior of the agency may diverge considerably from the original legislative intent. The incremental process also gives great weight to the opinions of established client groups; but—almost tautologically—it tends to result in legislation that will be implemented very well. It is roughly equivalent to adopting the operative goals as the formal goals of the organization.

The goals of the legislation may be displaced by the goals of the professionals who dominate the agency or by the goals of clients. The goals of a prison may shift toward those of the prisoners or the guards (or conceivably the criminologists) rather than remaining those of the citizenry.

SLOW ADAPTATION TO EXTERNAL CHANGES

Whether a bureau adjusts rapidly enough to changing external conditions will always be subject to dispute. The accusation of failure to adapt can include the inefficiency of failing to innovate more quickly, discussed previously. It can also include the failure to change operations to correspond with new conditions.

Agencies should certainly adapt to changes in the policies established by legislation and to relevant changes in technology. Whether they should also adapt to changes in public sentiment, professional fashions, and the relative strengths of pressure groups is a moot point. In the strict hierarchical model they should not, but since hierarchical control is inadequate, it could be argued that the bureaucracy should respond directly to such outside controls. The charge of unresponsiveness to changed conditions, therefore, generally implies either some notion of direct representation by bureaucracy or is synonymous with such failures as lack of innovation, failure to conform to changes in policy, or, perhaps, dereliction in the duty of proposing changes in legislation.

FAILURE TO COMPLY WITH STANDARDS OF DUE PROCESS IN ADMINISTRATIVE BEHAVIOR

Much of the literature on administrative discretion and administrative law is concerned with the problem of arbitrary behavior of bureaus in their relations with individuals or firms. Such failure to comply with fair procedures is a serious concern in view of the opportunities for favoritism and harassment that are frequently available to agencies.

FINAL NOTES ON SOURCES OF FAILURE

An attempt to summarize the preceding chapters would accomplish little. The hypotheses, such as they are, can serve as a list of the major topics covered, but, in view of the less than fully rigorous derivation of most of them and the problems with terminology inherent in such a wide-ranging survey, the hypotheses are of little value in isolation from the discussion accompanying their initial development.

This recital of bureaucratic failings presents a sharp contrast to the general assumption in the literature of public finance that legislation will be implemented in the form in which it is passed by the legislature. The general verdict—that bureaucracies can fail—is not of much use, however; for the alternative to the implementation of legislation by bureaucrats is anarchy, which has its own disadvantages.

Unfortunately, the attempt to develop more specific conclusions encounters a number of problems. Governments engage in a variety of activities including regulation and control of private businesses or individual citizens; direct provision of services to individuals; grants and loans of funds to citizens and other governments; and collecting and disseminating information of various types. The type of activity, various characteristics of the environment, and the form of organization, among other factors, must have some influence on the likelihood for success.

Although it might be possible to organize the various hypotheses according to the type of government activity cross-classified by environment and type of failure, it seems doubtful that this undertaking would be worth the effort at the present stage of development. The various bodies of literature surveyed have already provided an unmanageably large collection of low-level generalizations. Although the development of a more general framework would simplify analysis, it seems doubtful that greater theoretical refinement is valuable in the absence of a firmer empirical grounding.

Accordingly, the next part of this book presents 11 short case-studies of bureaucratic failure. It is not possible to construct a rigorous test of 75 hypotheses using 11 case studies. The analysis here is at a considerably earlier stage of inquiry. The case studies are presented, first, as useful illustrations of the sorts of problems that do occur during the implementation process and, second, to check, in a subjective way, whether the eclectic theoretical and speculative inquiry of Part I appears to be headed in a useful direction.

PART II

Cases of Bureaucratic Failure

CHAPTER **6**

HUD Houses the Poor[1]

The Housing and Urban Development Act of 1968 established a program to subsidize mortgage payments for families of low and moderate income—the Section 235 homeownership assistance program.[2] Although the Federal Housing Administration (FHA) had insured home mortgages since 1934 and rental housing for the poor had been subsidized since 1937, the direct subsidy for homeownership was a new activity for the Department of Housing and Urban Development (HUD).

The program set the family's payment for mortgage, taxes, and insurance at 20% of its income. The government paid the rest of the mortgage bill to the lender. Eligibility was restricted to families below a maximum income that varied with family size and geographic location.[3] The

---

[1]This chapter is based largely on U.S. General Accounting Office, "Weaknesses in Administration of the Program to Correct Defects in Housing Insured Under the Section 235 Program," Report RED–75–340, 19 March 1975. I am also indebted to Tobias Gottesman (Housing Management) and George Hipps (Housing Production and Mortgage Credit), both of HUD, for their assistance.

[2]Section 101(a) of the Act (P.L. 90–448) contained the provisions that became Section 235 of the National Housing Act, as amended. These provisions are found in 12 USC 1715Z.

[3]To qualify for the program the adjusted family income (total family income minus 5% minus $300 per minor child) could not be more than 135% of the local limit for admission to public housing. The minimum down payment was $200.

amount of the mortgage was restricted, as was the maximum subsidy on a mortgage of a given size. Family incomes were to be reevaluated periodically and the subsidy adjusted accordingly.[4] Although the legislation was oriented toward new construction or extensive renovation, some funds could be used to subsidize the purchase of existing houses.

The program as outlined had one defect that early observers noticed.[5] Since the subsidy filled the entire gap between the family's housing budget of 20% and the actual mortgage payment, the family had little incentive to find a less expensive house or to bargain down the price of one that was priced below the mortgage limit.[6] This inherent problem with the legislation was exacerbated by HUD's failure to provide field offices with a consistent policy on whether the statutory limit was the amount to which all were entitled, or whether the field office was to limit the mortgage to what was necessary to buy a modest house according to local standards and prices.[7]

By the summer of 1970 more ominous reports were reaching Congress. On September 29, 1970, the House Committee on Banking and Currency voted (35 to 0) to have its staff investigate the situation. The resulting report opened with a scathing attack:

> The Department of Housing and Urban Development and its Federal Housing Administration may be well on its way toward insuring itself into a national housing scandal.
>
> The Federal Housing Administration is insuring existing homes that are of such poor quality that there is little or no possibility that they can survive the life of the mortgage. . . . FHA has approved housing for the 235 program which, within months after purchase, has been condemned by municipal authorities.[8]

[4]A later GAO study showed that HUD failed to check the incomes reported by participants, thus encouraging widespread cheating. The GAO report was summarized in the *Cleveland Plain Dealer*, 10 Sept. 1975.

[5]See, e.g., Henry J. Aaron, *Shelter and Subsidies* (Washington:The Brookings Institution, 1972), p. 139; and Harrison G. Wehner, Jr., "Sections 235 and 236:An Economic Evaluation of HUD's Principal Housing Subsidy Programs" (Washington:American Enterprise Institute For Public Policy Research, Evaluative Studies 8, June 1973):6.

[6]If the family expected its income to rise enough to end the subsidy, it would be interested in keeping the cost down. Similarly, if it expected its income to fall, it would want to keep the minimum required payment (the payment necessary to amortize a mortgage calculated with a 1% interest rate) as low as possible.

[7]U.S. General Accounting Office, "Opportunities to Improve Effectiveness and Reduce Costs of Homeownership Assistance Programs," Report B171630, 29 Dec. 1972:34–40.

[8]U.S. Congress. House. Committee on Banking and Currency, "Investigation and Hearing of Abuses in Federal Low- and Moderate-Income Housing Programs," Staff Report and Recommendations, Committee Print, Dec. 1970, appended to "Hearing on HUD Investigation of Low- and Moderate-Income Housing Programs," 31 March 1971. Hereafter this document is referred to as "Abuses."

The remainder of the report included descriptions of shoddy new construction and far worse abuses in existing slum properties, apparently with the complicity of FHA appraisers in some instances. Speculators had purchased decaying slum buildings for less than $10,000 apiece, added some cosmetic rehabilitation, and sold them under the 235 program a few days later at markups ranging from $7650 to $18,200. It appeared that in some cities the slum landlords had used the program to unload houses that had outlived their usefulness. Furthermore, in the urban slums and other localities where the FHA had little experience in appraising property values, the sales at inflated values under the 235 program established the comparable values at which other properties were appraised.

The outrageous profiteering was just one indication that HUD did not have the capacity to administer the program. The most sensitive tasks were performed by the appraiser. When a prospective purchaser had decided on a house, the appraiser would inspect it to determine whether it was a good financial risk for FHA; that is, in the event of foreclosure, would the property sell for more than the amount of the mortgage? If the appraiser happened to notice defects threatening the integrity of the dwelling or the safety of the occupants he was to require their correction. (In questionable cases, such as judging the seriousness of cracks in a foundation, he could call on architects, engineers, or other professionals in the HUD field office.) Once the seller had been notified of defects requiring correction, it was necessary for either the appraiser or the lender to certify that the repairs were made.

The journeyman appraiser may be hired with no background in the work. He is trained on the job, mainly by accompanying another appraiser during a 9-month period. He is supposed to be closely supervised by a more senior appraiser, who has the authority to commit the FHA to guarantee the loan. The bribery cases found in the investigations of the 235 program make it clear that the appraiser is in an exposed position because of the profits involved in individual transactions and his relative independence of supervision in the field. Furthermore, the report suggests that "many of the appraisers feel that their only future lies in the possibility of 'good jobs' with the mortgagees or the real estate firms...."[9] so more subtle pressures than outright bribery were at work to break down professional standards of conduct. In addition, at times of peak workload the HUD field offices often relied on contract appraisers, who were paid a fee of $25 per appraisal, and who, with their lack of

[9] *Ibid.*, p. 6.

long-term connections to the federal government, were even more susceptible to external pressures.

The report also suggests a general laxity of administration including the failure of headquarters to impose consistent guidelines on the field offices or to find out what was happening in the field. Such allegations are difficult to substantiate, but it is clear that HUD was under strong pressure to move quickly into this new area and that it communicated this pressure to the field offices by reallocating funds quickly from offices that spent slowly to those that spent quickly.[10]

The most serious social problem disclosed by the report, and the point to which Congress was most sympathetic, was the plight of those who found their houses crumbling around them. HUD treats the appraisal as an internal task performed for its own benefit, not as a warranty of quality, and had won suits in court earlier against buyers who wanted to treat the appraisal as a warranty by the FHA.[11] Nevertheless, many of the poorly educated purchasers of Section 235 houses were encouraged by the sellers to believe that the FHA was certifying the houses and would even repair defects. As the stories accumulated, both in the staff report and in the press, of low-income families unable to finance the repairs necessary to make their houses livable and unable to sell them for enough to pay off their mortgages because of the inflated appraisals, Congress passed Section 518(b) authorizing HUD to pay for correcting the defects.[12] The law stated that if the owner of a used house applies before the deadline

> The Secretary is authorized to make expenditures to correct, or to compensate the owner for, structural or other defects which seriously affect the use and livability of any single-family dwelling which is covered by a mortgage insured under section 235 of this Act . . . [provided] the defect is one that existed on the date of the issuance of the insurance commitment and is one that a proper inspection could reasonably be expected to disclose. The Secretary may require from the seller of any such dwelling an agreement to reimburse him for any payments made pursuant to this subsection.

[10]GAO, "Opportunities to Improve Effectiveness and Reduce Costs," p. 12.

[11]See, e.g., U.S. v. Neustadt 366 U.S. 696.

[12]Section 104(b) of Public Law 91-609 "Housing and Urban Development Act of 1970" (31 December 1970) amended the National Housing Act by adding Section 518b. See 12 USC 1735(b). The "Housing and Community Development Act of 1974" (22 Aug. 1974) amended 518(b) to read "structural and other defects which so seriously affect use and livability as to create a serious danger to the life or safety of inhabitants . . ." thus tightening the limits on the types of defects that will be repaired. But the same act broadened the program to include some other dwellings insured by HUD. As the law was worded on 22 Aug. 1974, no new applications under 518(b) could be accepted by HUD after 22 Aug. 1975. The deadline for applications was subsequently extended to March 1976 "after red tape consumed seven months of the one-year program" (*The Cleveland Plain Dealer*, 28 October 1975, p. 4-A).

Thus Congress reacted to the difficulties HUD encountered in administering Section 235 by giving it Section 518(b) to administer as well.

Secretary Romney's initial reaction to the Staff Report was to acknowledge the problems, claim they had been solved, and require dwellings insured by FHA to comply with local building codes.[13] By mid-January, however, he realized that the problem was serious and ordered HUD's Office of Audit to review the program.[14] A random sample of 1281 houses indicated defects in 26% of the new houses and 43% of the existing houses. About 6% of the existing houses had defects so serious that they should not have been insured. HUD officials gave four reasons for the problems: (a) Poorly trained appraisers sometimes did not notice defects or know how they should be repaired; (b) the new program imposed such a heavy workload that appraisals were rushed; (c) supervision was inadequate; and (d) some HUD personnel advocated the view of caveat emptor as a result of long association with builders and bankers.[15]

It is thus apparent that shortly after the enactment of the 518(b) repair program HUD personnel were generally aware of the types of problems with the administration of Section 235 subsidies that had inspired it. Because these were programs that had attracted considerable attention from the press and Congress, HUD officials must have been alert to the importance of running the 518(b) programs as well as possible to avoid further attacks. Furthermore, many of the same people were involved in both programs.

When Congress passed 518(b), it required homeowners to notify HUD of defects within one year of the insurance of the mortgage, or by December 31, 1971, for houses insured before the Act became effective on December 31, 1970. Since the correction program applied only to defects "that existed on the date of the issuance of the insurance commitment and ... that a proper inspection could reasonably be expected to disclose," HUD was put in the difficult position not only of deciding whether a defect present at the time of the complaint "seriously affected the use and livability" of the dwelling, but also of judging whether it was both present and obvious at a much earlier time. Since the Section 235 program had gone into effect in the summer of 1968 and defects on

---

[13]Statement and testimony of George Romney, Secretary of HUD, 16 Dec. 1970, appended to "Abuses." In many cases it was not feasible to require compliance with local building codes, since these were designed to apply to new construction; and in any event cities often have too few inspectors to check all FHA commitments.

[14]"Audit Review of Section 235 Single Family Housing," 10 December 1971. The findings are summarized in GAO, 1972.

[15]GAO, 1972, pp. 26–27.

the earlier commitments could be reported until the end of 1971, HUD would sometimes be guessing how a house had looked 3 years earlier, even if complaints were investigated promptly. Distinguishing poor initial condition from the results of poor maintenance or abuse was not simple even under the best circumstances. Furthermore, the volume of complaints could be expected to be greatest in precisely those field offices where, because of excessive workload, poor management, ineptness, or corruption, the departures from regulations in the Section 235 program had been most serious. With this as a somewhat ominous background, we can now consider what the actual implementation of 518(b) involved.

For a homeowner to have a defect corrected under 518(b), he first had to recognize that it was a defect and then request assistance from HUD. How he was to know enough to do this is a problem that Congress had not seen fit to deal with. HUD did not notify owners of Section 235 homes directly because, it claimed, they could not be selected from the full file of FHA mortgages. Hence, in June 1971 (when half of the 1-year application period had already passed), HUD prepared a notice that could be sent to eligible homeowners by lenders who might have their files in better order.

Once a HUD field office received a request for assistance from a homeowner, it had to follow procedures similar to those followed in repossessions after defaults on insured mortgages. "These include inspections of the house to identify defects, issuance of specifications for the repairs, solicitation of bids, selection of contractors, execution of purchase orders or contracts, and the inspection of repairs."[16] HUD has a goal of 70 days for this process under other programs. The 518(b) program involved several difficulties, however. First, as noted previously, identification of defects eligible for repair (a task assigned to one of the same group of appraisers who had performed the original insurance appraisals) involved considerable judgment. Second, contractors, who were not eager to undertake the miscellaneous small repairs, delayed completion. Third, after the 518(b) guidelines were available on April 9, 1971, sellers of houses under Section 235 were required to agree to reimburse HUD for expenses incurred in correcting 518(b) defects. This imposed the additional step of notifying the seller of the eligible defects and giving him the opportunity to respond before proceeding with the repairs.

To check on the performance of the 518(b) program, the General Accounting Office selected a random sample of 101 cases from 6 field

[16]GAO, 1975, p. 7.

TABLE 6.1

Defects in Inspected Houses, Six Cities

City	Number of houses checked by the GAO	Average number of defects per house approved as eligible for repair by HUD	Average number of additional defects that HUD should have approved	Percentage of approved repairs not correctly completed	Average number of days needed to complete repairs
Cincinnati	10	14.6	2.8	25	209
Cleveland	20	11.5	0.7	16	350
Columbus	20	4.4	1.6	42	134
Detroit	19	14.7	0.7	13	413
Seattle	20	5.6	1.1	18	315
Washington	12	18.9	1.1	33	345
Total sample	101	10.9	1.2	22	298

SOURCE: U.S. General Accounting Office, "Weaknesses in Administration of the Program to Correct Defects in Housing Insured under the Section 235 Program," RED–75–340, 19 March, 1975, pp. 7 and 10.

offices (Cincinnati, Cleveland, Columbus, Detroit, Washington, D.C., and Seattle) covering the entire experience with the program through June 1973. The 6 offices (of a total of 77) were *not* chosen randomly, so generalizations to the entire program must be made cautiously. These offices accounted for 40% of the 518(b) expenditures; and, therefore, were probably relatively poor at administering both Section 235 and Section 518(b). The results of the GAO analysis are summarized in Table 6.1.

The most striking feature of the table is the time it took to complete the work, which ranged from an average of 134 days in Columbus to 413 days in Detroit to repair "defects which seriously affect the use and livability" of dwellings. The actual elapsed time on particular cases, among the 101 sampled, ranged from 18–791 days. Despite the obviously increasing difficulties in judging eligibility of defects as time passed, the program was accorded such low priority that the backlog from the initial flood of applications received in the summer of 1971 was not worked off until early 1973.

The GAO review included a physical inspection of the 101 properties with the assistance of HUD inspectors. These results, too, are shown in Table 6.1. Three striking findings emerged from this reinspection tour. First, many of the defects approved for correction were not properly repaired. Second, many eligible defects were not identified in the original inspection. Finally, none of the corrected defects was considered to be ineligible on the reinspection. The last finding is particularly puzzling, for surely in a program that involved so many individual judgments about borderline cases in complex situations one might expect to find that at least one approval in nearly 1100 was an error in favor of the homeowner.

Although differences in judgment were certainly involved in the finding by the inspectors of many eligible defects not previously approved for correction, inconsistent procedures among field offices were also at fault. HUD guidelines required the inspection report, following a request for assistance, to note all eligible defects, whether or not the homeowner had listed them. One of the six field offices, however, did not authorize any repairs unless the homeowners reported the defect. Another office refused to reimburse homeowners for defects repaired before the inspection, despite the explicit language of the legislation. It seems likely that an alert headquarters staff could have discovered such departures from prescribed procedures with the assistance of a good system of statistical reports from field offices, but HUD apparently did not accumulate much statistical data on 518(b).[17]

From a managerial viewpoint the most disturbing aspect of Table 6.1 is that 242 of the 1090 defects authorized for correction were not properly corrected. At this stage of the process the subjective problem of deciding on the eligibility was no longer an issue. The sole task was to write up adequate repair specifications and see that they were carried out inexpensively and quickly. Yet even in this well-defined task the failure rate approached one fourth. Three of the six field offices investigated by GAO did not always require an inspection of the repairs before payment of the contractor. The failure rate in those offices was 32%, compared with 15% where inspections were required. One office did not prepare repair specifications, simply copying the inspection report, instead. In other cases authorizations were verbal. Two of the six offices failed to require competitive bidding when the estimates exceeded $2000, although HUD regulations required them to do so.[18]

The evidence of widespread managerial failure crops up repeatedly in an examination of the Section 518(b) program. This is particularly disconcerting in view of the certainty that the program would be closely monitored after the problems with Section 235. Since field offices apply agency regulations incompletely and inconsistently, fail to follow routine contracting procedures, and do not follow HUD procedures for

[17]*Ibid.*, p. 3.
[18]*Ibid.*, pp. 10, 23, 25, 26.

collecting overdue claims, headquarters does not seem adequately to control the field offices.[19] This impression is heightened by HUD's inability to supply GAO with relevant data about local operations.

The consequences of the lack of effective control were particularly serious during this era when legislation attempted to extend the concern of the FHA from insuring mortgages on the homes of the middle class toward subsidizing mortgages for families with low income. Many FHA personnel were unenthusiastic about Section 235 and must have been even less pleased with Section 518(b), which was initiated by Congress without any concern for its administrative feasibility. The subsequent extension of 518(b) in the 1974 legislation was also opposed by the agency. Congress asserted that any failures in the programs were due not to defects in legislation, but to the incompetence of HUD and the perversity of the White House and OMB.[20]

Yet the fact remains that Section 235 moved many FHA personnel into a situation where they were forced to swim well beyond their depth. If a program inherently pits the combined forces of a poorly trained appraiser and an uneducated impoverished family, desperate for better housing, against ruthless slumlords, the program should be designed so it can be successful under those circumstances. To design a program that would work only if the cast of participants were different is the height of folly.

When Congress attempted to repair the damage done under Section 235 by adding Section 518(b), the difficulties were compounded. The appraiser who inspects property to determine eligibility for repairs is required to make a large number of unique, complex, and subjective judgments. Repair and renovation projects can be carried out most efficiently by an owner who has the technical knowledge, as well as the incentive, to make large numbers of correct decisions quickly. Hence they are not suitable for bureaucracies where the choice is generally either to be rigid ("bureaucratic") or to be slipshod.[21] Yet having said this it is still difficult to see why the lapses in the Section 518(b) program

---

[19]*Ibid.*, p. 28.

[20]U.S. Congress. Joint Economic Committee. Subcommittee on Priorities and Economy in Government, "Housing Subsidies and Housing Policy," Committee Print, 5 March 1973, pp. 2-7.

[21]For an account of the problems encountered in attempting a rehabilitation project under the very best circumstances see John L. Lineweaver, "Rehabilitating Houses for Lower-Income Buyers:Putting FHA 235j to the Action Test in Oakland, California," in *Federally Assisted Low Income Housing Programs:Three Case Studies*, Research Report 37 (Berkeley:The Center for Real Estate and Urban Economics, University of California, 1972), pp. 63-100.

did not take the form of excessive rigidity with concomitantly higher costs.

Several different types of failures occurred in the implementation of the Section 235 and Section 518(b) programs, so the explanations for failure could be expected to show similar variation. The fiascoes of the original appraisals—approving derelict hulks with major defects and accepting outrageous valuations—can be adequately explained by the combination of inexperienced and uninterested appraisers exposed to bribes and other outside pressures and constrained to commit funds quickly. Similarly, errors in determining eligibility for the Section 518(b) repairs can be ascribed to the inherent difficulty of the task and the qualities of the people to whom it was assigned. The remaining problems cannot be explained either on the basis of common sense or with the aid of the literature surveyed in Part I. In view of the absolute certainty that the behavior of HUD in implementing Section 518(b) would be subject to the closest possible congressional scrutiny, as well as much press coverage, it is inexplicable that the higher levels of HUD failed to collect information, insist that field offices give Section 518(b) special care, and detect and correct major interoffice variations in the application of rules and regulations. Similarly, theory cannot explain the failure of field offices to require that routine bureaucratic procedures be followed for writing repair specifications, obtaining bids, and inspecting work before payment. The standard procedures can be cumbersome, but they are routine, well understood and deal with readily observable activities. The procedures are designed to reduce the chances of corruption, which surely must have been a significant consideration after the unfortunate beginnings of this program.

CHAPTER 7

Fisheries Loan Fund[1]

The basic problem of the fishing industry is the "tragedy of the commons."[2] Any individual entering the industry gains as long as he catches enough to pay for the time, materials, and equipment he uses. However, each new entrant fishing from the common stock of fish decreases the catch of everyone else. If entry is unrestricted, it continues until the average boat earns no profit. For some fisheries, entry will still be profitable for the individual fisherman even when additional fishing effort actually produces a decline in the total catch. Although the tonnage harvested may continue to increase for some species, the

---

[1]This chapter is based mainly on U.S. General Accounting Office, "Need to Establish Priorities and Criteria for Managing Assistance Programs for U.S. Fishing-Vessel Operators," Report B-177024, 22 Feb. 1973. I am also indebted to Mr. Joseph W. Slavin, Associate Director for Resource Utilization of the National Marine Fisheries Service (NMFS), for providing additional information. The NMFS is part of the National Oceanic and Atmospheric Administration of the U.S. Department of Commerce.

[2]Anthony Scott developed a thorough statement of the problem for fisheries and other resources in *Natural Resources:The Economics of Conservation* (Toronto:McClelland and Stewart, 1973 [1st ed. 1955]). The same framework for analysis was used by the U.S. Commission on Marine Science, Engineering and Resources (known as the Stratton Commission), in its report, *Our Nation and the Sea:A Plan for National Action* (Washington:U.S. Government Printing Office, Jan. 1969).

additional yield to the industry is not worth the cost of the additional fishing effort.

The tragedy of the commons, as a problem involving a discrepancy between private and social costs and benefits, can be solved only by restricting entry through government or other collective action. In the case of ocean fisheries, however, the jurisdiction is often split among various governments. Traditionally, states have regulated fishing within 3 miles of their shores, which is not satisfactory for those fish that travel widely. The federal government had very limited authority in the 3–12 mile zone at the time of this case. A few international agreements (negotiated with immense difficulty and delay) dealt with such particular issues as whales. Beginning in 1977 the United States has asserted jurisdiction over fisheries within 200 miles of the U.S. coast.[3] Whatever the implications of such unilateral action may be for international relations, it has some potential for dealing with the fundamental problem of fisheries management in a way that the stop-gap measure described in this chapter could not.

In addition to the difficult problems of a common resource subject to divided jurisdiction, the fishing industry has traditionally been characterized by low wages. Moreover, it faced increasingly severe foreign competition after World War II. Whereas the weight of the U.S. commercial catch showed a practically horizontal trend after 1938, the weight of imports increased steadily from 13.4% of total commercial supply in 1945 to 57.4% in 1970.[4] The growth in imports combined with the chronic depression in much of the domestic industry resulted in appeals for tariff protection and other forms of assistance.[5]

One specific source of competitive disadvantage is the high cost of fishing vessels. Since the earliest days of this nation, the domestic shipbuilding industry has been protected by the requirement that vessels registered in the United States *must* be built in the United States.[6] One result has been that unsubsidized international cargoes are carried in vessels registered in foreign countries, but that escape is not open to

[3]The Fishery Conservation and Management Act of 1976 (P.L. 94–265) was analyzed by Donald L. McKernan in *Washington Public Policy Notes* (Seattle:University of Washington, Institute of Governmental Research) 4, No. 3, 1976. Implementation problems are discussed in U.S. General Accounting Office, "Enforcement Problems Hinder Effective Implementation of New Fishery Management Activities," Report CED–79–120, 12 Sept. 1979.

[4]Stratton Commission, p. 89; GAO, 1973, p. 22.

[5]See, e.g., the hearings of the Senate Commerce Committee, Subcommittee on Merchant Marine and Fisheries and the House Committee on Merchant Marine and Fisheries.

[6]John G. B. Hutchins, *The American Maritime Industries and Public Policy, 1789–1914:An Economic History* (Cambridge:Harvard University Press, 1941), pp. 57–60.

either the coastal trade or the fishing industry, both of which are limited to vessels of U.S. registry. Since ship construction is often twice as expensive in the United States as elsewhere, the Stratton Commission recommended outright elimination of the burdensome requirement.[7] In the absence of political support for such a move, however, Congress has continued its long series of attempts to offset some of the worst effects of the basic law by special subsidies and prohibitions.

The foregoing problems of the industry have been compounded, in some fisheries, by a decline in the stock of fish. This has sometimes resulted from overfishing, but in certain fisheries it has been caused by pollution, obstructions in rivers, or other factors—some of which are not fully understood. States have often reacted to the symptoms of overfishing by regulating the amount of time the fishery is open or the type of equipment that can be used. Such regulations, even when based on adequate biological knowledge, are inherently costly and tend to perpetuate excess capacity and obsolete techniques. They are also hard to enforce in view of the individual fisherman's overwhelming gain from breaking them. The alternative of restricting entry to the fishery, however, has little political appeal, especially when split jurisdiction means that those outside the state or country will take whatever fish one jurisdiction denies to its residents.

The economic weakness of the fishing industry attracted congressional attention in 1956. Congress had 2 years earlier passed the Saltonstall–Kennedy Act (P.L. 83–466) to subsidize research and marketing of fish. This had met with widespread approval, but the continuing evidence of excess capacity, widespread obsolescence, and growing imports prompted a new flurry of bills and hearings.[8] These dealt with a number of issues including reorganization of the federal bureaucracy dealing with sport and commercial fishing, tariffs, and training of fishermen, as well as a proposal for lending money to fishermen.

The loan proposal seemed to be supported principally by Warren G. Magnuson of Washington (Chairman of the Senate Committee on Interstate and Foreign Commerce) and the California tuna fishermen. Some moderate support was expressed by other parties and occasional statements of opposition were heard, but most participants in the hear-

[7]Stratton Commission, p. 98.
[8]U.S. Congress. Senate. Committee on Interstate and Foreign Commerce, "Fisheries Legislation," Hearings on S. 2379 et al. (84th Congress, 2nd Session), 19–26 March 1956. U.S. Congress. House. Committee on Merchant Marine and Fisheries. Subcommittee on Fisheries and Wildlife Conservation, "Establishment of a National Policy for Commercial Fisheries," Hearings on H.R. 8001 et al. (84th Congress, 2nd Session), 10, 21, 22 May and 8 June 1956.

ings ignored the loan provision in their concern with what seemed to be more significant issues. Opponents generally were either reluctant to see increased government intervention in the industry or were concerned about overcrowding and excess capacity.[9] A spokesman for the Gloucester fishermen, for example, favored loans, but noted that so many fishermen lost money that banks would not lend on the security of a fishing vessel for fear of coming into its possession in the event of default. He added that even the Small Business Administration (SBA) could see no way to lend when 97 of every 100 boats showed losses.[10]

The Eisenhower administration opposed most aspects of the proposed legislation including the loan plan. Assistant Secretary of the Interior Wesley A. D'Ewart in his letter to Senator Magnuson dated 22 March 1956, after pointing out that the fishing industry rarely used SBA loans, questioned whether additional federal lending authority was necessary.[11] A few weeks later when the House held hearings Mr. D'Ewart, along with other administration officials, firmly opposed loans because subsidies would worsen the already serious overcrowding in the view of the administration and the fishermen.[12]

After hearing many reactions to the various bills, the Chairman of the House Committee, Herbert C. Bonner of North Carolina, introduced a new bill, H.R. 11570, which was to become the Fish and Wildlife Act of 1956. The loan provision was not present in H.R. 11570.[13] Called to testify on the new bill, Assistant Secretary D'Ewart stated his agreement with certain aspects of the bill, then, after opposing one aspect of the reorganization, stated:

> I would like to offer two additional general observations of H.R. 11570. These are what might be termed errors of omission, rather than commission. First, the bill makes no mention of the extension of the Saltonstall–Kennedy Act, one of the most constructive pieces of legislation pertaining to the commercial fishing industry that Congress has ever enacted. Secondly, there is no provision in the bill for a fisheries loan fund, something sorely needed by the industry. I believe that any legislation upon which we must rely to help the commercial fishing industry regain its rightful place in our American economy must include both a loan fund and an extension of the Saltonstall–Kennedy Act....

[9]U.S. Senate, "Fisheries Legislation," pp. 9, 134, 201, and 233.
[10]*Ibid.*, pp. 274–279.
[11]*Ibid.*, p. 181.
[12]U.S. House, "Establishment of a National Policy," p. 32. Statement of D'Ewart to the Committee, 10 May 1956.
[13]It did include the provision that the Undersecretary of Fish and Wildlife shall "make such recommendations to the President and the Congress through the Secretary with respect to credit relief and other measures as he deems appropriate to aid in stabilizing the domestic fisheries [Section 6 (2)]."

The fisheries loan fund included in the administration's proposed bill calls for initial capital of $10 million, which would operate as a revolving fund. The fund would be used to make loans for the maintenance, repair, and equipment of fishing vessels. Loans made from the fund would carry rates of interest of not less than 3 percent and could be made for periods of up to 10 years. This would be of tremendous benefit to commercial fishing vessel owners.[14]

The administration thus managed to forget its earlier philosophic and economic opposition to the loan program, despite the lack of any strong public support for loans either in the House or among most fishermen! When the Fish and Wildlife Act of 1956 (P.L. 84–1024) became law, it included the Fisheries Loan Fund, authorizing loans at not less than 3% interest, for not more than 10 years.

The concern of fishermen that the availability of soft credit might encourage entry was met by restricting the authorization to: "loans for financing and refinancing of operations, maintenance, replacement, repair, and equipment of fishing gear and vessels, and for research into the basic problems of fisheries [Section 4 (a)].

Section 4 (a) was interpreted as precluding the use of the Fisheries Loan Fund to finance new entry into the industry.[15] It could be used to enable existing fishermen to continue and to upgrade their equipment, but not to enable a new entrant to a fishery to finance the purchase of a used vessel from a fisherman who was buying a new one. This interpretation was clearly consistent with the House report accompanying the bill, which stressed the problems of overfishing and resource depletion, as well as "inability to secure adequate financing to upgrade vessels and equipment to keep pace with new developments in technique . . ."[16] The loan fund thus began operations with a dual purpose of encouraging upgrading of vessels and of helping existing fishermen to stay in the industry. The opposition that had surfaced in the hearings quieted down as the program operated.

The program, administered for the newly formed Bureau of Commer-

---

[14]U.S. House, "Establishment of a National Policy," pp. 241–242. Statement of Wesley A. D'Ewart, 8 June 1956.

[15]"Under the present law, the existing loan law, a loan can be made for new and used commercial fishing vessels only when the vessel is to be used as a replacement for a vessel that is then operating in the fleet or has been lost." Testimony of Mr. Donald L. McKernan, Director, Bureau of Commercial Fisheries, Dept. of Interior, in the Hearings before U.S. Congress. House. Committee on Merchant Marine and Fisheries. Subcommittee on Fisheries and Wildlife Conservation, "Miscellaneous Fisheries and Wildlife Legislation—1965," 27 May 1965 (89th Congress, 1st Session), p. 11.

[16]House Report No. 2519 to accompany H.R. 11570, 28 June 1956 (1956 *U.S. Code Cong. & Adm. News*, p. 4590). The abbreviation stands for *United States Code, Congressional and Administrative News* (St. Paul, Minnesota:West Publishing Company, annual).

cial Fisheries by the Small Business Administration, was credited with keeping many fishermen in the industry who would otherwise have been forced out.[17] When the program came up for renewal in 1958, the general reaction to it was favorable. The committee was impressed by the tight management of the program (the low level of losses) and the obvious benefits to particular fishermen.[18]

By 1965 the combination of bureaucratic and political pressures had shifted the program in a direction that was completely opposite to its original justification. Because the law was changed to correspond with practice, however, it cannot be said that the agency gave Congress something other than what the legislation required. The law, as noted, had the dual objectives of helping fishermen upgrade their vessels and assisting existing fishermen to stay in the business. Whereas the first objective made more sense in an overcrowded industry, the second was much easier to implement. In practice about 60% of the loans were for refinancing vessels or for operating expenses, and even the remaining 40% for new vessels and vessel improvements may have included much routine upgrading.[19] During the hearing on an amendment in 1965, the Director of the Bureau of Commercial Fisheries, Donald L. McKernan, defended the loan fund entirely in terms of assisting individual fishermen to remain in the industry. The amendment, moreover, eliminated the requirement that the old vessel be removed from the industry if a new vessel was to be financed—a provision originally inserted to quiet the fears of overcrowding. The explanation for the change was twofold. First, with a subsidized loan on the old vessel, the buyer would be able to pay a higher price; this would provide the seller with more money to use as a downpayment on the new vessel. Second, the assistance in financing the purchase of used vessels would attract younger men into the fishing industry.[20] Although the first argument is correct, the second is illogical. Since fishing vessels have very little value for other purposes, the price of an old vessel will be determined by its capitalized earnings in fishing. Subsidizing the loan for the purchase of the vessel enables the

---

[17]U.S. Bureau of Commercial Fisheries, *Report* for the Calendar Year 1957, pp. 23–24.

[18]House Report No. 2629 (Committee on Merchant Marine and Fisheries) "Fisheries Loan Fund Increase" (1958 *U.S. Code Cong. & Adm. News* 5144). By 1965 bad debts were less than 1% of outstanding loans because of intensive servicing, which included technical assistance and helping the hard-pressed borrower find a buyer for his vessel.

[19]U.S. Bureau of Commercial Fisheries, *Report* for the Calendar Year 1958, pp. 20–21; and 1959, pp. 24–25.

[20]McKernan, Director of the Bureau of Commercial Fisheries, U.S. Congress. House. Committee on Merchant Marine and Fisheries. Subcommittee on Fisheries and Wildlife Conservation, "Miscellaneous Fisheries and Wildlife Legislation—1965" Hearing on Fisheries Loans, 27 May 1965 (89th Congress, 1st Session), p. 10.

seller to obtain a higher price, but leaves the new entrant in exactly the same financial position as he would have been had he paid a higher interest rate on a smaller loan. Even if the argument had been correct, however, it implied that the fishing industry would benefit from new entry, which was certainly a doubtful proposition in many fisheries.

The new law did require that, before lending money to increase the fleet, "the Secretary must determine that the operation of the vessel in the fishery will not cause any economic hardship to the already efficient operators operating in that fishery." It is not clear what this provision means because, unless the fishery is almost completely untapped, adding a fishing vessel will decrease the catch of all others combined, as well as reduce the selling price of the fish if the total quantity caught increases.[21] Thus an increase in the fishing fleet is almost certain to cause an economic loss to those already in the fishery, but neither loss nor hardship is the appropriate economic criterion for fisheries management.

Congressman Thomas M. Pelly (Washington) voiced the concern about overcrowding in the hearings, but the agency showed more concern for treating fishermen equally and maintaining the price of existing vessels.[22] The latter, although economically inconsistent with upgrading the fleet, developed into a goal of the agency:

> At the present time the fisherman with the older vessel cannot obtain a loan for replacement with a larger, more modern vessel because he is unable to find a purchaser who has a means of financing the purchase of the older vessel. If he sells it as a commercial fishing vessel, he will be ineligible for a loan under the fisheries loan program because he is not replacing a vessel that has actually left the fleet or is lost. Most such vessels are not easily adaptable to other uses.[23]

Individual fishermen saw the extension of the loan fund to used vessels as a device to permit them to sell their boats at a higher price and thereby obtain a larger downpayment for a new vessel.[24] More disturbing than the myopia of individual fishermen was the alacrity with which

---

[21]Convenient summaries of the economic issues and references can be found in U.S. Commission on Marine Science, Engineering and Resources, *Marine Resources and Legal–Political Arrangements for Their Development* (Vol. 3 of the Panel Reports), 1969, pp. VII, 61–70; and Anthony Scott, *Natural Resources*, pp. 61–64, 70, 173–179.

[22]"Miscellaneous Fisheries and Wildlife Legislation—1965," 27 May 1965, pp. 13–14.

[23]Letter from Secretary Udall to the House Committee on Merchant Marine and Fisheries, 29 June 1965, in support of the amendment (1965 *U.S. Code Cong. & Adm. News*, pp. 2330–2331).

[24]U.S. Congress. Senate. Committee on Commerce. Subcommittee on Merchant Marine and Fisheries, "Fisheries Legislation, 1965," Hearings, 11 and 12 May 1965 (89th Congress, 1st Session) on S. 998 (Fishery Loan Fund Extension) *et al.*, p. 109.

the committees and the agency leaped to the support of a measure that was designed to increase the overcrowding of fisheries. As if to hammer home the point, Udall emphasized: "In addition to the need to upgrade and modernize the commercial fishing vessel fleet, which is the principal objective of this program, there is also a need to attract younger men to the fishing industry."[25]

The problem of overcrowding, however, did not disappear as quickly as Congress shifted the goals of the legislation. The Stratton Commission was very much concerned with the problem of excessive capital and labor in many fisheries.[26] The old Bureau of Commercial Fisheries (BCF) was aware of the problem inherent in subsidizing entry into over-crowded fisheries;[27] but it was not until 31 July 1973, that the National Marine Fisheries Service, successor to BCF, published the Conditional Fishery regulation to deal with it.[28] Even after that delay in establishing the procedures, the designation of conditional fisheries took years. When a fishery is designated as *conditional*, the subsidies administered by NMFS are not available to expand capacity. "Substantially equivalent" harvesting capacity must be removed from that fishery "within one year after the delivery of the new vessel." It can either be removed from all fishing, or displaced to a fishery not designated as conditional.

With the adoption of the new policy the administration of the NMFS subsidy programs in conditional fisheries returned to the standards that prevailed in all fisheries during 1956–1965. This restriction of capacity limitation to specific fish in specific areas is appropriate because many fisheries are not overcrowded, even according to the strict criterion of economic theory. Nevertheless, the effectiveness of this approach depends on the speed with which overcrowded fisheries are placed on the conditional list and the slow pace observed so far is not very encouraging.

The fisheries loan fund is not currently operating—a moratorium having been declared in March 1973 pending new legislation. Similarly, the construction-differential subsidy, under which the United States paid half the cost of building new vessels, ended in 1972. These were replaced by two programs having roughly similar economic effects with smaller direct impact on the federal budget, both subject to the conditional fishery rules. The Fishing Vessel Obligation Guarantee program provides a very strong government guarantee for loans made by banks for construction, reconstruction, or reconditioning of fishing vessels.

[25]Statement by Secretary Udall, ibid., p. 112.
[26]Stratton Commission, pp. 92–97.
[27]*Ibid.*, Panel Reports, 3: VII–55.
[28]50CFR251.

With the guarantee, such loans become about as riskless as Treasury obligations, and hence will be made by banks at relatively low interest rates. The Fishing Vessel Capital Construction Fund program permits, in effect, that funds paid into a Capital Construction Fund account are deductible from taxable income and thus provides the largest benefits to the most profitable firms.

While the legislation underwent the full cycle from unpredictable start through foolish middle age and back to its starting point, the program was apparently administered in a tight, business-like way. Although the GAO turned up one example of a questionable loan approved by headquarters against the recommendation of regional investigators,[29] the general approval of the program combined with very low loss rates suggests that it was administered fairly and honestly. The problems that did develop did not involve corruption or poor administration of the program itself, but rather the use of it in such a way as to help individual fishermen, without improving the condition of the industry as a whole.

The agency took understandable pride in the low loss rate of the Fisheries Loan Fund. Losses were generally under 2%, a figure which at first glance looks remarkably low in view of the stress in the hearings (and the provision in the law) that loans be made only to fishermen who find "credit not otherwise available on reasonable terms." That is, one would expect recipients either to have poor personal credit records or to be engaged in ventures with little commercial promise. The application for a loan had to be accompanied by proof of refusal of credit from a bank, generally the applicant's bank of account. When it is recalled, however, that the loans were made for periods longer than customary at interest rates substantially below those prevailing in the unsubsidized market, it is clear that refusal of a bank to lend on equal terms did not necessarily imply that the applicant was uncreditworthy or the project unsound.[30]

The agency did take positive action to prevent defaults. This consisted most notably of technical advice and assistance to fishermen who were approaching financial difficulties, as well as efforts at refinancing where that seemed appropriate. The former, especially, attracted favorable attention in the hearings as an indication of the agency's expertise.[31]

[29]GAO, "Need to Establish Priorities and Criteria," 1973, p. 13.

[30]The 1956 law specified an interest rate of not less than 3%. This was raised over the years, generally hovering in the vicinity of the prime rate, which was considerably less than the rate at which banks would ordinarily lend to fishermen. In the 1965 amendments, the interest rate was set at the average market yield on U.S. Treasury securities of comparable maturity plus a service charge. The rate determined in this way was 8% in 1973 (38FR28836).

[31]U.S. Congress. House. Committee on Merchant Marine and Fisheries. Subcommittee

TABLE 7.1

Fisheries Loan Fund Applications and Approvals

Time period	Applications received		Applications approved	
	Number	Average amount ($)	Number	Average amount ($)
1956–1958	514	34,593	278	25,816
1959	150	21,865	77	15,314
North East Region				
1970 and 1971	52	20,755	33	21,480
South East Region				
1970	23	30,865	14	34,121
1971	39	22,488	14	26,057

SOURCES: U.S. Bureau of Commercial Fisheries, *Report* for the Calendar Year 1958, pp. 20–21; *ibid.*, 1959, pp. 24–25; U.S. National Marine Fisheries Service, *Report* for the calendar years 1970 and 1971, p. 35.

The low loss rate was not achieved by rejecting large numbers of loan applicants. Table 7.1 summarizes the rejection rates and loan sizes for a few years. It can be seen that more than half of all applications received were approved. The paucity of outright rejections (some of the applications not approved were in process, ineligible, or withdrawn) suggests the possibility that the market for subsidized fisheries loans was saturated. If so, the agency could exert little control over the emphasis of the program by deciding which loans to accept.

Nevertheless, the approved applications tended to be smaller than the average of all applications received in the early years of the program. Half of the loans, it was reported in 1965, were for less than $10,000.[32] Little modernization of the fishing fleet could be accomplished with loans of that size, but the program seems to have been subject to the same pressures toward diffusing the benefits widely and thinly that characterized other programs including Accelerated Public Works (Chapter 8) and Model Cities.[33] The tendency toward approving many small loans became explicit agency policy in 1969: "In order to prevent the exhaustion of funds available for these loans and to assure that these

on Fisheries and Wildlife Conservation, "Jellyfish—Fisheries Loans," Hearings, 9 and 19 March 1970 (91st Congress, 2nd Session), pp. 10–16.

[32]U.S. House, "Miscellaneous Fisheries and Wildlife Legislation—1965" p. 16.

[33]Edward C. Banfield, "Making a New Federal Program:Model Cities, 1964–68," pp. 125–158 in Allan P. Sindler, ed., *Policy and Politics in America:Six Case Studies* (Boston:Little, Brown, 1973).

funds will assist the largest number of vessel operators possible, it is necessary to restrict the size of loans (to $40,000)."[34]

The Committee was somewhat concerned that the arbitrary limit would make it impossible for the agency to finance anything more than the transfer of ownership of used vessels and some slight renovation. It was pointed out that although a mackerel boat could sometimes be purchased for as little as $35,000, entry into many fisheries was much more expensive, with a shrimp trawler selling for $100,000, and others ranging up to a tuna boat at $1.8 million.[35] The inherent problem is that upgrading and modernizing the fleet generally involves adding vessels of increased capacity.[36] This requires that some existing vessels be forced out of the fishery. But taking such drastic action is politically impossible, as well as being contrary to the 1965 law, which prohibited loans that would "cause economic hardship or injury to the efficient vessel operators already . . . in that fishery."

In addition to political pressures to spread the benefits thinly, an agency is also under pressure to present evidence of success to Congress. This may have resulted in unnecessary assistance to fisheries that were profitable enough to attract capital on the open market. The agency claimed modernization of the Pacific tuna fleet as one of its most significant achievements.[37] This absorbed much of the funding available for vessel construction subsidies. The Panel Report of the Stratton Commission, however, denied the necessity of such aid.[38]

The basic problem in the Fisheries Loan case was the legislation, rather than its implementation. The two cannot be entirely separated, however. The breadth of the original legislation gave the agency enough leeway to operate a small loan program for fishermen. This was consistent with the legislation, but it did not satisfy the legislative goal of modernizing the industry. As the agency accumulated experience with the program, it encouraged the evolution of the legislation in the direction of the functions it could carry out well. Since the 1965 amendments ignored completely the fears of overcrowding that were so prominant a part of the original discussion, further modification in the form of the conditional fisheries designation was necessary. The financial assistance programs of the National Marine Fisheries Service, however, remain oriented toward aiding individual fishermen, rather than revitalizing the industry.

[34]*Federal Register,* 20 September 1969.
[35]U.S. House, 1970 Hearing, "Jellyfish—Fisheries Loans" pp. 30–31.
[36]Stratton Commission, p. 97.
[37]See, e.g., U.S. House, 1970 Hearings, "Jellyfish—Fisheries Loans" pp. 10–16.
[38]Stratton Commission, Panel Reports 3: p. VII-55.

CHAPTER 8

Accelerated Public Works

When Congress passed the Public Works Acceleration Act of 1962, it wanted the money to flow quickly into the depressed areas to provide an immediate increase in employment.[1] In the preceding year it had established an agency to design long-term solutions for chronically depressed areas.[2] The public works legislation, however, was an attempt to put people to work immediately both to combat the lingering recession and to produce useful public facilities. Congress felt strongly enough about the necessity for rapid action to specify, among other things, that a substantial portion of each funded project "be completed within one year of initiation or acceleration."[3]

Passage of the legislation involved the technical judgment that implementation could proceed quickly enough for the act to be helpful in solving the short-term unemployment problem. The House report on the bill presented at length the evidence that a large number of public works projects were planned and ready for rapid initiation.[4] The minor-

[1]P.L. 87–658 (76 Stat. 541) enacted 14 September 1962.
[2]The Area Redevelopment Act (P.L. 87–27), 1 May 1961.
[3]P.L. 87–658 Sec. 3(f).
[4]U.S. Congress. House. Committee on Public Works, House Report No. 1756, 2 June 1962 (1962 *U.S. Code Cong. and Adm. News*, pp. 2524–2525).

ity report contained a cogent statement of the contrary view; that is, designing sizable projects takes so long that any appreciable increase in employment occurs too late to be useful.[5]

Despite such doubts, the bill was passed and delegated to the Area Redevelopment Administration (ARA), the agency established to administer the Area Redevelopment Act little more than a year earlier. The new agency was having difficulties enough in organizing and staffing for its quite different principal responsibility of long-term development when the new, and much larger, temporary program was assigned to it.[6] The normal problems involved in starting up a new agency had been compounded by a very strict limitation (a total of five) on the number of supergrades (the top three civil service ranks). Furthermore, its task was complicated in certain respects by the decision to function as a small coordinating agency, reimbursing other agencies for various technical services. Although this alleviated the problems of staffing, it also weakened the agency's control over the timing and quality of work. Much of the planning for Accelerated Public Works (APW) also had to be coordinated with the Public Health Service or the Community Facilities Administration of the Housing and Home Finance Agency.

Whatever the reasons, the average processing time was 188 days, from application to final approval, for public facility projects during the first 8 months of fiscal 1963. The effect of additional experience had also been disheartening: between fiscal 1962 and the first two-thirds of fiscal 1963 the ARA's own processing time increased from 35 days to 64, whereas that of the Community Facilities Administration grew from 97 to 103 days.[7]

Despite the problems encountered by his agency, Administrator William L. Batt, Jr., recognized the necessity for prompt action to satisfy Congress: "We are looking for speed, speed, and more speed."[8] He got it. The Agency's prompt commitment of the initial appropriation of $400 million was rewarded by a supplemental appropriation of $450 million.[9]

The speedy commitment of funds was particularly impressive in view of the tortuous course through which applications passed. Areas eligible for APW assistance applied to the agency directly responsible for the

[5]Ibid., p. 2549, "Minority Views on H.R. 10113."

[6]Sar A. Levitan, Federal Aid to Depressed Areas:An Evaluation of the Area Redevelopment Administration (Baltimore:The Johns Hopkins Press, 1964), pp. 31–34.

[7]Ibid., pp. 44–45.

[8]Address to Accelerated Public Works Conference, U.S. Department of Commerce Auditorium, 26–27 September 1962, as quoted in Conley Hall Dillon, The Area Redevelopment Administration:New Patterns in Developmental Administration (College Park, Maryland:Bureau of Governmental Research, University of Maryland, 1964), p. 75n.

[9]Dillon, The Area Redevelopment Administration, pp. 75–77.

particular type of facility. Sewage and water facilities, for example, were funded through the Community Facilities Administration, whereas hospitals were the responsibility of the Public Health Service. Much of the processing of applications, therefore, took place in the local offices of the various agencies. The application then proceeded through a programming review by a joint conference of all participating agencies, after which it was reviewed by the ARA to ensure compliance with the APW law. After these reviews, the project went through the standard procedure for the granting agency, which generally next involved approval by the head of the agency. The grant agreement was then drawn up and sent to the applicant. Once the applicant signed, the project was initiated.[10]

The areas that were eligible for assistance under APW included:

(1) those areas which the Secretary of Labor designates each month as having been areas of substantial unemployment for at least nine of the preceding twelve months; and

(2) those areas which are designated by the Secretary of Commerce under subsections (a) and (b) of Section 5 of the Area Redevelopment Act as "redevelopment areas."[11]

The term substantial unemployment was defined as 6%. The redevelopment areas of section 5(a) were areas of substantial and persistent unemployment, that is:

1. where the Secretary of Labor finds that the rate of unemployment, excluding unemployment due primarily to temporary or seasonal factors, is currently six per centum or more and has averaged at least six per centum for the qualifying time periods specified in paragraph (2); and

2. where the Secretary of Labor finds that the annual average rate of unemployment has been at least—

(A) 50 per centum above the national average for three of the preceding four calendar years, or

(B) 75 per centum above the national average for two of the preceding three calendar years, or

(C) 100 per centum above the national average for one of the preceding two calendar years.

The Secretary of Labor shall find the facts and provide the data to be used by the Secretary in making the determinations required by this subsection.[12]

---

[10]U.S. General Accounting Office, "Assistance Under the Public Works Acceleration Act to Areas no longer Burdened by Substantial Unemployment," Report B-153449, 26 June 1964, pp. 3-4. The remainder of this chapter relies heavily on this source.

[11]P.L. 87-658 Sec. 3(a).

[12]P.L. 87-27 Sec. 5(a).

Section 5(b) gave the Secretary of Commerce more discretion in set-ting the detailed procedures and measurements, but was essentially aimed at including as redevelopment areas the nonurban depressed areas that did not qualify according to the unemployment rate standards prescribed in 5(a), but that, nevertheless, seemed depressed when one examined family incomes, the rate of outmigration, and proportion of population receiving public assistance.

When the General Accounting Office reviewed the operation of the APW program, it found two persistent problems. First was the reluc-tance of ARA to end or diminish the access to financing of any area once it had become eligible. The second was the continuation of the pressure to spread the benefits of the program widely at whatever cost in effec-tiveness in aiding depressed areas.

The passages quoted from the legislation indicated two ways to be-come eligible for APW assistance. One was to qualify as a redevelop-ment area by having a chronic problem of quantity or quality of em-ployment; the other was to encounter a period of acute unemployment. Since the act specified that the goal was to reduce unemployment, one might expect that aid under the act would be limited to areas of high unemployment. This turned out to be generally the case, but only be-cause of the persistence of high unemployment rates in particular areas, not because of the way the act was administered. The ARA adopted several procedures that had the effect of ensuring that a grant would be awarded, regardless of the unemployment rate in the area in question, as long as the area had been eligible when serious processing of the application began.

Specifically, the determination by the Secretary of Labor that an area had an unemployment rate exceeding 6% in 9 of the past 12 months involved relatively few elements of judgment.[13] The lists of areas newly designated and terminated were published monthly in "Area Labor Market Trends." The ARA received informal word of impending termi-nations 10–15 days prior to publication and shared this with the various agencies administering grants.[14] The advance notice was *not* used for

---

[13]This statement is not strictly true. In fact, the empirical basis for estimates of unem-ployment at the local level is very weak. A considerable amount of judgment is necessary in establishing the techniques for estimating local unemployment rates from the scraps of data available. At the time of this program, however, there did not seem to be any evidence that political considerations had influenced the estimating techniques. The other significant question is the choice of boundaries for the local labor market. By gerrymander-ing boundaries one can find high unemployment rates in any part of the country at any time. The choice of boundaries, which did become a political question in this program, is discussed in the following.

[14]This account is from GAO, Report B-153449, 26 June 1964, "Assistance under the Public Works Acceleration Act", p. 20.

the purpose of suspending further action on projects from areas where unemployment was no longer a substantial problem. Instead, the ARA adopted the policy of proceeding with any project that had been approved by the joint conference before the formal declaration of ineligibility. [15] Although areas lost their eligibility only rarely (only 69 terminations among the 1300 eligible areas were recorded by 15 November 1963), 85 grants went to areas that had lost, or were about to lose, eligibility when the aid that was supposed to reduce unemployment began.

The GAO also found evidence that the ARA used the information about impending terminations to speed processing. [16] Moreover, the Community Facilities Administration, which administered about half of the grant money, departed from its own written regulations by continuing processing when areas lost eligibility before the project had been publicly announced. The GAO report cites several cases in which grants were programmed during the interval between informal knowledge that unemployment was no longer serious in a labor-market area and the formal termination of eligibility.

The procedure was more complex in the redevelopment areas. There, the Secretary of Labor supplied information about labor-market conditions, but the Secretary of Commerce determined which areas were to lose eligibility. Since the Area Redevelopment Act focused on long range programs for economic growth, in contrast to the immediate relief of unemployment expected under APW, it is apparent that designation as a redevelopment area and removal of that designation must involve longer-term considerations than the unemployment rate at one moment. The legislative provisions do indicate the use of the unemployment experience of up to 4 years, as well as the even more persistent income records, as the basis for designation. Similarly, the regulations for terminations refer to "a significant reduction in the rate of unemployment" that "has continued for a reasonable period of time." The time period between certification by the Department of Labor that the area no longer met the unemployment criterion and termination of designation by the Secretary of Commerce ranged from 7–13 months with an average of 10. Although the long lead may be appropriate for projects requiring long-term planning it was clearly inconsistent with the goal of APW. Thus, for example, on September 12, 1963, the ARA was still urging the CFA to approve a project for an area that was dropped from the "substantial and persistent unemployment" list more than a year earlier.

[15] *Ibid.*, pp. 4–5.
[16] *Ibid.*, pp. 7–9.

The time lag between the change in labor market conditions and the date of termination ranged from 7–13 months in the cases studied by the GAO.[17] Such lags are particularly significant when combined with the evidence that ARA speeded processing although termination of eligibility was imminent. Since legislation called for spending a substantial part of the APW money within one year, the fact that projects could still be approved from 7–13 months after unemployment had subsided indicates that the countercyclical impact specified by Congress was not being realized in practice.

The minority report of the House Committee on Public Works emphasized the technical problems of completing plans, engineering studies, land acquisition, and processing of applications, as well as the lag between letting the contract and hiring many people. In retrospect the report overstated the engineering problems while ignoring the more significant bureaucratic obstacles to a countercyclical public works program. The rapid exhaustion of the initial appropriation indicates that the preliminary stages of implementation took little time. The speed with which the funds were allocated might even cause a sceptic to inquire whether the federal funds were not—despite an express requirement to the contrary—replacing state and local funds in projects that would have been completed anyway.

The major failure involved not the expected delays in implementation, but rather the continued aid to areas that no longer qualified according to the spirit, if not the letter, of the legislation. What explanations can be found for the continued aid to relatively prosperous areas, despite the repeated assertions that funding was inadequate to finance large numbers of projects in areas that remained depressed? The three explanations that suggest themselves relate to the characteristics of the bureaucracy, the political context, and the availability of alternative uses for the funds.

The response of the ARA to the criticisms of the GAO emphasized the necessity for coherent long-range planning, which precluded the possibility of turning public works projects on and off in response to fluctuations in unemployment.[18] This would imply that a countercyclical program of the sort specified by Congress was difficult or impossible for bureaucracy to implement, perhaps because of the pressures within the organization to salvage the work that had already been done on the

[17]U.S. General Accounting Office, "Accelerated Public Works Assistance Approved for Areas Under Consideration for Termination of Eligibility," Report B–153449, 9 October 1964, p. 6.
[18]GAO, Report B–153449, "Assistance under the Public Works Acceleration Act", June 1964, p. 12.

application. For particular units within the agency, the output is, after all, not jobs created in depressed areas, but applications approved or grants awarded.

A more optimistic appraisal is that the APW program could have been administered well, but not by ARA. An agency that specialized in planning long-term development projects was simply not prepared to subordinate those interests to a program aimed at offsetting short-run cyclical fluctuations. That was the agency's defense, "Planning for economic development is a long-term process... [so] the seven to 13 month period of administrative delay shown in our report is a reasonable period of time for terminating an area's eligibility."[19] Levitan even argued that the agency's focus on long-term development improved the effectiveness of APW, but it did contravene congressional intent.[20]

Whatever the factors involved, it seems clear from subsequent history that the effort to hurry grants to areas that were about to lose eligibility was part of a highly persistent pattern of behavior. After the Area Redevelopment Administration succumbed to an accumulation of political problems, it was replaced by the Economic Development Administration.[21] Faced with the necessity of expending a full year's funds in the few months following its organization, the agency did not have time to develop explicit criteria for ranking, accepting, and rejecting projects. Observers noted, however, that the agency strongly favored projects from the two extreme types of areas—those closest to losing eligibility and those most depressed. Specifically, "110 of the 364 projects funded during the first year of operation were located in areas that were declared ineligible after the annual designation review."[22] To the extent that the concentration on relatively prosperous areas reflects a conscious choice of strategy, rather than being a byproduct of bureaucratic administration or a response to political pressures, it would seem to be an example of displacement of goals. That is, it might be attractive to help areas that are almost prosperous enough to remove from the depressed category, because with a small amount of help they will no longer be depressed. The agency can then claim credit for the success. If success is defined not as helping areas across the "line," but as aiding economic development, then it might prove worthwhile to concentrate on the less

---

[19]Quoted in GAO, "Accelerated Public Works Assistance," October 1964, p. 19.
[20]Levitan, *Federal Aid to Depressed Areas*, p. 158.
[21]E.D.A. was established by P.L. 89-136 "The Public Works and Economic Development Act of 1965," 26 August 1965.
[22]Raymond H. Milkman, Christopher Bladen, Beverly Lyford, and Howard L. Walton, *Alleviating Economic Distress:Evaluating a Federal Effort* (Lexington, Massachusetts:D.C. Health, 1972), pp. 21-22, 30-31.

favored. A cost-benefit analysis is, of course, appropriate, but the results will depend on what is chosen as the measure of benefit.[23]

The Area Redevelopment Administration had been beset by severe political difficulties since its inception, and the Accelerated Public Works program certainly shared in them. The basic problem with ARA was that it originally purported to focus on a very small number of chronically depressed areas. Senator Douglas was aiming at helping 40–50 cities when he proposed the legislation.[24] In order to attract enough support in Congress, however, the criteria for eligibility were greatly extended or left open for administrative determination. Before the lines were finally drawn, the ARA found itself with more than 1000 counties (one-third of all those in the U.S.), including nearly one-fifth of the U.S. population, in its jurisdiction. It was not possible to extend meaningful assistance to so many areas with the limited budget available, so ARA was put in the difficult position of deciding which areas and which projects would be favored.

One device adopted by the ARA administratively to distribute the benefits widely and attract more widespread support was to designate the most nearly depressed area in each state as a redevelopment area, even if it did not meet the explicit criteria. The GAO was highly critical of this practice.[25] But the agency asserted it was carrying out congressional intent: "the Secretary shall endeavor to distribute the projects widely among the several States, so far as is feasible and proper..."[26] Although the agency's reading of the letter of the law seems quite strained, it was obviously in keeping with its spirit. The Public Works and Economic Development Act of 1965 confirmed the bureaucratic modification of the preceding law by enacting it.[27]

The agency increased its administrative discretion by rounding out and splitting up labor market areas. The boundaries of a labor-market area are indefinite, at best, so the fact that the Administrator of ARA chose to retain some flexibility is not too surprising. He could round out redevelopment areas by adding contiguous counties. Alternatively, in the event that a labor-market area did not qualify as a redevelopment area, it might be possible to separate the central city or a declining

[23] *Ibid.*, pp. 30–33. Many of these arguments are presented in connection with the "worst first" policy tried later.

[24] For a discussion of the legislative and administrative history of ARA, see Levitan, *Federal Aid to Depressed Areas*, esp. pp. 1–29 and 54–69.

[25] U.S. General Accounting Office, "Unauthorized Assistance to Seemingly Nondepressed Areas Under the Public Works Acceleration Act and the Area Redevelopment Act," Report B–153449, 24 August 1964.

[26] P.L. 87–27 Sec 5(b).

[27] P.L. 89–136 Sec. 401(d).

industrial portion of the area that would qualify. The Detroit area, for example, was recovering from a severe recession in 1961 and 1962. By July, 1963, it no longer met the criteria for substantial and persistent unemployment. On February 20, 1964, the Detroit area lost its designation as a redevelopment area. The regulations, however, had been changed on December 31, 1963 to permit splitting, so the city of Detroit became eligible on the day that the area became ineligible.[28] Such administrative discretion to favor particular geographic areas invites political pressure, especially when the stakes are high. APW certainly met that criterion since it provided up to 50% (in some cases 75%) of the cost of approved projects. Levitan states that the rounding-out concept was adopted specifically to enable the ARA to placate congressmen who had promised their constituents ARA assistance.[29]

The agency was as reluctant to revise the formula by which funds were allocated as it was to terminate the eligibility of particular areas.[30] The ARA had used a slightly obsolete estimate of the number of unemployed in each district to prorate the funds available under the initial appropriation. When funding was renewed the following year, the same factor was used for each district, although the relative number of unemployed in various areas had, of course, changed. It is possible that this was just an accidental oversight amidst the mass of work that had to be done, but it seems puzzling that the spokesman for the agency would then lie by saying that more recent data were not available unless more basic factors were involved.[31]

Both the ARA and the APW programs were subject to much political pressure. This seems inevitable in programs financed from general tax revenues that offer large benefits to particular areas. It is possible, of course, that under different circumstances; for example, with more time to organize the agency and write regulations, and perhaps with a different administrator, the political pressures might have been blunted. But of their existence in this case there is no doubt.[32] It must also be stressed that the laws as written—both ARA and APW—left a great deal of discretion to the bureaucracy, not just about technical matters but even concerning the interregional distribution of benefits. Congress rec-

---

[28]GAO, "Accelerated Public Works Assistance," October 1964, pp. 9–15.

[29]Levitan, *Federal Aid to Depressed Areas*, p. 63.

[30]U.S. General Accounting Office, "Inequitable Allocation of Accelerated Public Works Among Eligible Areas," Report B–153449, 17 May 1965.

[31]*Ibid.*, p. 10.

[32]In addition to Levitan, *Federal Aid to Depressed Areas*, see U.S. Congress. House. Committee on Public Works, "Hearings on Public Works Acceleration Act," 15–18 October 1963 (88th Congress, 1st Session), pp. 42–44.

ognized the political sensitivity of the matter and could not bring itself to grapple seriously with it.

These problems were more severe for APW than one might expect in standard "pork barrel" programs for two reasons. First, the maneuvering over eligibility determined whether an area was ever going to have a chance at getting anything. Second, the program was temporary, hence it was not possible to mollify losers by promising them something in a later round.

The preceding discussion presupposes the existence of an excess demand for ARA and APW funds, but that assumption may be incorrect. According to Milkman et al., "the lack of feasible project applications was a major problem confronting EDA administrators in the fall of 1965."[33] If in fact the project backlog, publicized by the administrators and mentioned in the GAO reports, was nonexistent, then the problem with the whole agency was simply excess funding, rather than favoritism in selection, political influence, or failure to terminate areas no longer eligible.[34]

[33]Milkman et al., Alleviating Economic Distress, p. 19.
[34]For a discussion of the alleged large backlog of worthy projects see U.S. Congress. House. Committee on Public Works, "Public Works and Economic Development Act of 1965," Hearings, 10–14, 18, 19, 26 May 1965 (89th Congress, 1st Session), p. 32.

CHAPTER **9**

Grading of Processed Fruits and Vegetables[1]

Whereas the preceding cases dealt with programs offering subsidies to selected individuals or geographic areas, this one deals with the grading activities of the Agricultural Marketing Service (AMS). The U.S.D.A. shield and grade designations are familiar to consumers from a variety of food products. The originating legislation was not consumer-oriented, however, but was designed to improve the marketing process by providing general standards of quality and information about whether specific lots of food meet those standards. Such information could, of course, also benefit consumers both directly and by reducing the spread between farm and retail prices. The two major faults found by the General Accounting Office in the administration of the program were the resistance by the AMS to informing the Food and Drug Administration (FDA) of adulterated products discovered during the grading process and the continuation of grading at plants failing to correct sani-

[1]The main source for this chapter is U.S. General Accounting Office, "Processed Fruits and Vegetables:—Potentially Adulterated Products Need to Be Better Controlled—Sanitation in Some Plants Needs Improvement," Report B–164031(2), 21 Feb. 1973. I am also indebted to David A. Patton, Deputy Director, Fruit and Vegetable Division, Agricultural Marketing Service, for providing additional information. Prior to 2 April 1972, the activities described here were carried out by the Consumer and Marketing Service.

tary deficiencies. Although it would be natural to attribute these faults to the fact that processors pay the costs of the grading service, a comparison with the far worse problems encountered in grain and poultry inspection, where the institutional arrangements are quite different, suggests that the problem is more complex.

The grading services of the Department of Agriculture are authorized by the Agriculture Marketing Act of 1946 (7 U.S.C. 1621), which was aimed primarily at improving "the marketing and distribution of agricultural products."[2] The grade of a product can be judged by the characteristics that can be observed by the consumer when he opens the can, by the safety and sanitation of the processing plant, or by the level of the more subtle contaminants such as pesticides, molds, or heavy metals. The AMS emphasizes observable characteristics; but it also imposes sanitary standards for in-plant grading. More sophisticated testing for trace contaminants, with the exception of some mold counts, is not routinely done by the agency. Once the AMS grader assigns a grade of A, B, or C, the packer can use the grade certification in his advertising, and thus the consumer can tell what quality to expect in the marked package.

The grading criteria and methods require an entire volume (765 pages) of the *Code of Federal Regulations* (7 CFR 52.1 to 52.87) to give enough detail on the hundreds of different fruit and vegetable products of the recognized commercial processes such as canning, freezing, and drying. The overall quality designation is based on a variety of characteristics applied in ways specified for each product. These characteristics may include size, shape, texture, color, freedom from blemishes, viscosity and flavor of syrup, and the quantity of foreign materials of various kinds including weeds, decayed product, paint, metal filings, insects, and mud balls. The characteristics graded are primarily those relating to taste and visual appeal, rather than health. The buyer who knows how to interpret the grade will not be surprised when he opens the can, but will not have any additional information, except a feeling of security that the product was packed under sanitary conditions.

The entire grading program for processed fruits and vegetables is voluntary, as specified by the legislation (7 U.S.C. 1622(h)). If a food processor chooses to have his product graded, he can request continuous in-plant grading of output produced while at least one AMS grader is present in the plant, or in-plant pack certification, in which the grader

---

[2]U.S. Congress. Senate. Committee on Agriculture and Forestry, Senate Report No. 1843, 26 July 1946 (quoted in 1946 *U.S. Code Cong. Service*, p. 1587). Regulatory activities are mentioned, but they are distinctly secondary to marketing and distribution.

attests only to the quality of output produced when he is on duty, although the plant may also operate at other times producing uncertified output. Either the producer or some other financially interested party may request certification of a particular lot. For this purpose, the AMS grader draws a random sample from the lot, examining the product alone without regard to the conditions under which it was produced. Similarly, the AMS will grade products taken to an AMS office, but cannot certify either the conditions of the plant or whether the products graded are representative of any lot.

The party requesting the grading must pay the costs. Continuous in-plant grading, on which the rest of the discussion will focus, thus represents an outright cost to the processor, as well as subjecting his processing operations to continuous scrutiny. In return he has the right to use not only the grade designation, but also the shield with the words "packed under continuous inspection of the U.S. Department of Agriculture."

About 30% of canned fruits and vegetables and 70% of frozen were packed under all forms of certification in 1975, down from 35% and 75% respectively, in 1970–1972. Of those entitled to use the USDA shield, moreover, a large proportion do not. This raises the question of why a food processor would want to pay for a certification of quality that he does not use, as well as why more use is not made of it. Despite some fears by the AMS, alternative grading agencies, which might be sponsored by states or trade associations, have not developed. The industry does have two alternatives of its own, however. The first is the individual brand name: the packer, distributor, or retail chain that owns a brand name will want consumers to associate the name with a constant level of quality. The brand name may be more valuable to the packer than a U.S. Grand A label, and certainly more so than a U.S. Grade C. The other choice in the channels of trade is to use testing procedures similar to those employed by AMS, but without going through the formality of appealing to third party certification. It is conceivable that the existence of AMS standards keeps the informal processes of grading more orderly.

The grader may be very useful to the processor in his own efforts to maintain standards, as well, according to an AMS spokesman. No one wants his best customers to be killed by botulism or even frightened by flies. In the rush to pack large quantities of product cheaply and quickly from perishable raw produce that may be marginal in quality, the quality control department of the firm may find the grader useful in strengthening its position against the demands of production and field men. The grader does not enter the plant as an adversary, therefore, but rather as an ally of those within the firm who want to maintain quality, ever alert to point out problems before they become too serious.

The Food and Drug Administration is also concerned with food processing, but with the objective of preventing the distribution of adulterated foods, rather than improving marketing by standardizing grades. According to the Federal Food, Drug, and Cosmetic Act, food is adulterated if it (a) "consists in whole or in part of any filthy, putrid, or decomposed substance," (b) "is otherwise unfit for food," or (c) has been prepared, packed, or held under unsanitary conditions whereby it may have become contaminated with filth or may have been rendered injurious to health."[3] At the time of the GAO study, the FDA had only 210 inspectors to cover the 60,000 food establishments in the United States.[4] With more serious health hazards to worry about, they could spend little time on fruit and vegetable processing.

The AMS graders are ideally placed to extend the reach of FDA inspection. Only the processor can know more about the conditions under which the food has been packed. The Food, Drug, and Cosmetic Act was designed to take advantage of such information accumulated in other government agencies by requiring them to make their records available for FDA inspection. Nevertheless, when the GAO began its investigation, the AMS did not routinely supply any information to the FDA, having agreed in 1953 to provide grade and quality information only on lots specifically identified by the FDA.[5] Not until a quarter-century after the grading programs began was the flow of information from the Department of Agriculture to the FDA finally initiated.

The individual grader has only a few weapons to force a reluctant processing-plant management to follow proper sanitary procedures. When the processing problems can actually be identified in the product (rodent hairs, insect parts, etc.), the product may no longer meet grade standards. Some sanitary problems, however, are not evident in the product. The grader reports all deficiencies to the firm in his daily written report. Major and critical deficiencies are also reported orally immediately to management. When the overall condition is unsatisfactory, the grader notifies the area officer, who is to meet with plant management when major or critical problems prevail for long periods. These procedures rely entirely on the voluntary response of management. If persuasion does not work, the grader can temporarily suspend grading by marking the product Grade Not Certified and, as a final step, the area

[3]21 U.S.C. 342 (a) (3–4).
[4]GAO, *Processed Fruits and Vegetables*, pp. 9–10.
[5]*Ibid.*, p. 15.

officer can recommend to headquarters the withdrawal of grading service, but only headquarters can take such drastic action. The AMS does not like to threaten and punish, it would much prefer to restrict its services to plants that are willing to cooperate in attempting to pack high-quality products. The individual grader is left with no middle ground between perfunctory notification of problems (from which few plants are ever entirely free) and the drastic refusal to certify grade; although the boundary between acceptable and unacceptable processing depends upon a subjective judgment.

Withdrawal of grading services, although it obviates the problem of policing the recalcitrant, is not fully satisfactory either. Not only does the termination of service remove whatever chance the AMS might have to raise the quality of food processing in that plant, it also results in a direct reduction in the AMS budget. The AMS is as subject to the pressures of its customers as is any business. It is vulnerable to the same sorts of accusations (whether justified or not) as the magazines that give seals of approval to their advertisers and the traveling trenchermen who recommend restaurants. When 40 plants cancelled their grading contracts around the time of the GAO investigation, the agency ceased hiring graders for about 2 years and laid off 30. This painful managerial task would surely be made more severe by any additional withdrawals or by applying sufficient pressure to firms to induce them to cancel. Grading services are withdrawn from 3 or 4 processors (of the roughly 300 receiving in-plant inspection) in a typical year, but the relationship between severity of grading and voluntary cancellation of the grading service is not known.

Fear of cancellations was one of the reasons why the AMS opposed giving the FDA more information. (Whether the fear was warranted is not fully established by the 40 cancellations mentioned previously, since the charges for the grading service have also increased with higher federal salaries and other costs.) The AMS had traditionally maintained somewhat higher standards than the FDA. Hence, a product could be denied the low grade of C without necessarily implying that it was unfit for human consumption by FDA standards. The processor could still market it for human consumption, without any indication that it had been inspected and found unsuitable for a grade designation. This avoided penalizing those processors who had voluntarily submitted to, and borne the costs of, the grading and quality improvement program.

It must be noted, as well, that "adulterated" is an ambiguous term until specific criteria are established. In a practical sense, zero is a small positive number; that is, food is never completely free of foreign material, a fact that is recognized by the FDA as well as the AMS. Furthermore, such adulterants as bits of paper, weeds, and well-pasteurized insects pose only esthetic problems; in such cases it seems harsh to impose severe penalties for a slight variation from an arbitrarily chosen permissible level. Some processing failures, moreover, although posing sufficient potential hazard to be considered unacceptable—reprocessing of product spilled on a clean floor, for example—may, nevertheless, result in a wholesome product nearly all the time. Most significant of all, of course, is the fact that processors who refuse to purchase grading service from the AMS will not be penalized for any lapses in processing technique except those that show up in the products.

The situation at the time of the GAO investigation, however, did have its unsatisfactory aspects. The FDA, at the request of the GAO, tracked down 31 lots of food that had been considered substandard by the AMS for reasons that would have classified them as adulterated (and therefore unfit for distribution in interstate commerce) under Section 402 of the Federal Food, Drug, and Cosmetic Act.[6] Of the 31 lots, 3 had definitely been destroyed or used as cattle feed, 14 were still in distribution channels for human consumption, 2 lots had been reprocessed, 10 could not be traced, and 2 were seized by the FDA. When the consumer, therefore, bought processed fruits and vegetables not bearing the USDA shield, he had no way of knowing whether the product (a) had been graded with the processor not choosing to display the shield, (b) had not been graded but would have passed, (c) had not been graded and would not have passed, or (d) had been rejected. Brand names, of course, eliminate much of the risk, but the consumer would have them to rely on regardless of government activity.

The AMS could argue that its grades are an assurance of quality in an otherwise uncertain market and that if consumers look for the grade label, processors will soon begin to use it, but from this viewpoint some of the observations of sanitary conditions within plants using the USDA shield are even more disturbing. In an earlier study of a random sample of 97 plants, the GAO had found that 24% were operating under seriously unsanitary conditions capable of causing product contamination.[7] In the followup study of 34 plants chosen at random from those receiving continuous in-plant grading by the AMS, deficiencies were found in all plants, with 21 of the 34 plants having 10 or more deficiencies. At least 22 of the plants (probably more) had major or critical deficiencies. These included such problems as dirty equipment, slime,

[6] *Ibid.*, p. 14.
[7] *Ibid.*, p. 10. These plants were not limited to fruit and vegetable processors.

rust, condensation, flaking paint, and insects.[8] Some of these problems had been reported repeatedly by graders, with no apparent results. Despite such examples of continued failure to meet the basic sanitary requirements that are supposed to be the prerequisite for grading, during 1970 and 1971 AMS did not terminate any contracts for grading service because of unsanitary conditions. Only two plants were subject to temporary withdrawal of service—for 8 and 17 days—for unsanitary conditions.[9]

It would be natural to lay a large part of the blame for continuing sanitary deficiencies on the grader in the plant; for, as the only AMS employee on duty during the shift (unless the plant is very large), he is exposed to all the informal social pressures of the processing plant, while being isolated from fellow graders. He might even be offered bribes on occasion, and he will certainly become accustomed to the peculiarities of the plant that militate against compliance with good sanitary practice. The GAO report suggests that, despite such pressures, graders kept diligently reporting problems on which no action was taken. The onus for failure to act more aggressively must fall on either the area officer or his superiors. In any event, the area officer is supposed to visit each plant often enough to know of egregious problems of long duration, so the weak point of the system was not the in-plant inspection.

Some regulatory agencies have run into difficulties because of the technical complexity of the areas in which they operate.[10] That is not the problem in the present case, because the AMS has been able to develop meaningful criteria and techniques for grading and to encourage the improvement of processing techniques and equipment. Providing technical assistance to the industry to improve the quality of output and strengthening the position of those within the firm who are striving to maintain high standards are the functions that the agency appears to prefer.

Since the inspection function may be inconsistent with voluntary quality improvement, the AMS would prefer to concentrate its efforts on grading. Although the separation of the two functions may seem attractive, it is an impossibility for two reasons. First, any in-plant grading must necessarily be contingent on minimum sanitary standards for the packing process. Second, in the process of grading, the AMS does collect most of the information needed for inspection oriented at protecting

[8]*Ibid.*, pp. 22–24.
[9]*Ibid.*, p. 26.
[10]Regulation of pesticides (Chapter 10.) provides an example.

the consumer. Separating grading from inspection, therefore, could only mean returning to the situation that prevailed before the recent agreement with the FDA; that is, leaving the FDA in ignorance while food that the AMS knows to be adulterated is sold in the grocery stores. In the absence of a huge army of FDA inspectors, it is a practical necessity for that agency to rely on the information generated by others.

Any analysis of the problems of the processed fruit and vegetable-grading activities of AMS must scrutinize its peculiar financial dependence on the firms that it inspects. It would seem that only the most saintly dedication to the consumers' interests could persuade the AMS to push its clients so hard that large numbers would cancel their grading service. The only feature that makes the agency's role tenable is the fact that processors, also, have an interest in maintaining a reputation for quality. The fact remains, however, that the agency obtains its budget by selling its services to the firms. The firms must remain convinced that the costs of the service—including the fee paid to the agency, the costs of maintaining higher processing standards in the plant, and the greater risk of coming to the attention of the FDA—are less than the benefits. The most tangible benefit to the firm anticipated in the original legislation, the U.S.D.A. shield certifying quality to the final consumer, has not proved to be very valuable.

Dependence on its customers for support also frees the grading activities from taxpayer support and, therefore, from close congressional scrutiny except during periods of adverse publicity. This is not a highly visible program in normal times. Firms that do not like it can easily refuse to participate and the only public contact is with the grade labels, themselves, which do appear to label well the qualities of which the consumer is aware. The agency is, therefore, relatively safe from publicity except during episodes of consumer activism, muckraking, scandals, botulism scares, or other disasters.

The agency is thus, of necessity, oriented toward the industry, but this does not explain laxity in enforcing sanitary standards. The only segments of the industry to which the agency need be responsive are the clients or potential clients, who are presumably interested in high quality. Those who pay for a label must want it to be worth something, even if they might be inclined to cut corners occasionally in their own plants. Thus one would expect fairly general pressure from the industry participants and the agency to maintain the quality of the label, except where pushing too hard on the aspects of quality not seen by the consumer drives up costs either directly (e.g., by necessitating replacement of decrepit equipment) or indirectly through higher exposure to FDA regulation. The agency, with its grade label, is in essentially the same position as a packer or distributor with a brand name; that is, strongly motivated to maintain standards on those aspects of quality that will be evident to the consumer of the product, but reluctant to raise costs by setting excessively high standards for other aspects of processing quality. Deference toward its customers must certainly have contributed to the reluctance of the AMS to share its information with the FDA.

Before putting too much stress on the deleterious effects of a voluntary fee-for-service grading system, however, it is worthwhile to examine the compulsory poultry plant inspection activities of the Department of Agriculture. The descriptions of some conditions found by the GAO in its 1970–1971 inspection of poultry plants are reminiscent of Upton Sinclair's muckraking account of meatpacking at the turn of the century in *The Jungle*.[11] The Wholesome Poultry Products Act (21 U.S.C. 451) requires that all plants processing poultry for interstate or foreign commerce comply with the sanitary regulations of the Department of Agriculture. The federal inspector on duty in the plant has the authority to suspend inspection—and hence prohibit interstate shipment of the product—if sanitary conditions are bad enough. The inpsector, thus, has a powerful weapon that he can use without fear the poultry processer will retaliate by cancelling the inspection service. Nevertheless, in the 1971 review the GAO found that conditions were equally serious in 17 "bad" plants singled out for followup after an earlier study and in 51 randomly selected plants. At 40 of the 68 plants operations were suspended by the inspectors accompanying the GAO investigators.[12] The percentage of the randomly selected plants rated as unacceptable on the various aspects of sanitation ranged from 6 to 44.

Although conditions in the poultry plants have improved, some features of meat and poultry inspection are conducive to failure. In particular, by giving the inspector the authority to stop the plant at any moment when serious violations are detected, the legislation created conditions conducive to bribery and extortion. Comprehensive evidence of the extent of illegal behavior is not available, but one investigation suggested that it might be widespread in the New York City area.[13] The compulsory nature of meat and poultry inspection gives the inspector more

[11]U.S. General Accounting Office, "Consumer and Marketing Service's Enforcement of Federal Sanitation Standards at Poultry Plants Continues to Be Weak," Report B-163450, 16 Nov. 1971, pp. 19–32. After the GAO began its series of investigations of the inspection of food processing plants, the Department of Agriculture reviewed and reorganized its activities in the area. Meat and poultry inspection were transferred from the Consumer and Marketing Service to the Animal and Plant Health Inspection Service, and then in 1977 to the Food Safety and Quality Service.

[12]*Ibid.*, pp. 4, 16, 17. By 1977 conditions were much better; see U.S. GAO, "A Better Way for the Department of Agriculture to Inspect Meat and Poultry Processing Plants," Report CED-78-11, 9 Dec. 1977.

[13]Selwyn Raab, "Payoffs to U.S. Meat Inspectors Are Found Common in City Area," *The New York Times*, 5 April 1976, p. 1.

power, which he can use for extortion if he is so inclined, than does the most powerful sanction of the fruit and vegetable grader—denial of the grade label. Not only is the incentive to bribe larger for the meat or poultry plant, but the long-term penalties for selling subgrade products are also smaller. Meat and poultry products are usually anonymous by the time they appear in the grocery store, so the processor often does not have a brand name to protect. Most processing plants will have some violations, so a subjective decision is often necessary regarding the unacceptability of some sanitary lapse. Under such conditions detection of corrupt behavior is not easy.

It must not be concluded that some factor peculiar to government operation of grading services is responsible for the problems that have been observed, for the private agencies licensed by AMS to inspect grain have been subject to equally vigorous criticism.[14] The extent and magnitude of the problems with the grain inspection system far surpass anything encountered in the grading of fruits and vegetables. Although grain inspection is beyond the scope of this study, a few of the structural features are worth noting.

Like the AMS Fruit and Vegetable Division, the grain inspection companies are dependent for their income on one of the interested parties. The inspectors are employed by companies that operate grain elevators and export grain to certify the quality and quantity of shipments. Unlike the situation in fruit and vegetables, however, the possibilities for a conflict between self-interest and professional judgment are accentuated by the characteristics of the market. In contrast to the continuing relationships characterizing markets for processed fruits and vegetables, the grain exporter deals with buyers who are geographically remote, whose transactions are sporadic and irregular, and who frequently, as the recipients of heavy U.S. government subsidies, have been in a poor position to complain about quality. The transitory nature of the relationship is particularly noteworthy because it suggests the more general rule that, as the market moves closer to the anonymity of pure competition, the importance of more nearly perfect information becomes greater. That is, if one expects to deal with one customer for a number of years, it does not pay to cheat him on one transaction. If the market relationship is transitory, it may. Moreover, each transaction is so huge

[14]See, e.g., U.S. General Accounting Office, "Supplemental Information on Assessment of the National Grain Inspection System," Report CED–76–132, 16 July 1976, and a long series of newspaper reports during 1975 and 1976 including William Robbins, "Agriculture Investigation on Possible Grain Fraud Said to Find Bureaucrats Inept," *The New York Times,* 25 Sept. 1975, p. 33, and John Huey, "Grain-Inspection Job Hasn't Changed Much Since Scandals Broke," *Wall Street Journal,* 15 September 1976, p. 1.

that bribery may well be profitable for both the exporter and the inspector. The fruit and vegetable grader, by contrast, is rarely in a position where the gains to be made by falsifying a grade are commensurate with the value of his expected salary and pension rights as an honest civil servant.

The final appraisal of processed fruit and vegetable inspection must remain mixed. The performance was certainly better than that in meat and poultry inspection or grain inspection. The most important lapses were the toleration of conditions that should have led to the withdrawal of certification and the delay of many years in sharing information with the FDA. Yet a review of the three inpection programs raises the question of whether the brand identification of processed fruits and vegetables may not offer the consumer more protection and information about quality than does government certification. In view of the suggestions that are frequently made to extend certification to a variety of products and repair services, the question clearly merits some investigation.

CHAPTER **10**

Regulation of Pesticides[1]

Because of the serious externalities, pesticides should certainly be regulated by government. The technological problems, however, are considerable. The agency has also had trouble keeping track of a huge number of products and uses and coordinating action with other agencies. Furthermore, controversial decisions must be made among the contending claims of manufacturers, users, and environmentalists. The most puzzling feature of this case, however, is that the agency did not aggressively try to expand its budget.

The Department of Agriculture administered the Federal Insecticide, Fungicide, and Rodenticide Act of 1947 (7 U.S.C. 135), known as FIFRA, until December 1, 1970, when those functions were transferred to the Environmental Protection Agency (EPA). The legislation was strengthened by the passage of the Federal Environmental Pesticides Control Act of 1972 (7 U.S.C. 136, supplement II, 1972), known as FEPCA. Under these laws, pesticides are defined broadly to include insecticides, herbicides, rodenticides, fungicides, disinfectants, sanitiz-

[1]This case is based primarily on U.S. General Accounting Office, "Pesticides:Actions Needed to Protect the Consumer From Defective Products," Report B–133192 (23 May 1974). I am also indebted to Mr. Edwin L. Johnson, Deputy Assistant Administrator for Pesticides Programs, for his assistance.

ers, and plant regulators, so the agency is responsible for a wide range of products in a rapidly changing field. More significantly, public perceptions of what is environmentally acceptable have been changing rapidly. Most of the problems discussed in this chapter surfaced during the transition to the new organization and the expanded functions specified by FEPCA, but the agency was bedeviled by lost files and lax procedures throughout the 1970s.[2]

Under the new law all pesticides must be registered before they can be sold (the old law applied only to interstate shipments). Before they are registered, they must be shown to be safe and effective when used in the ways described and for the purposes indicated. The labels must comply with detailed regulations regarding the warnings about various hazards involved. In addition, the label for a product must correspond with the registration on file with the EPA, both in regard to ingredients (which must, of course, also correspond with what is actually in the package) and with regard to uses and hazards. There are, therefore, many possibilities for discrepancies among actual contents, registrations and labels, as well as between the wording of the label and the regulations concerning warnings. Clearly the agency must have some means for detecting violations and enforcing compliance.

A great many different products are covered under the provisions of the act. On June 30, 1972, about 32,000 pesticides, formulated from 1800 chemicals, were registered by the federal government. Guesses about the total number to be included under FEPCA ranged as high as 70,000 products of 10,000 firms, although by March 1977 only 34,000 pesticides were registered.[3] The new law required the agency to reregister all registered pesticides, and to register all those previously unregistered including those restricted to intrastate commerce. This was not supposed to be a reshuffling of existing papers, but a serious reexamination of each pesticide to see whether its use should be discontinued, restricted to licensed applicators, or limited.

This large task was supposed to be completed by October 21, 1976, but with slippage and delay at every stage in the process, it was evident to the GAO more than a year before the deadline that the schedule could

[2]U.S. General Accounting Office, "Delays and Unresolved Issues Plague New Pesticide Protection Programs," Report CED-80-32 (15 Feb. 1980).
[3]GAO, "Pesticides," 1974, p. 6; U.S. Congress, Senate, Committee on the Judiciary, Subcommittee on Administrative Practice and Procedure, Staff Report, "The Environmental Protection Agency and the Regulation of Pesticides," 94th Congress, 2nd Session (December 1976), p. 5; U.S. General Accounting Office, "Special Pesticide Registration by the Environmental Protection Agency Should Be Improved," Report CED-78-9 (9 January 1978), p. 1.

not be met.[4] All theories of bureaucracy imply that an agency receiving such a report would use it as leverage to obtain a larger budget. Yet the response of this agency was to deny the necessity for additional resources, "We are less certain than GAO that the statutory deadline of October 1976 cannot be met, or at least closely approached."[5] The agency first attempted to meet the dealine by sacrificing the depth and quality of review, but, after several years of intense internal and external criticism of the compromises necessary to meet even an extended deadline of October 1977, the agency finally conceded that the task could scarcely be completed before 1980.[6] The GAO has continued to accuse the agency of being understaffed.[7]

Laboratory capacity of the agency was inadequate for testing the safety and effectiveness of new registrations and checking all products on the market to ensure that the ingredients complied with both label and registration. In order to be perfectly certain of the latter, one would have to check each batch of each product. In the face of such an overwhelming task, it is necessary to resort to some sampling procedure. Unfortunately, the sampling procedure used by the agency resulted in the repeated testing of the same products, whereas others went completely untested.[8]

The agency chose products to be tested at the point of sale, rather than manufacture, ostensibly because evidence obtained at the point of manufacture could not be used to prosecute under the old law applying only to interstate commerce. Sampling at point of sale, however, requires more coordination than sampling at the manufacturing plant since the same products are available in hundreds or even thousands of retail outlets. The new law obviates this problem since all pesticides are covered; hence the agency has turned to sampling at the manufacturing plant. It should be noted in passing, however, that the penchant for legal correctness is puzzling since the agency did not refer a single case to the Justice Department for prosecution between 1959 and 1968, with the level rising after that to 250 in 1973.[9] Surely the routine sampling

[4]U.S. General Accounting Office, "Federal Pesticide Registration Program:Is It Protecting the Public and the Environment Adequately From Pesticide Hazards?" Report RED–76–42 (4 December 1975), p. 67.

[5]Ibid., p. 83, "Comments" of the Office of Pesticides Programs of the U.S. Environmental Protection Agency on the draft of the GAO report released 4 December 1975, and appended to it. The "Comments," dated 11 Sept. 1975, were submitted by Alvin L. Alm, Assistant Administrator for Planning and Management.

[6]U.S. Senate, "The Environmental Protection Agency and the Regulation of Pesticides," pp. 6, 11–12.

[7]GAO, "Delays and Unresolved Issues," 1980, p. 21.

[8]GAO, "Pesticides," 1974, pp. 9–13.

[9]Ibid., pp. 11, 27.

could have been performed informally at the plant. When a case had to be built to force a consistent violator to comply, that could have been a separate and easily manageable undertaking.

Even with the reliance on sampling at point of sale, it would hardly seem impossible to devise a reasonable sampling plan. Instead, the headquarters personnel divided the 32,000 pesticides into 82 categories, based on type, place of use, and ingredients; they then told their inspectors how many samples to collect in each category. The regional offices were supposed to be responsible for preventing duplication. In fact, however, in 29,000 samples collected over a four and one-half year period, only 7000 different products were represented. Furthermore, 253 pesticides were each sampled at least 10 times between January 1968 and June 1972, although they were not especially subject to violations.[10]

Imported pesticides are also regulated. The Bureau of Customs is supposed to notify EPA when pesticides arrive, a function that is particularly important with the shift of domestic sampling to the point of manufacture. During 1972, however, customs officials at only 47 of the 291 ports of entry were reporting pesticides to the EPA regularly.[11] Commissioner of Customs Vernon D. Acree explained, "At the time of enactment of FIFRA, the Customs Service reported shipments of pesticides and devices to the Pesticides Regulation Division, Agricultural Research Service. When EPA assumed administrative responsibility for pesticides, there was a temporary loss of contact between the agencies involved."[12] The two agencies eventually found each other, but the new regulations regarding cooperation that seemed imminent in September of 1973 were not issued until the June 28, 1974, *Federal Register*.

Even after contact was restored the problems with Customs did not end. The list that EPA gave to Customs to alert the agents to the most common pesticides filtered irregularly and sporadically into the hands of individual agents. The agents of the Houston district in September 1972, for example, reported only 2 of 21 shipments of chemicals on the EPA list. In 2 of the 4 offices of that district agents had not been given the list at all. In addition, there were various misinterpretations of instructions, some reluctance to assume the additional reporting burden, and some concern that the entire process would delay the release of shipments and hence add to the importers' storage costs.[13]

Despite the mishaps, Customs did manage to notify EPA of 1026

[10]*Ibid.*, pp. 10–11.
[11]*Ibid.*, p. 14.
[12]Letter to Charles P. McAuley, Assistant Director, General Government Division, GAO, dated 19 September 1973, reproduced in GAO, "Pesticides," 1974, pp. 51–52.
[13]GAO, "Pesticides" 1974, pp. 15–18.

shipments of pesticides during 1972. The EPA examined samples of 67 and found violations in 26, which might suggest that imports are worth watching closely. Because of various delays, however, 20 of the samples were collected after the pesticides had entered the channels of trade. When the Pesticide Enforcement Division completed its reviews, an average of 243 days after the release of the pesticides from Customs, 3 of the 11 shipments that were found to be in violation had already been sold out.

As this discussion has suggested, the pesticides group suffered confusion and administrative problems around the time of the transfer of functions from the Department of Agriculture to the Environmental Protection Agency. The various GAO reports indicate serious lapses in the filing systems, inability to retrieve information, and generally chaotic procedures. Despite the agency's explanation that these problems of transition to the new law and the new organizational structure would soon be solved, the Staff Report of the Senate Judiciary Committee found the problems still to be serious in 1976.[14] Even if it can eventually straighten out such problems, the question of what the EPA can reasonably certify about a pesticide remains.

If a consumer takes the present law at face value, he knows that any pesticide on the market is safe, effective, and properly labeled as to the hazards of use. It also does no more environmental damage than other pesticides registered for the same use. The question then arises as to how the EPA obtains the information necessary to certify these matters.

When a new active ingredient is presented for registration, the EPA requires a substantial amount of testing by the manufacturer. The records of the tests are examined by the agency, but the tests are not replicated. With proper record-keeping, the EPA can accumulate data relating to the safety of ingredients to the user and those nearby, and eventually it can collect the scraps of evidence that accumulate about environmental effects. When registrations are sought subsequently by different manufacturers or for different uses of the same, or a similar, active ingredient, the agency does not require replication of the earlier tests if they are still adequate by contemporary standards. Needless to say, the effectiveness of such an approach depends upon the quality of the information system used by the agency.

Problems can still arise regarding safety from a number of different sources. The testing is generally performed using the output of pilot

---

[14]U.S. Senate, "The Environmental Protection Agency and the Regulation of Pesticides," pp. 15–16 and elsewhere. The GAO report of 9 January 1978, also complained of delays in making decisions (p. 7) and writing guidelines (p. 17), as did the report of 15 Feb. 1980.

plants. Many of the chemical processes, however, are not fully controlled, so the change to full-scale equipment can result in contamination of the product with more harmful compounds. The same sort of problem can arise with any other changes in the manufacturing process as well. One of the functions of the agency's sampling and testing program is to detect such deviations, not only from the label and the registration, but also from the manufacturer's intent. Ingredients can break down after manufacture, too. This is one of the weaknesses of the new approach of sampling at the plant—problems that occur during storage will not be detected.

Problems may also arise with ingredients other than the active ones. Thus the registration spells out the entire contents so that when, for example, PVC was deemed to be too hazardous to use as a propellent, all pesticides containing the ingredient could be recalled. This poses two practical problems: one is the adequacy of the agency's information system, and the other is ensuring that firms, including the myriad of small and unsophisticated ones, know the regulations and comply. Another serious concern is the possiblity of *synergism* (complementarity); that is, that the adverse consequences of several ingredients combined in the same product may be more serious than the sum of the effects from each component. All of these possible problems suggest the importance of testing products in the form in which they are consumed, rather than relying on earlier tests of products with similar active ingredients. The quality of the testing by private firms has been questioned.[15] Indeed, many of the tests required by EPA regulations have either never been submitted by the firms or have been lost by the agency.[16]

At this point it is necessary to distinguish more explicitly the three functions of pesticide regulation. Traditionally the program has emphasized safety of the user and effectiveness against the pest. The more recent emphasis within the EPA is the environmental impact of the pesticides. Safety and environmental hazard are completely separate characteristics. DDT, for example, is very safe for the people by whom (or even on whom) it is used, but since it persists in the environment it builds up to the extent that it damages some birds and fish and arouses fears about the long-term effect on people. On the other hand, a pesticide can be hazardous to use but pose no threat to anyone outside the immediate neighborhood of its use. Until recently, chlorine was generally considered to be in this category. Safety and effectiveness are

---

[15] *The Cleveland Plain Dealer*, 10 April 1976, p. 10-A; *Wall Street Journal,* 16 August 1977, p. 8.

[16] GAO, "Federal Pesticide Registration Program," 1975, pp. 7–10.

primarily the concern of the individual user, but environmental degradation from a "safe and effective" pesticide is the perfect example of an externality. This places the regulation of pesticides in the public domain. If government does not take action to regulate these externalities, no one will.

Although safety, effectiveness, and environmental hazard are conceptually distinct problems, they shade together in a number of ways. All pesticides seem to inflict some external costs. If the problem is to minimize the total damage to the environment, one solution is to restrict administratively the uses of the most harmful substances to those for which no good substitutes are readily available. This is the approach embodied in the new law, which gives the agency the responsibility for registering not just products, but particular uses of particular products. The law provides stiff penalties for noncompliance not only by manufacturers but also by individuals who use an acceptable pesticide for nonregistered purposes.

Safety sometimes concerns not only the buyer of the product, but also his employees, consumers of treated crops, and the people living downwind or downstream. Such effects are of limited geographical extent, but they do fall upon people other than the immediate parties to the transaction, or involve serious imperfections in information, and thus suggest the possiblity that government action might improve welfare. The question of effectiveness has public aspects, since users will ignore environmental damage in weighing the costs against the benefits. Furthermore, since pests may develop immunity to pesticides, the effectiveness of the pesticide to one user may depend on use and misuse by others. This provides some justification for regulating and limiting use.

Some questions of effectiveness have public health aspects as well. Hospitals, government agencies, and food-processing establishments may be users. They, as well as consumers in general, will find life simpler if they can believe the claims of the producers of pesticides. If, for example, a hospital or dairy disinfectant does perform as advertised, then consumer welfare will undoubtedly be increased. In one sense this is no different from the advertising of any product, for with recent attempts to eliminate false and misleading advertising the government has, in effect, assumed the role of guaranteeing the claims made for all products. The task of the EPA with regard to pesticides, however, is more demanding. Since many pesticides impose some nonmonetary costs (e.g., degradation of the environment, risks to neighbors of the users, or accumulation of residues in food), the agency must decide which uses are cost-effective, that is, worthwhile *despite* the costs. It obviously cannot do so in the absence of some knowledge about effectiveness.

This leads to a crucial question: How much reliance can be placed on the implicit certification by the EPA that a product is effective when used as directed? The answer in a word is none, for a variety of reasons. The agency has limited laboratory facilities for testing that chemical composition agrees with the label and the registration and detecting some common contaminants. The biological laboratories test for acute toxicity to mammals, and sometimes fish and plants, but are limited in many ways even in testing safety. Biological tests are very expensive, particularly tests of chronic exposure to small doses. Furthermore there are no facilities for testing pesticides for use on pets and livestock.

Testing for effectiveness is more difficult than testing for safety. Such tests must be biological, of course; moreover, they should be field tests with all the complications and expenses that implies. The interesting question is not whether a rat bait is attractive to a laboratory rat, but whether Norway and black rats will actually eat it and die. They, like many other pests, are not raised commercially. Similarly, some pests are confined to particular regions, so the effectiveness of pesticides cannot be determined elsewhere. For statistical purposes the tests should be repeated many times if the results disagree with those presented by the manufacturer, especially since efficacy can vary from batch to batch.

When tests show that the pesticide does not work in the laboratory, but the company reports that people keep buying it, the EPA can accept the judgment of the marketplace rather than its tests. It puts the agency in the peculiar position, however, of attesting, not that a product works, but merely that since it remains on the market someone must think it works. That approach, also, makes it difficult for an equally ineffectual (according to laboratory tests) new product to compete with the existing ones. To avoid these problems, the EPA requires that manufacturers assume the burdens of testing by requiring them to submit evidence of efficacy, as well as of safety, with the application for registration. It is the quality of this information, however, that has recently been called into question. A good filing system would eventually detect slipshod or fraudulent safety testing, but since conditions vary so much, the information about effectiveness that the EPA can develop is limited. The agency might be better off abandoning such efforts entirely, in order to devote its resources to questions of safety and, especially, environmental effects. However, to end the grossly deceptive practice of pretending that the agency does certify effectiveness when in fact it cannot, the legislation must be changed to correspond with practice. Perhaps the labels of pesticides should bear the legend: "This product is believed safe when used as directed; it is illegal to use it otherwise; make your own guess about whether it works." But, as noted previously, the agency cannot avoid the problem that easily when it is required to weigh the effectiveness against the environmental cost of the product in particular uses.

If the product is a mouse poison or a moth killer, the consumer is the best judge of effectiveness. Pesticides, however, include such items as hospital disinfectants where the stakes are higher and the degree of effectiveness is less visible. Procedures for testing disinfectants are hard to devise because they seem to behave differently in actual service than they do in laboratory tests. The discrepancy between what the legislation promises and what the agency is able to deliver is particularly tragic when the disinfectants sold to hospitals are not effective against the microorganisms responsible for serious infections in hospitals. It is ironic, also, that agencies such as the Veterans Administration and the General Services Administration were awarding contracts for disinfectants at the same time that the EPA was requesting their recall for ineffectiveness.[17]

Although the agency was charged with the inherently difficult, but largely unavoidable, task of certifying effectiveness by the old law, the new law (FEPCA) added a provision that is, on its face, thoroughly unenforceable: "It shall be unlawful for any person . . . to use any registered pesticide in a manner inconsistent with its labeling".[18] This has created the problem of making registrations consistent with the way people actually use the products. Many minor uses have been cancelled inadvertently, despite the efforts of the agency to arrange a defense. If the amount used in a particular way is small, the manufacturer may not even know about it. Yet if the label ceases to reflect the ways in which a consumer uses the pesticide, he becomes a violator of the law. Furthermore, the usual patterns of innovation include the discovery of new uses for products by consumers. Under the current law that is an illegal activity.

Obviously the agency will devote most of its attention to the powerful pesticides registered for "restricted use." Yet the fact that a person now breaks the law by spraying wasps with a roach poison should give pause to civil libertarians. From the agency's point of view, the addition of another nonenforceable function to the efficacy provisions is scarcely likely to improve its performance. It is, rather, a distraction from the important public task of keeping the environmental externalities within

---

[17]GAO, "Pesticides," 1974, pp. 28–29, 36–37.
[18]PL 92–516, Sec. 12 (2)(G).

reasonable bounds and keeping the major problems of user and neighbor safety under control.

Environmental questions, unfortunately, seem to require a great deal of administrative discretion. They are too complex for a large body like the Congress to deal with, and too time-consuming or technical for Presidents to understand. The major questions, such as prohibiting use of particular ingredients, are sufficiently visible so that the major organized pressure groups are heard (which does not, however, guarantee that the decision is a correct one). The myriad small decisions that must be made by the agency are less visible to the public, but probably more important in aggregate. Foremost among these are the decisions regarding the quantity and quality of test data that will be regarded as acceptable and the rough weighing of nonquantifiable costs against unverifiable estimates of effectiveness.[19] Decisions must also be made about the severity of enforcement action to be taken against manufacturers and users. Such decisions have been hindered by the disarray of the files and the delays in writing final regulations.

The pesticides programs were subject to three distinct varieties of failure including confusion in routine internal operations, difficulties in coordinating activities with other agencies, and the technical problems of carrying out a difficult task. The confusion, lost files, failure to devise sensible sampling plans, failure to inform manufacturers when products failed tests, and similar procedural lapses suggest widespread incompetence and loss of morale at some stage in the agency's development. The difficulties the agency encountered in enlisting the cooperation of the Customs Service are less surprising. Customs, after all, had little to gain by performing the service for EPA, so, in the absence of aggressive persistence by the latter, not much cooperation could be expected. The technical difficulty of the task assigned to the Office of Pesticides Programs cannot be doubted. This fact makes if difficult to assess the extent to which performance matched the resources expended. Great burdens were added both by the new law and by changing public standards of the acceptable degree of risk to health and the environment from pesticides. But the obviously increasing workload and failure to satisfy congressional and other critics make still more puzzling the reluctance of the agency aggressively to seek out more resources.

[19]GAO, "Delays and Unresolved Issues," 1980, pp. 45–47.

CHAPTER **11**

Controlling Petroleum Prices[1]

The effects of price controls depend not only on the principles stated in the legislation, but also on the implementation. Opposition to controls can be based on their inefficiency or their inconsistency with one's ethical preferences for freedom of contract between buyer and seller. If one favors price controls, however, the argument must proceed to the level of regulations and enforcement, because advocacy of price controls—if it is rational—must be based on the conclusion that the gains in equity from controlling prices outweigh the losses in efficiency and in individual freedom. This requires judgment about the relative importance of equity, efficiency, and freedom, but it also requires a forecast of how the bureaucracy will make and enforce regulations. A close examination of the problems of enforcement may indicate some limitations on the circumstances in which price controls can actually achieve the purpose for which they are advocated.

Control of petroleum prices following the oil embargo of 1973 provides an interesting case study because the conditions of the industry

[1]This case is based primarily on U. S. General Accounting Office, "Problems in the Federal Energy Administration's Compliance and Enforcement Effort," Report B–178205, 6 Dec. 1974. I am also indebted to Harold Butz, Jr., of the Office of Compliance and Enforcement of the Federal Energy Administration for helpful information.

were consistent with the strongest theoretical arguments for price controls. Since most domestic oil at that time could be produced for less than $5 per barrel, existing wells would earn returns in excess of those necessary to keep them in production if prices were permitted to rise. Since old and new wells could easily be identified, it seemed possible to permit higher prices for new production without increasing profits on old wells. Furthermore, if, as was commonly believed, consumers would not reduce their use of petroleum products very much in response to higher prices, the inefficiency resulting from low prices would be small.

These same conditions, however, contributed to the highly charged political atmosphere in which the decisions had to be made. Effective price controls result in large changes in wealth or income, the prospect of which provokes strong political action. Nor did the feeling of crisis resulting from the Arab oil embargo make this an exceptional case, because controls are most likely to be adopted in times of crisis.

The Federal Energy Office (FEO) provides good examples of the problems that can afflict an agency caught up in political turmoil from its inception.[2] It was established to carry out the control of prices and allocation required by the Emergency Petroleum Allocation Act of 1973.[3] This act was considered during the summer and early fall of 1973 while reports of sporadic gasoline shortages and forecasts of heating oil shortages in the coming winter circulated widely. It was not passed, however, until the Arab oil embargo created the atmosphere of crisis that enveloped the new agency. Although the attempt to control allocation began after the embargo, prices of crude oil had been controlled by the Cost of Living Council on March 6, 1973, and petroleum products had been included under the various phases of the general price control

[2]Two books provide detailed accounts of the development of the law and policy. Mason Willrich, *Administration of Energy Shortages* (Cambridge, Massachusetts:Ballinger, 1976), stresses the legal aspects of controls on the allocation of fuels. He includes a detailed review of the statutory law and court decisions relevant to the various regulatory agencies. In his discussion of implementation of allocation controls by the Federal Energy Administration, Willrich describes the content of the regulations and the process by which the agency wrote them, rather than their impact on the outside world. Richard B. Mancke, *Squeaking By:U.S. Energy Policy since the Embargo* (New York:Columbia University Press, 1976), describes the historical background of the legislation and emphasizes the implications of various decisions.

[3]For the legislative history, see 1973 *U.S. Code Cong. & Adm. News*, pp. 2582 ff., which includes House Report 93-531 on the Emergency Petroleum Allocation Act of 1973. The Senate began consideration of the act on 5 June 1973. It was passed by the House on 13 November and the Senate on 14 November. The Federal Energy Office was established to administer the act by Executive Order 11748 on 4 December 1973. It became the Federal Energy Administration (FEA) after passage of PL 93-275 on 7 May 1974, and later became a cornerstone of the Department of Energy.

program since August 15, 1971. The FEO acquired the entire petroleum price control apparatus from the Cost of Living Council on December 26, 1973.

The administration had backed grudgingly into the area of price controls and its commitment to controls over allocation was even more tenuous. The Economic Stabilization Act Amendments of 1973 gave the President the power to impose mandatory controls on the allocation of petroleum products. He had chosen, instead, to rely on a voluntary approach to government controls, but the House Committee commented on a "noticeable deterioration in compliance" in endorsing the legislation to compel the President to issue mandatory allocations.[4] The House report asserted that the mandatory program was too complicated for the Committee to write and required administrative flexibility. Nevertheless, the President was required within 30 days to devise an allocation program including prices of products "or the methods for determining equitable prices of those products," and to extend this to the producer level (excluding small wells) without discouraging production. Congress thus turned over to an administration, many of whose leaders were philosophically opposed to such controls, the task of devising almost overnight a program that Congress recognized was too complex to deal with at all. The issues were inevitably politically charged, since many decisions would seriously affect the incomes of articulate interest groups and geographic regions. Furthermore, almost anyone who understood the petroleum industry well enough to control it was working for the industry. Since Congress, at least, phrased the issues in terms of the industry versus the people, such industry experts were bound to arouse suspicion even if they acted fairly.

The new FEO immediately transferred all compliance and enforcement responsibilities to the Internal Revenue Service (IRS), which had been enforcing the price control regulations of the Cost of Living Council. According to the agreement, the 300 auditors and investigators initially detailed by IRS to the FEO work would be increased to a total compliance staff of 1000 auditors, investigators, and clerical employees.[5] The large job of recruiting, training, and supervising the additional personnel did not begin until February, when the financial arrangements for the December agreement were completed. In the crisis atmosphere of the embargo, personnel were detailed from other agencies and hired from the street until the staff had grown to about 850 by the end of April.

---

[4]1973 U. S. Code Cong. & Adm. News, p. 2589.

[5]Gorman C. Smith, Acting Assistant Administrator, Regulatory Programs, Federal Energy Administration, Testimony before the U. S. Senate, Committee on Government Operations, Permanent Subcommittee on Investigations, 10 April 1975, p. 8.

The embargo had ended in March, however, and many administration officials were discussing the possibility of decontrol when the mandatory allocation controls expired—an event scheduled for February, 1975. Hence hiring was frozen at the April level.

The political decision to rely on rationing by inconvenience (explained in the following) imposed a very heavy burden on the compliance and enforcement people during the embargo. The basic rule called for freezing prices and all customer–supplier relationships, with equal percentage reductions for all customers as the effects of the embargo were felt. In the general case, therefore, these regulations seemed easy to understand and enforce, but the problems and exceptions rapidly assumed great importance. The anonymity of the gasoline market made it impossible to reduce the purchases of each motorist by a certain percentage and, as the situation evolved, service stations were actually *forbidden* to give preference to old customers, whereas dealers in other products were *required* to continue to serve old customers. The unhindered private market would have rationed the supply of gasoline by permitting the price to rise until usage was curtailed sufficiently. Similarly, a heavy tax would have reduced consumption without adding to the profits of suppliers. An alternative is rationing by fiat, restricting each individual to a specified number of gallons by some form of ration coupon or ticket system.

Once these and other organized techniques were rejected for political reasons, the only choice available was exhortation reinforced by inconvenience. The latter was achieved by reducing speed limits and closing gasoline stations on Sundays to make driving tedious and uncomfortable and , most important, by letting people fret in lines at gas pumps until driving ceased to be worth the effort. The technique was extremely costly in real resources including the time and pain of motorists and gasoline and other materials wasted in hunting for additional gasoline. This in itself was irrelevant to the political decision process, but the annoyance of motorists could very easily have become a serious political cost, as well, if reports of profiteering had been widespread.

The price controls were based on the principle of allowing changes in product costs to be passed through while maintaining margins fixed in dollar terms. With people waiting in line at gas pumps, however, it was a large and difficult task to prevent price increases. Even if posted prices were kept unchanged, various subterfuges would have undermined the effectiveness of the controls in the absence of vigilant compliance effort ("Pay $10 for a car wash, get 10 gallons of gas free," etc.). Since the retail gasoline shortage caused such inconvenience, created so many situations in which both the buyer and the seller would benefit from a price increase, attracted so much attention from the news media, and yet involved a myriad of transactions that left few paper traces after the event, the FEO devoted most of its compliance resources to insuring that the 200,000 (or more) gas stations in the United States did not raise their prices above the level determined by the agency to be correct.[6]

Although this was a large job because of the large number of gas stations and complaints, each case was relatively easy. The "investigators," who comprised 60% of the compliance force recruited by the IRS, had experience and training somewhat below that required for a CPA. They were fully competent to audit service stations after relatively short training.

By the end of June when the agreement with the IRS ended, the Federal Energy Administration, as successor to the Federal Energy Office, took full control of a compliance and enforcement group of about 850 people admirably equipped and located to audit gas stations.[7] Unfortunately for the agency, that job was no longer necessary. With the restoration of normal supplies following the expiration of the embargo, reports began to emerge of suppliers pressuring gas stations to promote gasoline more vigorously at the prevailing prices. Oil companies even refused to take some of the price increases allowed by the law, preferring to sell more gasoline instead. Thus, aside from checking on occasional complaints and working through a backfile from the days of shortage, the compliance force had lost its mission.

Although the market solved the enforcement problem at the retail level, the agency still had to continue the formidable task of ruling on allowable costs at earlier stages of production. FEA regulations permitted firms to keep a record of allowable cost increases that in fact were not passed through to the consumer as price increases. This bank of unrecaptured costs could be used to pay overcharges discovered by the agency or to raise prices in excess of costs whenever market conditions permitted. (The actual regulations were, of course, much more complex than the principle described here. Implementation required a host of

---

[6]Policing retail price ceilings is more rewarding for compliance officials than is the policing of allocation regulations. The former allows the compliance official to create the impression that he is protecting the general public from a few greedy firms, whereas the latter involves judging the competing claims of two consumers to the same products.

[7]This may be an exaggeration. When the IRS era ended, some regions did not yet have permanent directors for compliance and enforcement for the retail and wholesale level. Also, IRS had not provided FEO enough information to enable the latter to assess the effectiveness of the work that IRS had done (GAO, "Problems in the FEA's Compliance and Enforcement Effort," p. 13). Nevertheless, the problems at the retail level were so minor in comparison with those at the producer and refinery levels that the agency appeared to be successful in carrying out its assigned task at that level.

interpretations about which costs could be banked and the circumstances under which the bank could be drawn on.)

The attempt by the government to maintain two controlled prices for domestic crude oil, in addition to the higher price of imported crude, also required enforcement activities or the implicit threat of action. The Cost of Living Council had established the basic pattern of the crude oil price controls in 1973 by freezing the price of existing production (*old oil*) while exempting new wells to maintain an incentive for development. Small wells were exempt from the controls and, for added incentive, one barrel of old production was released for every barrel of new production.[8] The separate ceilings would have given refiners with a relatively large domestic supply a significant advantage in cost compared with refiners dependent on imported crude. To avoid this, the FEA required equalizing transfers of crude oil during the embargo and of money at other times.[9] Among the results of the complex regulations required to achieve these objectives were incentives for refiners to overstate costs and for producers to devise ways to convert old oil into the higher-priced categories.[10]

Since the number of domestic producers of crude oil is in the vicinity of 10,000, spanning the entire size range of firms, the task of ensuring compliance is a sizable one. The number of refiners is much smaller—200 companies with 250 refineries—but some are very complex companies. In addition to the usual problem of distinguishing cost from profit, the large oil companies pose the peculiar problems associated with attributing costs to the domestic stages of vertically integrated firms with operations in many countries. It was thus clear that the compliance effort, if controls were to be continued after the embargo, should take on a different character. The routine work of auditing gas stations had to yield to more complex tasks.

Between April and September of 1974, however, the continuation of the controls at all was subject to questioning within the agency.[11] Since

[8]The actual regulations can be found in 6 CFR 150. Crude-oil prices are far more complex than this quick sketch reveals; the actual regulations had to come to grips with variations due to quality, location, and conditions of sales, all of which can provide opportunities to circumvent the basic control.

[9]The entitlement program has been described by Mancke, *Squeaking By,* pp. 34–35, and Willrich, *Administration of Energy Shortages.* A study by Charles E. Phelps and Rodney T. Smith, "Petroleum Regulation: The False Dilemma of Decontrol" (Santa Monica, California: The Rand Corporation, January 1977; Report # R–1951 RC), indicates that the net effects of the price control and entitlement programs include increased dependence on imported oil, large transfers of profits within the industry, but not lower prices for consumers.

[10]For some insight into the problems that have surfaced, see Walter S. Mossberg and Jerry Landauer, "Energy Agency Alleges Oil-Price Manipulation by Middleman Firms", *Wall Street Journal,* 22 Sept. 1978, p. 1.

[11]Gorman Smith, Testimony, p. 9.

the administration was on record in favor of decontrol, and the allocation authority was due to expire in February 1975, some thought that launching a major new compliance effort was hardly worthwhile. In addition, many peple inside and outside the agency doubted the wisdom of relying on controls after the embargo ended. Congressional pressure and the extension of the Emergency Petroleum Allocation Act for another 6 months brought some remission to the formal debate. Considerable damage had already been done to morale, however, with the result that experienced personnel transferred back to their original agencies—an unusual privilege written into the legislation.[12] Qualified replacements were hard to recruit under such conditions of uncertainty. As a result of these problems, when the compliance effort finally did shift toward refineries and producers, the agency found itself with "the wrong people, in the wrong place, doing the wrong thing," in the words of an agency official.

The effort to upgrade the average skill level, train personnel in the different problems encountered in auditing refiners and producers rather than gas stations, and move personnel from the major population centers of the Northeast, where the gas stations are concentrated, to the producing areas of the Southwest had not been completed more than a year after the embargo ended. As late as August 1975 the FEA was publicizing the assignment of still more inspectors to check gas stations.[13] Although the plans called for 143 people to audit producers by December 31, 1974, and 212 by June 30, 1975, the agency had no one working on that task in December and only 93 by the following October. Staffing of the refinery audit program also slipped behind schedule, although not quite as badly. The wholesale and retail compliance effort was reduced substantially, because personnel were shifted to the utilities and propane investigations, which generated publicity exceeding their economic significance.

The problems that the GAO found in its December 1974 study (one of a series, reflecting the special scrutiny to which the agency has been subject by Congress) are primarily related to the problem of shifting the compliance effort from the retail level to refiners and producers. At the time of the GAO investigation: (*a*) "There was almost no direct audit of crude oil producer operations"; (*b*) "little audit effort had been directed. . . at the wholesale level"; (*c*) "the audits of refiner operations

---

[12]As an indication of the turnover experienced by the agency, 1265 separations of personnel occurred during calendar 1975, when the average payroll of the agency was 3276 (U.S. General Accounting Office Report B-178205 (24 May 1976)). The separation rate for all government agencies hovers around 1.5% per month (U.S. Civil Service Commission, *Federal Civilian Workforce Statistics,* monthly).

[13]*Portland (Maine) Press Herald,* 6 August 1975, p. 4.

were not completed"; (d) regulations had not yet been completed; and (e) "organizational disputes within FEA hindered the refinery audit effort."[14] Points (d) and (e) suggest that the top leadership of FEA had never really mastered the problems. The ad hoc decision making of the crisis atmosphere in which the agency began seemed not to have been straightened out by the time of the GAO study. One part of the problem may be that the top officials of the agency were forced to devote a great deal of effort to justifying past behavior before innumerable congressional committees and to building support for the agency's continuation.[15]

Auditing a major oil refiner is a large and complex task. It is hardly surprising, therefore, that neither the IRS nor the FEA was able to complete the work on schedule. Of the 200 refiners, 125 were required to submit reports, including cost information, to FEA. These monthly reports were used by the firms to compute permitted cost increases since the base month of May 1973.[16] In order to make the price-control exercise meaningful, the agency had to perform some audit to ensure that: (a) the costs passed on to customers were "allowable"; (b) the profit margin did not exceed the limit; (c) price increases were uniform to all customers; (d) the company maintained historic and consistent business practices (with regard to various discounts, extra charges, deliveries, billing dates, etc.); and (e) the behavior of the firm did not subvert the intent of the FEA regulations. During its administration of the compliance effort before July 1974, the IRS assigned 64 auditors to the 31 largest firms to accomplish all this! The IRS was supposed to complete the audit of the period from May 1973 through January 1974 by May 31, 1974. FEA was then to complete auditing the first half of 1974 by September 30 of that year. Needless to say, the schedules were not met. Checks by the GAO indicated that the auditing work was extremely sketchy, a fact well recognized by the auditors doing the work, who frequently did not have time even to pursue the discrepancies they observed.[17]

The magnitude of the task prevented a very thorough job, but the failure of FEA to establish and clarify regulations added to the problems

[14]GAO, "Problems in the FEA's Compliance and Enforcement Effort," 1974, p. 3.

[15]By June 1975, however, the agency had been able to find time to adopt Energy Ant as a symbol of energy conservation. (The UPI release, including picture, appeared in the *Portland Press Herald*, 26 June 1975.) In the Spring of 1975 inquiries were being conducted by 14 separate congressional committees. One official guessed that about 40% of the time of headquarters staff was devoted to answering questions about past activities, which made planning for the future very difficult.

[16]GAO, "Problems in the FEA's Compliance and Enforcement Effort," 1974, p. 7.

[17]*Ibid.*, pp. 8, 22.

of enforcing compliance with them. The oil industry is very complex and regulations made in ignorance of its complexities have had to be redone numerous times. Firms have also organized their legal structures and transactions to take advantage of variations in tax laws in different countries, and it would be surprising, indeed, if such mechanisms were not also suited to circumventing clumsy controls.

One of the standard problems in a vertically integrated firm is estimating appropriate transfer prices between different stages of production. When transactions occur between parties with common interests: for example, when a domestic refiner buys crude from a foreign affiliate, the prices established by the transactions are suspect. This is an acute problem in determing allowable costs for the purpose of setting a price ceiling. Yet this problem is not unique to the FEA. The IRS must deal with it every year when companies pay taxes on domestic profit, and may have an incentive to overstate the costs of buying oil from foreign subsidiaries. Even within the United States, the IRS had a great deal of experience with the same problem since the sales price of oil by the producing subsidiary influenced the amount that could be deducted from profits to allow for depletion. Despite these precedents for solving what is admittedly a complex problem, the FEA in April of 1975 had still not been able to tell companies what transfer prices it would accept for October 1973 and succeeding months![18]

Similarly, prices can vary among different classes of purchaser. This has posed the problem of defining class of purchaser in order to ensure that the oil companies do not move customers into a class that can be charged a higher price. The FEA did not publish rulings on the matter until June 18, 1974, and they were so incomplete and ambiguous that they had to be revised on March 3, 1975.[19]

A problem more frightening to anyone with traditional concern for civil liberties was raised by the fact that some of the orders issued by the FEA during the embargo were impossible for the firms to obey. In the words of the General Counsel of the Federal Energy Administration,

> Since it was physically impossible for many suppliers to comply with these orders fully, judgments had to be made as to whether at least a good faith effort was made to comply. If good faith was apparent, FEA made no effort to collect a civil penalty, even though technical violations of the injection orders had occurred. However, FEA recently compromised $450,000 in penalties against two companies that did partially comply with the injection orders but could not demonstrate to FEA's satisfaction that

[18]Robert E. Montgomery, Jr., General Counsel of the FEA, Statement before the U.S. Senate, Committee on Government Operations, Permanent Subcommittee on Investigations (10 April 1975), p. 3.
[19]Ibid., p. 5.

they had made every reasonable effort to comply. The best available evidence in those cases indicated that the companies were not entirely innocent, but was not strong enough to show that their violations were willful.[20]

The complexity of the problems that contributed to the vacillation and delay in establishing enforceable regulations also contributed to the cumbersome administrative procedures applied to violations that were detected. In compliance work at the retail level a substantial amount of discretion can be left with individual agents and regional offices.[21] This is not possible in the refinery audit program where problems and regulations are complex, the amounts of money can be very large, the auditor is confronted by top quality corporate accountants and lawyers, and questions of policy and precedent are frequently involved. If compliance cannot be gained by a voluntary price rollback and refund of overcharges, the agency issues a Notice of Probable Violation (NOPV) or, where the degree of certainty is greater or the violation is being repeated, a Remedial Order (RO). Before an NOPV is issued to a company, however, it undergoes review by the auditor's supervisor, the regional compliance office, the regional counsel's office and the national compliance office. If the national compliance office issues the NOPV, it is then reviewed by the General Counsel's Office, before wending its way back through channels[22]

This slow and involved process attracted much criticism, but in the absence of clear regulations the agency had to exercise care in the settlement of particular cases if it was to arrive at a uniform national policy. It seems likely that here, as in the HUD (Chapter 6), LEAA (Chapter 15), and EPA (Chapter 10) cases, the interposition of regional offices between the field and headquarters added to the delay and confusion, but the general outlines of the clearance process probably could not have been simplified without causing problems worse than delay.

If the firm chooses not to act on a Notice of Probable Violation, the agency can issue a Remedial Order. The firm can appeal that administratively, and then through the courts, or obey it. Alternatively, it can ignore it, forcing the agency to turn the case over to the Justice Depart-

[20]*Ibid.*, attachment on Civil and Criminal Penalties, pp. 2–3.

[21]It may be argued that this delegation of authority was somewhat overdone at the inception of the program: "During these first six months and for some time thereafter, there were no published standard compliance procedures. The investigators were operating in a crisis environment with locally established procedures and some national guidelines" (Gorman C. Smith, Testimony, p. 36).

[22]Montgomery, Statement before the U.S. Senate, p. 21; Phillip S. Hughes, Assistant Controller General of the United States, Statement before the U.S. House, Committee on Interstate and Foreign Commerce, Subcommittee on Oversight and Investigations (8 May 1975), p. 9.

ment, which can take the matter to court for civil penalties and restitution, or criminal penalties. Since court proceedings are expensive for both parties, there is a strong incentive to avoid them.

Although imposition of civil penalties requires the agency to refer the matter to the Justice Department and thence to the courts, the agency does "compromise" civil penalties prior to referring them to Justice. This is common administrative practice, although it was not specifically authorized for the FEA. Under this procedure, the agency informs the company of the maximum amount for which the company is liable, and then accepts or rejects compromise offers depending on such factors as "(1) the egregiousness of the violation; (2) the resources of the company; (3) the extent to which the company profited by the violation; (4) the likelihood that the government can prove its case in court; and (5) whether prosecution of the case in court... would be a productive use of FEA's limited manpower and resources."[23] This procedure is not only perfectly proper, it is also inevitable given the number of cases and the expense of litigation. It also means that the assessment of penalites, in fact, is subject to a very great degree of administrative discretion, as is the very decision, made at the level of auditor, to track down some violations and skip others in the limited time available.

The existence of administrative discretion should be no surprise. As Ernest Gellhorn points out, "Agencies, like district attorneys, have almost unlimited negative discretion."[24] Since the tasks assigned by the legislation always exceed the capacity of the agency, some discretion is inherent in the choice of cases to pursue and in the vigor with which a particular case is attacked. Nevertheless, every opportunity for discretion is also an opportunity for bribery, political influence, or harassment, and charges (whether justified or not) of differential treatment of various firms have been made.[25] Administrative discretion is evident in the wording used to differentiate cases: If the firm appears to have made an innocent mistake, the agency tries to get the firm to mend its ways and refund excess charges. If the firm "willfully violates any order" it is subject to criminal penalties. If the violation was neither innocent nor willful, civil penalties are sought, and generally compromised.

The FEA was undoubtedly slow in writing clear and consistent regulations and in checking that refiners and producers complied with them. It is not so clear, however, whether the poor record of the agency in

---

[23]Montgomery, Statement before the U.S. Senate, attachment, p. 1.

[24]Ernest Gellhorn, *Administrative Law and Process in a Nutshell* (St. Paul, Minnesota:West Publishing, 1972), p. 71.

[25]See, e.g., *The New York Times*, 17 November 1975, p. 20; *Washington Post*, 4 May 1975, p. 1.

completing its task was due to the difficulty of the task or to the particular people to whom it was assigned. The two are not entirely unrelated because it may be doubted that a temporary agency riven by political controversies could have attracted many of the solid, professionally oriented bureaucrats who keep other agencies from floundering. At the same time such a fluid situation in a politically visible area may be particularly attractive to the ambitious and unscrupulous individuals who create the problems in Tullock's model of bureaucracy.

The external setting of Washington during the embargo must also be kept in mind. Morbid concentration on the minute-by-minute development of the latest crisis shortens the politically abbreviated time horizon still further, so the failure to write regulations or plan the redeployment of forces a month or two ahead is not surprising. Even the lower ranks of the hierarchy, who usually carry out the meaningful long-range planning, were simply too caught up in the press of events to look ahead. What little foresight the top levels of the agency have shown has been focused, naturally enough, on organizational survival, rather than the accomplishment of its legislated objectives. That sometimes meant the deployment of limited manpower into whatever area attracted publicity (e.g., the propane and utilities investigations), rather than concentrating on the fundamental work of the agency. Yet this response seems inevitable when the legislation authorizing the agency is about to expire. Proposals to subject all agencies to similar pressure with "sunset laws" should be given close scrutiny.

The dispute between Congress and the President on the importance of controls clearly exacted its toll from the agency as is indicated by the vacillation and delay already noted. Congress did not really trust the FEA leadership to exercise the vigorous control policy it wanted, but refused to write—the excuses for delay were built into the inconsistent wish list that passed as legislation. The subsequent close scrutiny by congressional committees worsened the problem by absorbing appreciable amounts of top-level time.

Beyond these special factors, however, the experience of the FEA provides some general lessons. The most basic point is that the vast outpouring of bureaucratic motion expended on the control program brought few benefits to the American public. The high level of banked costs is clear evidence that markets, not controls, were holding product prices down. In the absence of controls, prices would have gone up temporarily during the period of the embargo, thus curtailing consumption to the same extent that rationing by inconvenience did—but without the inconvenience. The allocation controls were made necessary only by the price controls and were never either effectively issued or enforced. The controls on crude-oil prices have transferred profits from producers to refiners, thus decreasing the incentive for domestic production.

The reasons why such a program cannot succeed in a crisis of short duration are self-evident. The routine delays in shifting personnel because of a 2-month lag at the Civil Service Commission or in settling the details of an agreement with the IRS or Customs are enough to eliminate the reasons for emergency action. As the form of the emergency shifts, resources cannot be shifted because they are specialized to a particular job, locked into a particular region, or are in the wrong box in the budget. Finally, the complexities of this particular industry mean that the agency cannot regulate it effectively without developing substantial expertise of its own, the costs of which are high.

CHAPTER 12

The Housing Investment Guarantee Program[1]

The foreign aid bill, as it emerged from Congress in 1961, included a program that had not been present at all when deliberations began. Section 224 of P.L. 87–195 authorized the Agency for International Development (AID) to guarantee mortgages for housing projects in Latin American countries. The act specified that:

> In order to stimulate private home ownership and assist in the development of stable economies, the authority conferred by this title should be utilized for the purpose of assisting in the development in the American Republics of selfliquidating pilot housing projects designed to provide experience in rapidly developing countries by participating with such countries in guaranteeing private United States capital available for investment in Latin American countries.

The projects were to be "of types similar to those insured by the Federal Housing Administration and suitable for conditions in Latin America [22 USC 2184b]." The U.S. government would guarantee the repayment of mortgages made by U.S. investors. Although the law did not limit the

[1]This case is based primarily on U.S. General Accounting Office, "Low Income Groups not helped by Agency For International Development's Housing Investment Guaranty Program," Report B–171526 (25 Nov. 1974). I am also indebted to Peter M. Kimm, Director, Office of Housing, U.S. Agency for International Development, for his assistance.

income of the home buyer, the analogy to the FHA suggests a target of middle-class housing. However the report also mentioned "accruals of technical skills, . . . low-cost housing, infrastructure development— these are the slowly materializing benefits in many countries of American aid."[2] In any event, Congress was apparently pleased with its work, because by 1962 the ceiling was raised from $10 million to $60 million. The Committee remarked that, "Low- and medium low-cost housing is among the most urgent of consumer needs in Latin America."[3]

Congress certainly intended, therefore, to increase the supply of housing that could be purchased by people of modest means. The desirability of such action was defended because of both the need for more decent housing and the virtues of home ownership. In keeping with the technical assistance aspects of foreign aid, the original projects were awarded, by competitive bid, to U.S. developers and involved U.S. builders, as well as lenders, who could transfer building technology to the underdeveloped countries.

The legislation appears quite stupid on the surface. Since people everywhere manage to house themselves according to local conditions, resources, and incomes, it was patronizing to assume that U.S. builders and developers could make major contributions to the state of building technology. The overwhelming differences in relative costs and other conditions facing builders and the notable inability of the U.S. construction industry to produce new housing at a price that people of low income can afford made the argument especially dubious. One might also question the wisdom of teaching developing countries how to divert more capital from industry and agriculture into residential construction. To the extent that the program merely channeled additional funds from the United States into Latin America and resulted in cheap housing because of the low interest rate, the U.S. government was conferring an extraordinary benefit on the few initial owners of the houses. In the natural course of events, they would probably turn out to be privileged in other ways, as well.

The legislation was thoroughly rational from the viewpoint of its supporters, however. The program at its inception was endorsed by the National Association of Home Builders, which wanted the government to open up a foreign market at a time when the domestic industry was depressed.[4]

---

[2]U.S. Congress. Senate. Committee on Foreign Relations, Report on the Foreign Assistance Act of 1961, Senate Report No. 612 (1961 *U.S. Code Cong. and Admin. News*, p. 2477).

[3]Senate Report No. 1535 on Foreign Assistance Act of 1962 (1962 *U.S. Code Cong. and Admin. News*, p. 2045).

[4]U.S. Congress. House. Committee on Foreign Affairs. 87th Cong. 1st Session, *The International Development and Security Act*, Hearings on H.R. 7372, Part III, pp. 1217–1219.

The program required a public guarantee, but not a public appropriation. The borrower paid an annual premium, in addition to the mortgage rate, ranging between one-half of 1% and 2% of the outstanding loan. Most of this was available to the agency for operating expenses after meeting current losses. Even with the guarantee fee, the rate to the homebuyer was only one-half to one-quarter of the prevailing rate in many countries because of the comparatively low mortgage rates in the United States and because of the guarantee of repayment. With such low interest payments, a builder from the United States could sell a home that was expensive by local standards because of superior quality or high contruction costs. More recently, proposals originated by foreign governments have superseded the initiatives of U.S. builders and developers, but the low interest rate still provides someone with a valuable benefit.

Congress not only devised the program it also took the initiative in raising the amount of loans authorized for guarantee from $10 million in 1961 to $250 million by 1964. The role of the agency was mainly that of passive recipient of applications for guarantee. Whereas aiding the construction of fairly expensive housing did not seem consistent with AID's focus on development and alleviation of poverty, assistance for low-cost housing, a secondary purpose of the original act, was considered by the bureaucracy to be impossible to implement. The prevailing wisdom of the 1960s held that only heavy subsidies could help the poor move from the slums into decent housing. With the general scarcity of resources for housing, this made it seem impossible to help more than a small minority of the poor.

By 1965, however, the top officials of the agency had announced a new focus for the program that was consistent with the other policies of AID and seemed realistic in view of the capabilities of the agency. Specifically, AID sought to phase out the "pilot and demonstration" program in favor of the general approach of building institutions within the countries that would then work toward solving the local problems. David E. Bell, Administrator of AID, in testifying in support of the amendments pointed out that "up to this point the special housing guarantee program for Latin America has consisted of a series of projects in which American organizers, American funds, and sometimes American builders have built projects in a number of Latin American countries."[5] This approach had resulted in certain problems, including the failure to have any impact beyond the immediate projects build. Furthermore, Bell noted, "We have felt that the income levels that were reached by this housing have been too high. We want to focus the program in such a

[5]*Ibid.*, "Hearing on the Foreign Assistance Act of 1965," p. 32.

way that it will reach middle and lower income families much more than it has in the past and will be much less a program of housing for the relatively well to do." He added that, "The intention would be that the great bulk of this authorization would be aimed at middle- and low-cost housing."[6]

Deputy Administrator William S. Gaud similarly stressed the importance of institutions and low-cost housing, "What we want to do is to encourage the growth of credit institutions. We want to encourage the growth of labor movements. We want to encourage particularly the building of more low-income housing than we have been able to do so far."[7] (Mr. Gaud did not explain how the labor movements would improve housing.)

Some were not as enthusiastic about the change in emphasis of the programs as were the bureaucrats. Former representative Sibal, testifying for the Committee For International Housing Through Private Investment, stressed the importance of the existing programs in teaching mass-production homebuilding and the conquest of institutional barriers to mass markets while providing "homes for democracy" by housing the solid middle class.[8] Representative James G. Fulton tried to press an extra $50 million on Deputy Administrator Gaud to continue the pilot and demonstration housing, but Gaud refused, "We think the time has come to put an end to this business of building houses as houses."[9] The minority report vehemently opposed the change:

> We view with alarm the steps AID is taking to change the Latin American housing guarantee program, which a representative of the American homebuilding industry has testified will throttle the program. This program, authorized as a pilot project in 1961, was unique in two ways: (1) it provided an opportunity for American private enterprise to demonstrate its building know-how in areas where housing was a most primary need, and where the construction of modestly priced private homes would be discernible evidence of our own democratic institutions; (2) it has been accomplished thus far without any expenditure of appropriated funds and could even produce a return to the Federal Treasury if handled properly. Any difficulty the program has faced so far is due to bureaucratic redtape on the part of the AID organization. It evoked great interest on the part of American builders and lenders. We understand that AID has a huge backlog of applications. Now the limitation in the amendment severely curtails the program. Instead of continuing and expanding the effort to stimulate private homeownership, it is believed that it will effectively prevent American private homebuilding industry from further participation. Worse

[6]*Ibid.*, p. 33.
[7]*Ibid.*, p. 1142.
[8]*Ibid.*, pp. 411–428. Sibal did not explain why the government needed to perform the traditional role of the entrepreneur or why anything more than a single demonstration of the profit potential was necessary.
[9]*Ibid.*, p. 1152.

still, the amendment requiring particular emphasis on guaranteeing funds loaned to institutions could very well result in a greater administrative boondoggle and construction of fewer homes.[10]

Despite the agency's protests that the self-liquidating pilot or demonstration housing projects were no longer needed, "the committee specifically provides continuing authority for supporting this program, which is now being carried on so successfully."[11] Thus what the agency had proposed as a change in the emphasis of the program became a mere supplement to the existing one, for which the agency still had no enthusiasm, but which the committee was determined to retain for its own reasons.

The law as modified in 1965 permitted guarantees for loans in any of the following categories: (a) private housing projects similar to those insured by the FHA; (b) loans that assist in developing institutions engaged in Alliance for Progress programs, including cooperatives and free labor unions; (c) housing projects for lower income families; (d) projects that promote the development of savings and loan associations or other institutions for mobilizing savings; or (e) housing projects with 25% local financing and a maximum unit cost of $8500.[12] There was no requirement that each of these five categories be represented, but only that the projects guaranteed fall into at least one of them. The 1969 law added the responsibility

to facilitate and increase the participation of private enterprise in furthering the development of the economic resources and productive capacities of less developed friendly countries and areas, and promote the development of thrift and credit institutions engaged in programs of mobilizing local savings for financing the construction of self-liquidating housing projects and related community facilities.[13]

At this time, also, AID created an Office of Housing to carry out the program.

When the General Accounting Office reviewed the performance of AID in carrying out the housing program, the ambiguity and generality of the legislation left room for dispute regarding the success of the agency. The housing built was not cheap enough for low-income buyers to afford, but the law did not specifically require it to be. The range of costs of the houses guaranteed by the program in various Latin Ameri-

[10]1965 U.S. Code Cong. and Adm. News, House Report No. 321, Minority Views, pp. 2988–2989.
[11]Ibid., p. 2961.
[12]P.L. 89–171, Sec. 224.
[13]Foreign Assistance Act of 1969, Title III, Sec 221.

TABLE 12.1

Potential Buyers of Houses Guaranteed by AID, Latin America

	Cost of house		Percentage of urban families that can afford cheapest house
Country	Lowest ($)	Highest ($)	
Argentina	3000	11,120	52
Costa Rica	3928	7500	32
El Salvador	7000	11,477	13
Guatemala	5500	8289	24
Honduras	3350	8719	30
Nicaragua	6000	10,322	13
Panama	8290	12,732	38
Venezuela	5700	19,128	28

SOURCE: U.S. General Accounting Office, Report B–171526, "Low-Income Groups Not Helped by Agency for International Development's Housing Investment Guaranty Program" (25 November, 1974): 9.

can countries is shown in Table 12.1, as is the percentage of the urban population in each country that could afford the cheapest house. The decision regarding the minimum income necessary for a family to afford the house was made by the country concerned. The results show very clearly that even the cheapest houses built under the program were available only to the higher reaches of the urban income distribution. Only in Argentina could the top 52% qualify. The income figures are not very reliable, and may well be biased downwards as the agency contends, but the overall situation is worse than the figures in the table indicate for several reasons. First, urban incomes are higher than rural incomes, so by national standards in the less-developed countries the top quarter of the urban population is a very high income group. Second, the comparison in the table is based on the cheapest house sold; the more expensive ones were restricted to an even narrower market. Third, many of the actual purchasers of the houses had incomes higher than the minima imposed to ensure that the mortgage would be repaid.[14]

The situation in Thailand was even more extreme than that in Latin America. A project launched in Bangkok in 1966 was accessible to only the top 5–7% of that city's income distribution. The project was judged

[14]GAO, "Low Income Groups not helped by Agency," 1974, p. 13.

to be a success, however, because the objective was not to house the poor of Bangkok, but rather to demonstrate that high volume production and marketing combined with low downpayments and 20-year mortgages could make new housing accessible to a previously unserved segment of the population.[15]

The houses built were not mansions. They might be purchased by highly skilled blue-collar workers, school teachers, or low-level bureaucrats in government or big private firms. Although it may seem peculiar to assist such moderately successful people to buy homes in countries beset by severe poverty or offering advantageous alternative investments, the performance of the agency was consistent with the legislation.

Top agency officials, however, had clearly spelled out the objective of providing housing for people of lower income in their testimony on the 1965 changes. The agency had thus failed to implement its own announced policy objectives. It is possible that AID officials simply lied to the committee in making the statements quoted previously, but it seems more likely that they were not in control of the way that the program actually was run. The response of the Housing Office to the GAO report probably provides a better indication of the policies pursued at the operating level than do the statements of the AID administrators:

> Prior to 1973 lower-income housing was one of five legislative objectives, and while considered highly desirable, it was also judged to be a least likely target for HIG resources, since conventional wisdom was that highly concessional resources were needed to reach this group.

> Since 1973, A.I.D. has given much higher priority to housing for lower-income groups, and has taken substantial steps to convince LDC's that they should make policy changes which will lead to better housing for lower-income groups, and that these can and should utilize HIG resources for this purpose.

> The 1974 revision of this policy makes it absolutely clear that lower-income housing is the HIG priority, and that a principal consideration in all new HIG financing is the degree to which the interests of lower-income groups is served by the proposed financing. An analysis of new projects will confirm this emphasis.[16]

The key point is that the agency, having acquired the expertise to carry out a certain type of project, stayed close to what it could accom-

---

[15]*Ibid.*, pp. 24–25.

[16]A.I.D. Comments on GAO Report Dated 25 November 1974, titled "Low-Income Groups Not Helped by Agency for International Development's Housing Investment Guaranty Program" (B–171526)," unpublished, no date, p. 2. A more recent GAO study, "Agency for International Development's Housing Investment Guaranty Program," Report ID–78–44, 6 September 1978, confirms that the agency has made substantial progress toward its own more coherent and rational goals since 1973.

plish successfully. An objective specified by top officials that was thought to be impossible—housing the poor decently without an immense subsidy—was pushed aside in favor of the familiar.

The agency did, of course, refine its procedures as experience accumulated. Some early projects were initiated in a haphazard way by builders, and the form of the investment guaranty to the U.S. lending institution sometimes put the agency in the difficult position of having to collect from agencies of foreign governments, or foreclose on homeowners, in the event of default. Furthemore, currency devaluations by the foreign country often produced losses for the U.S. lender that the agency had to cover. These problems have been overcome in the new guarantees, which are arranged directly with the foreign government agency and are repaid in dollars to the lending institution. Nevertheless, the mistakes of earlier years continue to create losses in some projects because of the duration of mortgage loans. More significant is the drain on top-level energies brought about by lack of forethought in the early years of the program. To cite one example, poor administration of a housing project contracted in 1968 in Senegal eventually involved both the U.S. Ambassador and the Minister of Finance of that country.[17]

In the years since the GAO began its investigation, the agency has confronted most of the issues discussed here. It has gradually come to use the income generated by the housing guarantee program to support a program of technical assistance to less-developed countries in devising national housing policies. During the late 1960s and early 1970s the agency concentrated on assisting the development of savings and loan associations and similar directly relevant institutions. This was part of its congressional charge, and also appears to be a sensible way to approach the housing problem. It is also a difficult task in which to rate the degree of success. More recently the agency has turned its efforts toward encouraging such institutions to make small loans for simple shelter. Current policy is to direct most guarantees, as well, to those below the median income in the relevant area.

If the agency succeeds in assisting countries to devise coherent and feasible housing policies, and if it can show poor countries that the attempt to provide subsidized housing for the poor is not only ruinous but unnecessary, then it will indeed have accomplished something. Succeed or not, the agency has given Congress better than it deserves from the initial casual and irresponsible legislation. One can argue that it should have done this more quickly, just as one can criticize particular actions by the bureaucracy since the program began. When the bureau-

---

[17]GAO, "Low Income Groups not helped by Agency," 1974, p. 45.

cracy acquires the policymaking function by default, as occurred here, the underlying assumption (that diversion of resources into housing is good for the less developed country) is never scrutinized, but the internal pressures toward professional performance can move the program in a useful direction. The one indisputable failure of the agency was the inability, for nearly a decade, of the top administrators to shift the emphasis of the program. Thus actual behavior was consistent with the legislation, but not with what the Administrator of AID claimed he was doing.

CHAPTER **13**

Revenue Sharing for Vocational Education[1]

The experiences of the Office of Education (OE) in administering the distribution of funds under the Vocational Education Act illustrate some problems of revenue sharing. Vocational education is the responsibility of the states and local school districts. The federal government provides supplemental revenue ($388 million for Part B of the Vocational Education Act in 1973 when state and local expenditures were almost six times as large). The federal aid is distributed among the states according to a formula based on population in various age groups, provided that the states comply with the other provisions of the act. At the time of this case, the act was administered by a small organization, the Bureau of Occupational and Adult Education (BOAE), within the Office of Education of the Department of Health, Education, and Welfare.

This form of federal involvement with vocational education began with the Smith–Hughes Act in 1917 (20 USC 11), but it has much in common with the more recent approaches to special revenue sharing, in which the federal government turns over funds to the state and local

[1]This case is based primarily on U.S. General Accounting Office, "What is the Role of Federal Assistance for Vocational Education?" Report MWD-75-31 (31 December 1974). I am also indebted to Dr. William F. Pierce, Deputy Commissioner for the Bureau of Occupational and Adult Education of the U.S. Office of Education, for his assistance.

bureaucracies to carry out some specified range of functions.[2] Vocational education was singularly favored during the long years while the issue of federal aid to education was debated so acrimoniously. The result of the special treatment was a special organization, resistant to external influences and not very responsive to local, state, or federal control. Public vocational education is typically a separate program at the local level funded by the state office of vocational education, rather than the local educational authorities. The state vocational education bureaucracy focuses its attention on both the state legislature and the federal funding agency, which, in turn, looks to its friends in Congress. Since the whole apparatus constitutes a strong organization with formidable political support, the friends in Congress can receive their rewards at the polls.

Federal aid to vocational education was extended and enlarged by the George–Barden Act of 1947 (20 USC 15i note), but the modern era begins with the Vocational Education Act (VEA) of 1963 (20 USC 1241). While the topic of "manpower" was subject to voluminous, if not incisive, discussion in the 1960s, the objective of vocational education was shifting from training a few for highly specialized occupations to a broader preparation of all for the "World of Work."

The amendments of 1968 (20 USC 1241 *et seq.*) clarified congressional intent by setting aside specific proportions of the funding for the disadvantaged and handicapped, specifying the criteria that states must use in distributing funds among local education agencies, requiring certain types of planning and the collection of information for evaluation, and requiring coordination of various agencies engaged in training. The latter point was given still greater emphasis in the Educational Amendments of 1972 (P.L. 92–318, Title X), which called for "Federal funds to act as leverage to bring about comprehensive, coordinated planning and delivery of occupational education." These objectives may seem reasonable and modest enough, but implementation within the traditional structure of vocational education has posed serious difficulties that raise some fundamental questions of the overall public accountability of such a mixed collection of federal, state, and local bureaucracies.

At the most elementary level, these problems are illustrated by the results of the congressional requirement that at least 15% of the basic

---

[2]A lucid examination of the history of federal involvement with vocational education is provided by Grant Venn, *Man, Education, and Work* (Washington:American Council on Education, 1964). The more recent legislative history is sketched in GAO, "What is the Role of Federal Assistance for Vocational Education," 1974, pp. 2–3. Revenue sharing, as practiced in the 1970s, has undergone scrutiny in such works as Richard P. Nathan and Charles F. Adams, Jr., and Associates, *Revenue Sharing:The Second Round* (Washington: Brookings, 1977).

grants, as well as all the special funds appropriated for the purpose, be used "for persons . . . who have academic, socio-economic, or other handicaps that prevent them from succeeding in the regular vocational educational program." The intent of Congress, clearly, was to focus special attention on those who need it in order to learn. In other legislation, however, disadvantaged is defined as low income. Some state and local officials could not, or would not, comprehend the distinction and, therefore, allotted the funds on the basis of family incomes, rather than difficulty in learning.[3] HEW provided written guidelines and instructions, which repeated the wording of the law without offering any help in complying with it. The plans of the four states that the GAO studied also repeated the wording of the law without specifying how its requirements were to be met. When the GAO investigators checked what happened in the field, they discovered that the funds set aside for the disadvantaged were being used for regular courses by school districts in California and were allocated by the State of Michigan for unrestricted equipment purchases by school districts. In Ohio the procedures were correct on paper, but "the programs in operation were not the same as those described in the approved proposals."[4] In Pennsylvania the special programs for the disadvantaged were open to all and "only limited attempts were made to identify persons requiring special assistance."[5]

Once attention was focused on the problem, the agency improved its guidelines and instructions and the states expressed their willingness to impose tighter controls. Some indirect evidence suggests that the definitions, at least, have been tightened up.[6] The question remains, however, as to why a specific instruction from Congress was ignored or directly subverted at all levels of the hierarchy.

The act also required that the Commissioner of Education "shall collect data and information on programs qualifying for assistance . . . for the purpose of obtaining objective measurements of the effectiveness achieved in carrying out the purposes of such programs."[7] The regulations issued by HEW (45 CFR 102.4 [j]) were even more general than the legislation, but the reports actually required by HEW "consisted of summaries of the number of students graduating with major training in each of 10 types of employment fields and their employment status about four months after graduation."[8] The necessity for collecting in-

[3]U.S. General Accounting Office, "Training America's Labor Force:Potential, Progress, and Problems of Vocational Education," Report B–164031(1) (18 October 1972), pp. 22–31.

[4]*Ibid.*, p. 27.

[5]*Ibid.*, p. 28.

[6]GAO, "What is the Role of Federal Assistance for Vocational Education," 1974, p. 18.

[7]82 Stat. 1095.

[8]GAO, "Training America's Labor Force," 1972, pp. 32–33.

formation on every graduate effectively precluded the use of a sample survey to produce meaningfully detailed information, whereas the 4-month followup was too soon to be of any real use. Thus, those states interested in collecting useful information did it on their own, while at the same time complying with the federal requirement for meaningless data just to obtain funding.

Moreover, even the simple data required of the states were often inaccurate or incomplete.[9] The GAO noted, in particular, a strong tendency toward overstatement of enrollment and graduation figures, in most cases caused by the cumulation of the enrollments in individual classes as an estimate of the number of students in school. The followup data were based on such low response rates as to be useless without further field work. Nor had the statistical accuracy improved by the time of the GAO reinvestigation 2 years later.[10] Substantial discrepancies were found between the records kept by some states and the records reported to HEW. In many instances, moreover, the agency has failed to collect either the statistics necessary for the managerial purposes required by the act or for rebutting the allegations of the GAO.[11]

Although HEW distributes the funds among states on the basis of population in various age groups, within states the distributions to the local education authorities are supposed to be based on four general criteria: (a) manpower needs and job opportunities; (b) differences in vocational education needs; (c) relative ability to provide resources; and (d) relative costs of programs, services, and activities. The four criteria are described in some detail in the legislation, but Congress apparently could not decide on their relative importance because it provided no clue as to how these disparate elements were to be combined. The OE regulations require the states to take the four criteria into consideration, but also do not specify how. As implementation proceeded, the agency failed even to insist that the states use the four criteria.[12] In view of the vagueness of the law, a state could comply by distributing most of the funds as it chose, reserving a token amount to satisfy the remaining legislated criteria. Some states did not even comply in that sense, however, basing their distributions solely on population or one or two other criteria. In one state, moreover, the allocation was based on total school

[9]*Ibid.*, pp. 33–34.

[10]GAO, "What is the Role of Federal Assistance for Vocational Education," 1974, pp. 12–13, 72.

[11]U.S. Bureau of Occupational and Adult Education, "Review of GAO Report on Vocational Education, 'What Is the Role of Federal Assistance for Vocational Education?'" undated mimeo, pp. 2, 3, 24.

[12]GAO, "What is the Role of Federal Assistance for Vocational Education," 1974, pp. 37–39.

enrollment, so the districts did not have an incentive to expand the expensive vocational programs. One state plan stated that money for the handicapped and disadvantaged would be distributed according to need, but in fact projects were funded individually after a competitive assessment of merit.[13]

This problem originated in Congress, but the agency did not take action to improve the situation. The agency, itself, is responsible for failure to ascertain that the actual distributions were consistent with both the law and the formal plan of the state. It is difficult to know what to make of the defense by the bureau: "Morever, the assumption is made [by the GAO] that the *only* permissible interpretation of VEA is a literal one whereby the four funding criteria are applied verbatim *each* and *every* time a State distributes Federal vocational funds to an LEA."[14]

The possibility of a discrepancy between plan and action was not confined to the distribution of funds; the entire planning function appeared to be subject to deficiencies. The law requires the OE to review the plan of each state, to ensure compliance with the law, and to assure itself that the plan will be carried out. Furthermore, the commissioner is to stop payments to a state that fails to comply with its plan.[15] Congress obviously set great store by the planning process, because it specified in considerable detail what the plan is to include. The basic purpose is to encourage the state and local education authorities to survey labor markets and potential students, as well as all training resources both public and private, before shaping a coordinated and feasible approach to providing the services with as little waste and duplication as possible. The main problem is that meaningful planning of this sort is an immensely complicated process, most of which has to occur at the local level.

The state plans, which are the ones that the Commissioner must approve, would ideally be built up using knowledge that is available only at the local level. In some states, however, the local educators not only denied contributing to the state plans, they even professed ignorance of their existence. The impression appeared to be widespread that the state plans are merely paper—documents prepared in order to qualify for funding—but not used for operational purposes or to assess progress toward goals.[16]

The GAO report criticised the bureau for never having exercised its authority to cut off funds to a state for failure to submit an acceptable plan or to comply with the plan submitted. This raises some questions

[13]*Ibid.*, pp. 39–42.
[14]BOAE, "Review of GAO Report on Vocational Education," p, 17.
[15]20 U.S.C. 1263.
[16]GAO, "What is the Role of Federal Assistance for Vocational Education," 1974, p. 23.

about the limits to the bureau's power. Although no plans have ever been formally disapproved, an informal process of returning the plans for changes does occur. Whatever the differences between state and bureau officials, they have been settled by these informal negotiations without reaching the stage where a plan would have to be rejected. It seems questionable, however, that the bureau really has the political power to turn off the funds flowing to vocational education in any state. The pressures from Congress would undoubtedly prevent such drastic action, which suggests that the bureau actually has no other sanctions than the informal pressures it has been using.

More disturbing are the indications that no one took the plans seriously enough to see whether they were being followed. The BOAE argues that the HEW Audit Agency is responsible for policing the degree of compliance with agreed plans for expenditures.[17] The BOAE lacks both staff and inclination for such activities, preferring to concentrate instead on assisting the states. Nevertheless, a planning process that fails to compare actual performance with that previously planned is not very useful.

The BOAE and the GAO disagreed about the quality of the planning done by the states with the guidance of the bureau. Since quality of planning is the ultimate example of an unmeasurable output, the assessment of bureau performance is inevitably a matter of judgment. Moreover, the local education officials must perform most of the planning that matters, and they must do it without much help. The federal government cannot monitor the plans of every local education authority, nor does it try. The states are said to do little for local planning either.[18] This suggests that the federal and state agencies are engaged largely in expensive paper maneuvers, while the activity takes place at the local level entirely unaffected.

Congress especially wanted local education authorities to coordinate public vocational schools with the various other public and private sources of occupational education. Such coordination has sometimes resulted from local initiative, but in general each bureaucrat at the local level prefers to control his own resources and answer only to his own superior, so coordination of local resources must usually be enforced from above. The same state education authorities that have failed to assist in local planning have failed to help in coordinating local training resources. Indeed, state vocational education officials have no real in-

---

[17]BOAE, "Review of GAO Report on Vocational Education," pp. 9–10.

[18]GAO, "What is the Role of Federal Assistance for Vocational Education," 1974, pp. 23–25.

centive to require local vocational schools to coordinate offerings and facilities with manpower programs, community colleges, military training facilities, and private vocational schools. The result has been duplication of facilities and equipment, simultaneous initiation of courses by several schools to fill the same labor-market demand, and other evidence of fragmented decision making.[19] The problem of coordinating the activities of two adjacent school districts is quite similar, except that it would appear to be more readily within the power of the state education authority to reduce duplication of facilities and programs. The examples of successful coordination are scarce, however, and the problem is so difficult that the BOAE would prefer to leave its solution to the students:

> In voicing its concern about the lack of lateral planning at the local level and the possibility of redundant programs resulting in an oversupply of workers in particular occupations, GAO fails utterly to account for the "common sense" factor of the trainees. The economic acumen of the American Worker has considerable influence on the viability of occupational programs.[20]

The legislation requires that state plans include a statement that the LEAs have taken account of other available training resources. Neither the OE nor the states, however, checked to see whether this was done or helped the LEAs to carry out the law.[21]

The general lack of leadership by the state educational authorities in planning, coordination, and other functions is particularly disconcerting in view of the diversion of large amounts of federal funding to state administration.[22] The use of VEA funds to support the state's educational administration is not unlawful; for the VEA, unlike some other federal educational programs, sets no limit on administrative expenses. Furthermore, in a static sense it does not matter whether a state takes a certain amount of money for its administrative expenses entirely from its own tax revenue, entirely from VEA funds, or from some combination of the two. In a dynamic sense, however, it may very well make a difference to both the rate of growth of administrative expenses and the controllability of the state bureaucracy, as will be developed in the following.

The exact amount of federal funds spent by states for administrative expenses could not be determined by the GAO because the states did

---

[19]*Ibid.*, pp. 29–32, 47–56.
[20]BOAE, "Review of GAO Report on Vocational Education," p. 14.
[21]GAO, "What is the Role of Federal Assistance for Vocational Education," 1974, p. 48.
[22]*Ibid.*, pp. 10–13.

not tell the BOAE. Funds spent for ancillary services are reported, but this category includes such functions as "teacher education, supervision, planning, evaluation, special demonstration and experimental programs, and development of instructional materials, in addition to State Administration and leadership."[23] Some of the ancillary expenses are incurred at the local level. A later survey indicated that administrative activities at the state level consumed about 7.2% of total Part B funds, or about $173 million in 1973.[24] Total federal, state, and local spending for ancillary services, of which more than 80% is absorbed by administration, grew from $133 million in 1971 to $213 million in 1973—faster than total Part B expenditures, which increased from $1.8 billion to $2.4 billion in the same period.[25]

In order to determine whether too much is spent on administration one must know not only how much is spent, but also how the results vary with spending. The quantity and quality of administrative effort are notoriously difficult to evaluate. The National Advisory Council on Vocational Education and state directors of vocational education told GAO investigators that the federal funds had served to develop strong leadership at the state level.[26] The GAO report, however, did not reveal any state activity that could not have been carried out equally well by weak leadership. The coordination and planning functions in particular, where strong leadership might accomplish something, seem to have been left to the local level by default.

The GAO data indicate that some states used federal funds to finance existing administrative activities, thus freeing state tax revenues for other educational purposes. This was entirely proper under the laws as written, but it raises the broader question of accountability in revenue-sharing programs. The simplest point relates to the fungibility of grants. If, for example, an organization using funds for operations, administration, and construction receives a grant restricted to one of these, it will use the restricted grant for that purpose and shift some unrestricted funds elsewhere. Such behavior is common to rational individuals and administrators in all organizations, and is efficient in advancing the purposes of the recipient, if not the donor.

The implications for citizen control of the bureaucracy are more serious. Administrative expenses are the costs that make life more pleasant

[23]BOAE, "Review of GAO Report on Vocational Education," p. 10.
[24]Terrell H. Bell, U.S. Commissioner of Education, Statement before the U.S. House, Committee on Education and Labor, Subcommittee on Elementary, Secondary and Vocational Education (19 February 1975), p. 8.
[25]BOAE, "Review of GAO Report on Vocational Education," p. 3.
[26]GAO, "What is the Role of Federal Assistance for Vocational Education," 1974, p. 11.

for administrators. The bureaucrat has a personal incentive to have such costs grow. The growth of administrative costs is normally kept in check by the appropriations process. An agency that receives its administrative expenses from a higher level of government (or by selling services, insuring loans, or creating money) is insulated from the pressure of review committees. Since the behavior of the states was legal in this case, there was nothing the BOAE could do about it. There is no reason to suppose that it was unhappy about the expansion of state administration, however. A stronger state administration undoubtedly does a more professional job in preparing plans, filling in reports, and otherwise complying with good bureaucratic practise and the letter of the law. The state administrators also constitute the nucleus of a powerful interest group favoring more funding for vocational education.

The relevant congressional committees can retain some control over the direct activities of the bureau, but the members cannot be expected to acquire familiarity with the activities of 50 states and a myriad of local education authorities. By shifting the source of financing from the states to Washington, therefore, the increase in federal financing not only destroys local control, it weakens all representative control over bureaucracy.

In the case of vocational education, the shifts that have occurred recently have probably been marginal. Vocational education, with its long tradition of partial federal financing, was already insulated from public pressure. The parents of vocational high school students have probably been, on average, less articulate than the parents of other student groups, as well. Most important, the state bureaucracy has long had considerable power in vocational education. Some of the other forms of revenue sharing may reduce control more dramatically.

CHAPTER **14**

Improving the Management of Records[1]

Red tape and the excessive cost of paperwork are two of the traditional complaints about bureaucracy. What could be more natural, therefore, than for Congress to assign to the records-management expert of the government the task of policing the effectiveness with which other agencies manage their paperwork? A study prepared for the 1955 Hoover Commission included the guess that paperwork by the federal government cost $4 billion, or 6% of the total budget, in 1955.[2] If it is assumed that the percentage has remained constant, by fiscal 1979 paperwork cost $30 billion. Even a minor improvement could save a substantial sum. In addition, more efficient management of records offers the possibility of improving the quality of government service.

The National Archives and Records Service, a part of the General Services Administration, carries out a number of tasks related to paperwork, in addition to maintaining the national archives. The Office of

---

[1]This case is based primarily on U.S. General Accounting Office, "Ways to Improve Records Management Practices in the Federal Government," Report B–146743 (13 August 1973). I am also indebted to John H. Gant, Director of the Records Administration Division of the Office of Records Management of the National Archives and Records Service, for his assistance.

[2]GAO, "Ways to Improve Records Management Practices," 1973, p. 6.

Records Management sets policies relating to paperwork, provides consulting services, and inspects and evaluates agency programs for managing paperwork. It is the last function with which this chapter is concerned. The consulting activities, however, provide some indication of agency expertise. At the request of local, state, and federal agencies and foreign governments, the Office of Records Management provides technical assistance for tasks such as designing reports and reporting systems, establishing filing systems, microfilming, and managing correspondence. The fact that outside agencies pay for such assistance suggests that the agency has some competence.

In addition to providing consulting services, the National Archives and Records Service (NARS) is authorized by Congress to make comprehensive reviews of records management programs in other agencies. According to the legislation, "When the Administrator finds that a provision of... this title has been or is being violated... [he must inform the head of the agency, then unless corrective measures are taken, he]... shall submit a written report of the matter to the President and the Congress."[3] It is clear, therefore, that the agency is supposed to enforce its recommendations by reporting violators to the President and Congress. Yet although NARS had evaluated more than 40 federal departments, bureaus, and agencies since the program began in 1964, by 1975 it had not reported any for failure to comply with its recommendations. It was not until mid-1972 that NARS began to make the followup inspections that would enable it to discover whether its recommendations were followed. The followup on the first 4 agencies revealed that 3 had not made satisfactory progress in correcting deficiencies, which suggests that a large proportion of the agencies surveyed should have been reported over the years in order to comply with both the letter and the intent of the law.[4]

The evaluation program itself absorbs only a small part of the resources of the Office of Records Management. Of an office of somewhat less than 100 people, the inspection and evaluation group numbers 9 professionals and 1 secretary. It is divided into 2 teams, each of which works about 6 months on an agency; thus 4 inspection reports are completed each year. The consulting group, in contrast, numbers about 55 people and generated more than $1 million in revenue (of a total budget for the office of just under $3.5 million) in 1974 from its reimbursable work.[5]

---

[3]44 USC 2112.

[4]GAO, "Ways to Improve Records Management Practices," 1973, p. 14.

[5]U.S. General Services Administration, National Archives and Records Service, Office of Records Management, *Annual Report to the Archivist of the United States*, 1974, p. 39.

The agency explained its failure to report violators to Congress and the President very simply—it would have done no good. A persuasive and cooperative approach might assist an agency in overcoming problems, but what could reporting accomplish except to irritate the agency? Notifying the President must presumably be interpreted to mean the Office of Management and Budget (OMB), since the President should not be bothered with how much paper agency X uses and how it is filed. NARS is convinced that the OMB would not use information on the inefficiency of paperwork procedures in a given agency as a basis for tightening its budget. A report to Congress would presumably go to the committee that authorizes the activities of the culpable agency, rather than to the appropriations subcommittee where budget decisions are made. In any event, an agency spokesman expressed doubt that the procedure could accomplish anything.

It is possible to offer some other explanations as well. In the crudest sense, one might venture that the agency does not want to anger any of its actual or potential fee-paying clients or political supporters. A less offensive variation of that conjecture is that the inspection activity, as a minor function of an agency concerned with other matters, never received much managerial attention. Since the other agencies had to submit to evaluation, the market provided no check on the quality of the work, which might result in laxness and perhaps the transfer of the most capable personnel into the paying activity. Perfunctory execution could be expected of such an unpromising program imposed from above. Furthermore, since the activities of the agency are almost invisible to the public and far removed from the central concerns of politicians, the only control of any importance is the professional desire to do a good job. This might easily be overwhelmed by a feeling of futility at the absence of sanctions or lack of resources to do an adequate job.

NARS has strengthened its procedures since the GAO study to require that agencies respond in writing to evalution reports within 30 days; that the response contain an action plan for implementation which must be approved by NARS; and that a followup inspection be made by NARS 6 months after implementation of the action plans.[6] NARS is then required to report recalcitrant agencies to the President and Congress. It has also sought legislation giving the administrator of the General Services Administration the power to order an agency to implement regulations if his decision is endorsed by a board appointed by the President and confirmed by the Senate. Ironically, the net effect of trying to cut red tape may yet be to increase it!

[6]GAO, "Ways to Improve Records Management Practices," 1973, p. 17.

It is difficult to see how the changes or proposals will do any more than to guarantee that NARS will think about recommendations before making them and that someone in the evaluated agency will read them. Regardless of the mechanisms adopted, it is difficult to imagine the funds actually being cut off from an agency because it refuses to institute a reports-management program or a files-classification system. These are areas in which procedural delay, empty expressions of compliance, and general footdragging throughout the agency can prevent any action in the absence of strong incentives to follow the recommendations.

It is not unusual for an agency to ignore the directives or suggestions of another agency, or even of Congress, when the orders are phrased in general terms and are not central to the main tasks of the agency. For example, Congress passed legislation calling for the coordination of those federal activities having an impact at the local level (various grants and construction projects, etc.) with each other and with the plans of local governments. The implementation of this act, however, was treated somewhat haphazardly by the Office of Management and Budget, and often ignored altogether by the various agencies that should have been affected.[7] Similarly, the efforts to persuade agencies to submit cost–benefit analyses with their requests for budget increases have not been very successful.[8]

The case discussed in this chapter is a little more surprising, however, for the objective of NARS was not to force the agency studied to cooperate with another or to publicize an analysis that would have harmed its interests, but rather to improve its record-keeping procedures. This would save resources, and also might permit quicker and more flexible performance of the agency's functions. The head of the agency can sometimes benefit from making his organization efficient and it is to him that the recommendations of NARS were addressed.

The GAO suggested that the management of an agency could be motivated to comply by an indication of the savings that could be achieved by adopting each recommendation.[9] The most immediate objection to this argument is that the savings are difficult to estimate with any confidence. Even if the information were available, why should an estimate of the potential savings from an innovation motivate an agency to adopt it? Niskanen argues that in the usual case the bureaucrat is

[7]U.S. General Accounting Office, "Improved Cooperation and Coordination Needed among all Levels of Government—Office of Management and Budget Circular A-95," Report GGD–75–52 (11 Feb. 1975).

[8]U.S. General Accounting Office, "Civil Agencies Make Limited Use of Cost–Benefit Analysis in Support of Budget Requests," Report FGMSD–75–10 (14 Jan. 1975).

[9]GAO, "Ways to Improve Records Management Practices," 1973, pp. 12–13.

constrained by the budget, which means that he will have an incentive to adopt efficient methods in order to produce a larger output with which to gain a still larger budget from the sponsor.[10] Unless the excessive costs of paperwork served some other managerial purpose (e.g., they were a convenient form in which to hoard budgetary slack for the inevitable crisis or the excessive costs consisted of extremely attractive secretaries), the manager would have an incentive to adopt the recommendations. The incentive might not be strong enough, however, if the costs of the change, in terms of managerial time and effort were too high. The suggestion that the benefits of the change be made more explicit and noncompliance more visible and painful thus does seem like a correct (albeit weak) approach for motivating the budget-constrained bureaucrat.

The demand-constrained bureaucrat, however, has no incentive to eliminate inefficiency. Since the sponsor does not want more output and the bureaucrat does not want to cut his budget, the only question is what form the inefficiency will take. The head of such a bureau will resist efforts to make his paperwork more efficient, for that would require that the savings be used in other ways.

Within the agency the considerations would appear to be roughly similar. It is difficult to imagine that a bureaucrat could earn a more favorable opinion from his supervisor by reorganizing the files than by any number of other activities. The incentives for change will be strong only in response to internal pressures; for example, when rapid growth threatens to throw the whole system into chaos. In such a situation, an agency may turn to NARS for help. Without such an incentive, the attempt to encourage efficient paperwork practices hardly seems to be worth the effort. This was apparently what NARS concluded when it took its legislated charge so lightly. In the sense in which *bureaucratic failure* is used in this book, NARS offers a clear example of failure: It was ordered to report to Congress and the President those agencies that failed to implement its recommendations. It did not do so, even though the order could have been carried out. Rarely are bureaucratic failures so straightforward or so uninteresting. Yet it does raise the very important question of how to build incentives for technical efficiency into the bureaucratic structure.

[10]William A. Niskanen, Jr., *Bureaucracy and Representative Government* (Chicago: Aldine-Atherton, 1971).

CHAPTER **15**

The Pilot Cities Program[1]

With memories of riots and reports of rising crime rates as a background, Congress passed the Omnibus Crime Control and Safe Streets Act of 1968 (82 stat 204). The Law Enforcement Assistance Administration (LEAA) created by the act was charged with helping state and local governments fight crime. The new and poorly staffed agency was under great pressure to spend money quickly in order to show Congress that it was battling vigorously against crime.

The Pilot Cities Program begun in 1970 epitomized the bureaucratic failings of the unfortunate agency. In a striking refutation of the hierarchical model, however, the local teams accomplished something despite the lapses in national and regional administration. Furthermore, the way the money was spent in the field probably came closer to congressional intent than the program that the agency tried to impose, although that is a moot point in view of the vagueness of the law.

Under the standard LEAA procedures, state planning agencies received bloc grants that they used to finance both state and local pro-

[1]This chapter is based primarily on U.S. General Accounting Office, "The Pilot Cities Program: Phaseout Needed Due to Limited National Benefits," Report GGD–75–16 (3 Feb. 1975).

grams. The agency retained discretionary funds to finance projects that it believed to have national significance. Within the LEAA, the National Institute of Law Enforcement and Criminal Justice financed research and demonstration projects. The financing of the Pilot Cities Program from discretionary funds implies that it was supposed to have national significance, rather than just financing particular projects in particular cities. Nevertheless, throughout the life of the program its purposes were disputed. The three possibilities were (a) to seek out and evaluate innovations that might improve the criminal justice system; (b) to improve the criminal justice system of the pilot city; and (c) to work with the criminal justice community of the pilot city in accomplishing (a) and (b).[2] Eight cities were chosen to participate—San Jose, California; Dayton, Ohio; Charlotte, North Carolina; Albuquerque, New Mexico; Norfolk, Virginia; Omaha, Nebraska; Des Moines, Iowa; and Rochester, New York.[3] In each of these a Pilot Cities team established by a nonprofit institution, generally a university, was to receive $20,000 per month in operating expenses for 60 months. Each city was allotted $500,000 per year to finance demonstration projects, but proposals for specific projects had to be approved by LEAA. Presumably the team would analyze the local situation, discover ways to reduce crime or improve the administration of criminal justice, help the relevant agencies to write proposals for financing innovations, and keep track of the results.

It is difficult to be more specific about the agency's intentions because, since the LEAA did not provide many clues, participants had differing opinions. In particular, the agency had not come to grips with the possibility that the task of conducting research might be inconsistent with the task of improving criminal justice in the pilot city by adopting well known innovations.[4]

The Pilot Cities Program developed from a proposal by the American Justice Institute for a project in Santa Clara County, California, that would emphasize engaging local people to introduce innovations based on study of the local criminal justice system. The particular projects would not be described in advance, but would be based on study and planning. The agency wanted to generalize this proposal into a national

---

[2]Murray, Charles A. and Robert E. Krug, *The National Evaluation of the Pilot Cities Program: A Team Approach to Improving Local Criminal Justice Systems* (Report on Contract J–LEAA–016–74 by the American Institutes for Research for the U.S. Department of Justice, Law Enforcement Assistance Administration, National Institute of Law Enforcement and Criminal Justice: November 1975) p. 11.

[3]For a critique of the criteria for selecting cities and of the specific selections, see Murray and Krug, *The National Evaluation of the Pilot Cities Program* p. 34.

[4]*Ibid.*, Murray and Krug develop this point in their chapter XI.

program. Negotiations proceeded between January 1969 and May 1970, while the Agency remained in turmoil internally and seven different officials were responsible at various times for the one proposal. Differences were never fully resolved about the appropriate point at which projects must be described in full detail. The LEAA remained committed to specificity before funding, whereas the American Justice Institute retained its position that innovative projects can be described in detail only after research and planning.[5]

Although the differences were not actually resolved, Santa Clara was awarded a pilot-city grant in May 1970. By June of 1972 the other seven pilot cities had been awarded funding. Following the advice of LEAA, the remaining pilot cities used the vague wording of the Santa Clara grant in their own applications. Since the other teams had not struggled with the issues during negotiations, they did not know what the agency expected and several teams had no clear idea of what they wanted to do.[6]

Written guidelines often provide some indication of the objectives of the program; in this case, however, the guidelines were not circulated until January 1973—2½ years after the first grant and half a year after the last pilot city had received its first award. Furthermore, even when the "Guide for the Establishment and Management of LEAA Pilot Cities" was drafted and available, it was never officially issued. Some participants, therefore, did not treat the document very seriously.[7] The long delays involved in preparing the ground rules for the program suggest disagreement within the agency about what was supposed to be accomplished. The guidelines, as drafted, were based on what the teams were actually doing, rather than on prior program goals, and, since different teams were doing different things by then, the guidelines were necessarily quite general.

The vagueness and uncertainty in central control over the program did not necessarily mean that individual teams pursued their own goals. Many of the teams were so beset by indecision that they did not benefit from freedom. Santa Clara, with its clear goals, survived the uncertainties. Other cities had difficulties, especially in the choice between research and adopting ideas already tested elsewhere. The indecision was compounded by the discontinuities in administration of the program, because of personnel changes at LEAA headquarters, and by the effort to delegate administration of the program to the regional offices. In the

[5]GAO, "The Pilot Cities Program," pp. 6–7.
[6]Ibid., p. 10.
[7]Ibid., pp. 10, 11, 22.

absence of clear objectives, the results included vacillation, delay, and contradictory orders.

The following quotations illustrate the difficulties. In March 1970, the Director of the National Institute stated that:

> The projects in the pilot cities are mainly taken from *prior* research that has *proved* either on a research or demonstration basis, or both, that a certain kind of action is feasible and helpful. Therefore, in the projects we are primarily looking to implement *prior* knowledge rather than establish innovative ways that have not been tried before. As you will recall, the theory of the pilot cities is to put *existing* knowledge together in a package and implement it across the whole criminal justice system in these designated areas.[8]

Two years later a regional official wrote to the Omaha team director: "The focus of demonstration projects should be designed primarily to solve specific problems within the criminal justice agencies of the Omaha–Douglas county area and to benefit emphatically that immediate community."[9]

About a year later a University of Nebraska official tried to make this explicit by writing to the LEAA: "As I understand it, an agreement was reached among the pilot cities and the LEAA that projects funded need not be nationally innovative so long as they were innovative for the jurisdiction concerned." Although this appears to be a reasonable interpretation of the memo and the letter, the LEAA replied that "Innovation as you have defined its use for the Omaha pilot program would in our opinion adjust the program from national in scope to parochial in nature."

Thus, even in the middle of 1973, neither the teams nor LEAA officials were sure about what they were supposed to be doing, except that the teams were supposed to study the local conditions before recommending solutions. The extreme financial pressure under which the teams labored, however, generally prevented the rational approach of gathering data, establishing lines of communication with local agencies, and conducting research before devising proposals to obtain the project money.[10] Not only did the teams have $20,000 per month to spend for their own salaries and expenses in accomplishing those tasks, but they were also obliged to write good proposals for spending $500,000 per year on demonstration projects. Since these funds could not be carried over

---

[8]Quoted from a March 1970 LEAA memorandum in GAO, "The Pilot Cities Program," pp. 8–9. Underscoring supplied by GAO.

[9]Letter of 18 July 1972, quoted in GAO, "The Pilot Cities Program," p. 28, as is the rest of the exchange.

[10]*Ibid.*, pp. 15 ff.

beyond the end of the fiscal year, and LEAA was under pressure to show Congress how successfully it could spend money, the local teams had to write proposals before they had time to do any of the work on which the proposals were to be based.

This financial pressure did not bother the Santa Clara and Norfolk teams, which were already at work on the preliminary phases when the pilot-city grants were initiated. Other teams, however, found the proposal writing to be a heavy burden. The grant for Rochester, for example, became effective in March 1972, and research began in August with hiring completed in November. Yet in January 1973 the regional pilot-city coordinator wrote to the Rochester team to complain of the delay in preparing proposals and to urge that something be submitted immediately; research and innovation could wait![11] In April the team director was informed that any demonstration money not obligated by June 30 would be lost. Since $800,000 was at stake (the amount for March through June of the previous year having been held over), this was a serious matter. The team did succeed in writing its proposals, although the degree to which they were innovative and addressed to the particular circumstances of the pilot city must be open to some question.

Albuquerque was under still more extreme pressure. The grant was awarded in February 1971 and a director hired in April. In May an LEAA official informed the team that grant applications were due by the end of June. Then on June 6 the team was advised by an LEAA official to assist local agencies in applying for competitive discretionary funds, for which applications were due by June 17. The team did succeed in submitting applications for both categories of funds—without research, however, and often copied from other applications. LEAA rejected most of the applications, thus suggesting to the local agencies that the team was not competent. The pilot city projects were approved 6–10 months later and charged against 1972 funds, so the entire rationale for the rush was lost anyway.[12]

Most teams were similarly goaded. Those that tried to dash off proposals could not base them on the research, planning, and coordination of existing local agencies that were basic to the Pilot Cities Program. The strain of forcing research-oriented teams to turn out stereotyped proposals disrupted serious work and undoubtedly contributed to the turnover in staff that plagued most of the teams.

The lack of guidelines became more disastrous when the LEAA complied with the new federalism by giving regional offices more responsi-

[11]*Ibid.*, p. 16, includes the letter.
[12]*Ibid.*, p. 17.

bility. Regional officials knew little about the program and had few written clues when the boxes of records for each pilot city arrived in 1971. Each region was told to designate a pilot-city coordinator, but since the average tenure of a regional coordinator was less than 8 months between December 1971 and September 1973, the guidance varied not only between headquarters and region and among regions, but also over time within one region.[13] Since regionalization coincided with the introduction of a High Impact Anti-Crime Program involving efforts to reduce rape, homicide, robbery, and burglary in eight cities, it is not surprising that pilot cities received inadequate attention from the regions. The result of regionalization in this case, as in so many others, was to overlay another level of confusion on an already chaotic situation.

The problems of the Pilot Cities Program were partly attributable to the political atmosphere of crisis in the war against crime. Poor staffing has also been offered as an explanation,[14] but it seems to be another symptom of the problems. Similarly, the rapid turnover in staff in the LEAA and within some pilot-city teams contributed to the difficulties of establishing consistent policies; yet it is not clear why this particular program was plagued by such instability at the outset when success was still possible.

Another basic difficulty was the inability of LEAA to come to grips with the inherent nature of research and development. The expectation that research proposals could be developed almost overnight is one indication of this, as is the pattern of funding that provided no recognition of the acceleration in pace of research and development activities from an inexpensive start, with preliminary ideas and a literature search, to a far more expensive conclusion as technicians are employed to build and test hardware or trial runs are conducted. A more fundamental problem, however, was the attempt to combine freedom for pilot-city teams to originate research projects on the basis of local conditions and problems with a strict, secret, and variable research agenda devised by LEAA headquarters.[15] The inevitable result was frustration for the pilot-city teams that found one proposal after another rejected while at the same time the clues as to what might be accepted were constantly varied.

Despite the confusion and inattention at higher levels, the teams did manage to accomplish something for the local areas. The main complaint of the GAO was not that the funds were wasted, but rather that the

---

[13]*Ibid.*, pp. 20, 23.

[14]Phone conversation with James Gregg, Assistant Administrator of LEAA, 2 May 1975.

[15]Murray and Krug discuss this in chapter XI of *The National Evaluation of the Pilot Cities Program*.

projects funded were so similar to the projects funded from bloc grants. The fact that the teams could accomplish anything useful under such difficult conditions, however, serves as evidence of the strength of professional and other motivations working directly on individuals, as compared with the almost nonexistent hierarchical control. It is especially significant that the teams even managed to bring about some national coordination of data collection, which could not have been achieved hierarchically under the circumstances.[16]

Of equal interest is the fact that the political pressures that have operated in so many cases (e.g., model cities and the Area Redevelopment Administration) to expand the number of qualifying areas were apparently not felt in this case. There was some evidence of political maneuvering in the selection of Albuquerque, which did not meet the criteria for the program, over Tulsa, which did,[17] but in general the rewards of the program must have seemed sufficiently remote to preclude aggressive efforts to obtain them.

The Pilot Cities Program provided numerous examples of technical inefficiency by the bureaucracy in carrying out tasks that are supposed to be part of the bureaucratic routine. The political pressure to spend funds quickly certainly contributed to the agency's difficulties, but one cannot resist the feeling that a few strong and interested individuals might have changed the history of the program. The problems of running the program did not seem different in kind from those of running other research-oriented programs.

The failure of pilot cities was so generally recognized within LEAA that the agency readily accepted the GAO recommendation that the program be phased out. Even in its demise the ill-starred program evoked complaints of mismanagement. The results of a major outside contract ($309,000), designed in part to assist the regional offices to · monitor and evaluate progress of pilot-city teams and to provide feedback to the teams, were received as the program was being brought to a halt.[18]

---

[16]GAO, "The Pilot Cities Program," p. 36. Murray and Krug, *The National Evaluation of the Pilot Cities Program*, considered the San Jose and Tidewater teams, in particular, to have been successful because of their accomplishments in their local areas.

[17]GAO, "The Pilot Cities Program," p. 32.

[18]*Ibid.*, pp. 50–52.

CHAPTER 16

Corruption by Consultants[1]

Although this particular case is of no great importance in its own right, it is useful as an illustration of the conditions that are conducive to corrupt behavior, as described in Chapter 5. Furthermore, rumor has it that the process of awarding grants and contracts tends toward the type of behavior to be described here, unless all participants are scrupulously ethical.[2] This is a disquieting thought because of the tendency in recent years to restrain growth in federal employment by contracting out activities to the private and nonprofit sectors. Although hierarchical control worsens as the size of the bureaucracy increases, functions performed by outside contractors and consultants are even more difficult to control than those performed internally.

The Emergency School Assistance Program (ESAP) was initiated in August 1970 to provide grants to school districts and nonprofit agencies,

[1]The main source for this chapter is U.S. General Accounting Office, "Role of Three Consultants in Award of Emergency School Assistance Program/Community Groups Grants," Report B–164031(1) (21 Sept. 1973).
[2]Daniel Guttman and Barry Willner recount a number of the conflicts of interest and borderline cases in *The Shadow Government:The Government's Multi-Billion-Dollar Giveaway of its Decision-Making Powers to Private Management Consultants, "Experts," and Think Tanks* (New York:Pantheon Division of Random House, 1976).

organizations, or institutions to help meet the cost of desegregating primary and secondary schools. The part of the program dealing with everything other than school districts (i.e., community groups) was known as ESAP/CG and consisted of only a director, four program officers, and two secretaries. At the time of this problem (1971), ESAP/CG was located in the Office of Education of the Department of Health, Education, and Welfare.

The failures in this case were of two types: technical violations of bureaucratic regulations and procedures, and behavior that was apparently corrupt. Although the technical transgressions are of the type that must occur frequently in the rush to accomplish anything, they made the corrupt actions easier to effect and more difficult to prove. The technical violations included allowing consultants to perform ordinary agency operations; permitting consultants to request and rewrite proposals, and then dominate the panels that decided on funding them; failing to keep adequate records; and overpaying consultants because of payroll errors. The apparently corrupt behavior by the consultants consisted of their revision of grant proposals to include funds for consulting services to be provided by firms in which they or close associates had interests. When expressed in such a stark form, the behavior of the agency in permitting the technical violations seems as inexcusable as the corrupt behavior by the consultants themselves, yet neither is as far removed from standard practice as would at first glance appear.

In particular, the consultants were hired at a time when the small regular staff of ESAP/CG was under great pressure to spend funds quickly. It is natural, therefore, that the consultants would acquire more decision-making responsibility than was consistent with their function of advising, as specified in the Federal Personnel Manual. It is, after all, not unheard of for an energetic federal executive to shortcut the red tape of federal personnel procedures by making his selected appointee a consultant until the permanent appointment can be cleared. In this case, however, the director of the office carried the practice of cutting red tape to an extreme by making one of the consultants his acting deputy director with the authority to convene and chair the panels that reviewed grant applications.

As Chapter 5 suggested, it is the permanent relationship between the employee and the federal government that makes petty dishonesty unprofitable. Even so, the interactions between the government and the nongovernmental sectors are vulnerable to corruption because of the possibility of large payoffs. The rule of reserving grant decisions for regular members of the bureaucracy is, therefore, a sound one for decreasing the likelihood of corruption. It should be noted, however, that

TABLE 16.1

Budgets Revised by the Granting Agency

	Original budget		Revised budget	
School	Total ($)	Consultative services ($)	Total ($)	Consultative services ($)
Florida Technological	154,879	10,000	154,879	42,000
Prairie View A&M	158,487	1500	140,000	42,000
Southern University and A&M College	120,987	1200	223,000	45,000
Savannah State	60,000	—	110,000	24,759
Atlanta University	60,000	—	60,000	11,300
Millersville State	24,970	—	27,676	4250

SOURCE: U.S. General Accounting Office, Report B–164031 (1), 21 September 1973: 11.

in an area where technical expertise is important—as it tends to be in areas where the government contracts for services or awards grants— the bureaucrats in regular positions may identify themselves primarily with a profession and be mobile between government and private employment. Chapter 4 stressed the importance of such professional identification in maintaining the output of bureaucracies despite the failure of hierarchical control. This case, however, reveals the other side of the coin: Except in cases as blatant as this one, it is difficult for the layman to distinguish between the respect of one professional for another of great ability and a mutual exchange of favors among charlatans or thieves.

The most serious charge in this case is that the consultants working for ESAP/CG would approve grants only when they included large sums to be paid for the consulting services of their cronies. The failure of the agency to keep proper records made it impossible to determine who had participated in which decisions, but the pattern observed in Table 16.1 speaks for itself.

The spokesmen for the universities listed in the table indicated that the three consultants working at ESAP-CG would suggest both the increase in the funding for consultants and the name of the consulting firm to employ.[3] Since the GAO showed that the consulting firms were closely associated with the ESAP/CG consultants, the impropriety of the procedure seems beyond doubt. If the enterprise had been undertaken in a more subtle way, however, it might not have been distinguishable from the "old boy network." Once such arrangements have been in effect for a long time, it is simply understood that each proposal will

[3]GAO, "Role of Three Consultants," 1973, pp. 11–19.

include the services of reputable consultants. The reciprocity of favors is somewhat less direct, but the public may not receive any more output per tax dollar.

Buying a standard product at a competitive market price does not confer a favor on anyone, but most of the participants in the government grant and contract process probably view it as the dispensing of favors. The reasons why it does not approximate a perfect market include both the extreme difficulty in measuring output, the still greater difficulty in forecasting expected output, and the small numbers of potential buyers and sellers in most such transactions. The last characteristic, alone, means that the results will be negotiated, rather than determined by market forces, so it will be in the interest of the consulting firms to have some of their agents within the government agency. This is an extreme case, but other examples have surfaced of sellers attempting to write the government's purchase specifications.[4] Excessive influence by the seller over the buyer is corrupt, but often in highly technical areas it is necessary to obtain assistance from the selling firms—either as information from salesmen or as formal design contracts—so in this area, as well, the boundary between ethical and unethical behavior may be hard to draw.[5] Outright corruption of the sort described in this case is probably not common and each instance is easy to deal with once it is discovered. The gray areas are more troubling and are becoming increasingly common as the government grows in size and complexity.

[4]See, for example, the UPI item "Computer Probe, Contract Favoritism Described," *Portland Press Herald*, 18 August 1977, p. 44.

[5]For an example of an instance in which the agency could not be shown to have done anything wrong, but in which the GAO thought that it could have done more to promote competition, see U.S. General Accounting Office, "Contract Award by the Federal Power Commission for Developing and Installing a Regulatory Information System," Report RED–76–59 (2 April 1976).

PART III

Bureaucratic Failure and
the Agenda for Government

CHAPTER 17

Some Lessons from the Cases

The cases of Part II were chosen to illustrate a wide variety of government activities. Despite the heterogeneity, there were a number of characteristics common to several cases. At the same time, each case involved a unique combination of characteristics, and no single characteristic was present in every case. There is no universal key to failure.

The characteristics of the various cases are listed in Table 17.1. They span the full range from underlying causes of the difficulties to mere symptoms of problems. Each case is described by several of the characteristics—in no case less than five. At the other extreme, the Federal Energy Administration appeared to suffer from 21 of the 28 characteristics. The exact counts are unimportant because the characteristics differ in degree of overlap. Some programs had more severe versions of the same problem than did others, and considerable judgment is often involved in attributing a particular problem to a particular agency or program. It should also be noted that existence of one of these problems in some aspect of a program does not preclude success in other aspects of the program and perhaps not even in the afflicted aspect. In the remainder of this chapter, the name of each case is abbreviated. The table lists the abbreviations along with the chapter in which each was described. The 28 characteristics are arbitrarily divided into 4 groups: those

Characteristics of Cases

TABLE 17.1

Characteristics	6 HUD	7 FISH	8 APW	9 AMS	10 PEST	11 FEA	12 AID	13 VOC	14 NARS	15 LEAA	16 ESAP
Law											
1. Oversimplification		X			X	X	X				
2. Inappropriate sanctions				X	X			X	X		
3. Ambiguous goals							X			X	
4. Deleterious incentives	X	X				X					
5. Violation of liberties					X	X					
6. Budgetary independence		X		X			X	X			
Program											
7. Exploitation of beneficiaries	X										
8. Difficulty of task	X	X			X	X	X	X			
9. Incompetence of personnel	X			X		X					
10. Decisions at low level	X					X					
11. Corrupting structure	X					X					X

13. Complexity of transactions
14. Necessity of cooperation

Agency
15. Deference to clients
16. Incompatibility of task
17. Opposition within agency
18. Administrative deficiencies
19. Personnel problems
20. Delays in regulations
21. Regional variations
22. Excessive workload
23. Failure to expand
24. Displacement of goals

Environment
25. Haste to spend
26. Spreading the benefits
27. Threat of termination
28. Excessive expectations

239

pertaining to the underlying legislation; those inherent in the program; those peculiar to the agency; and those that describe the environment in which the program operated.

CHARACTERISTICS OF THE LEGISLATION

To suggest that implementation could be improved by having some staff agency rewrite bills presumes that minor tinkering with the wording could save the program. This distinction between the minor quirks of the legislation and the basic nature of the program lies behind the first grouping: characteristics of the law. Although the distinction is fuzzy, it is also important because of the frequency of *inadvertent legislation*. Of the 11 cases studied, at least 5 included sections that appear to have been written without any forethought. Such inadvertent legislation is most likely toward the end of the legislative process. If the President proposes a confused bill, Congress can straighten it out, but the brilliant legislative compromise or supplement in the final moments of debate may not receive much scrutiny. The HUD program is an example of inadvertent legislation. It was tacked on by Congress in response to the pitiful tales of HUD's performance under Section 235, without any concern for the fact that the people who had done so poorly with 235 would certainly fail with 518(b). The Fisheries Loan Fund was legislated without any serious consideration of the effects on anyone but the recipients of the loans. The AID housing program was added by Congress to help certain segments of the domestic housing industry. The NARS program was inspired by the universal hope for decreasing the costs of paperwork, but without considering how the hope would be realized. Finally, the FEA was directed to solve the problems that were admittedly too difficult for Congress to solve, including such contradictory objectives as controlling prices without decreasing the quantity supplied or increasing the quantity demanded.

Oversimplification

Legislation that is hastily drafted frequently ignores significant complexities of the real world. In particular, the fisheries legislation ignored the limits to the stocks of fish. In the pesticides case, the law set up the agency as the guarantor of the safety and effectiveness of commercial products, a task that far exceeded its capability. The FEA had to perform contradictory tasks, whereas the AID Housing Program had an expressed goal that seemed to be impossible.

Inappropriate Sanctions

The legislation may also provide the agency with inappropriate sanctions. If the punishment does not fit the crime, it is unlikely to be used. Likewise, if an agency has no rewards to dispense, it cannot buy correct action. Typically, as exemplified by AMS, vocational education, and NARS, the sanctions are so strong that they cannot be used by the agency to deal with ordinary daily business. At times, however, the law may not provide any sanctions. This is particularly likely when, as in the pesticides case, the law requires the cooperation of another agency, but provides no currency with which one agency can purchase the assistance of another.

Ambiguous Goals

Sometimes the goals specified in the legislation are ambiguous, rather than contradictory. The bureaucrat who knows exactly what he wants to do may use the ambiguity to pursue his own goals. The LEAA case (in which the ambiguity was created at high levels within the agency rather than by the legislation) may be more typical. When most participants are engaged in defensive maneuvers to avoid being caught on the wrong side of any issue, the organization accomplishes little. Alternatively, the agency may try a little of everything, as AID did in the early years.

Inefficient Incentives in the Private Sector

Some laws create incentives for someone to act in a way that is inefficient for society as a whole. Such inefficiency is an external cost of government. The inefficient behavior need not be limited to the private sector. Municipal governments, for example, have individually found it profitable to establish offices in Washington to compete for grants. From society's view, such an expenditure in dividing the limited funds is pure waste.

In the cases studied, HUD, FISH, and the FEA all created incentives for inefficiency. HUD weakened the rationing function of the market, thereby transferring expensive housing to people who could not maintain it. FISH increased the excess capacity in crowded fisheries. The worst incentives were created by the FEA when it established multiple prices for the same product. It immediately became profitable to drill new wells in old fields and to import more oil, so a mass of regulations had to be written to forestall the most egregious results of the incentives created.

Violations of Civil Liberties

The new pesticides law made it illegal to spray any insecticide on an insect not mentioned on the label. If the agency were to enforce the law, it would have to send an army of agents to spy on every citizen. Fortunately, the agency has been too busy with other tasks to take on this activity, but the law does require it to violate individual liberties.

The FEA, on the other hand, used its authority to regulate market transactions in a way that violated basic standards of justice. Regulations were kept secret until long after their effective date, and were sometimes impossible to obey even when published. The agency then used its own discretion in punishing departures from its laws.

Budgetary Independence

Establishing an agency with budgetary independence is not generally treated as a flaw in the legislation. Nevertheless, the theory suggests that budgetary independence is conducive to loss of hierarchical control because of the freedom from detailed budgetary review. Among these cases, FISH, AMS, and AID generated much or all of their own revenues by sale of services or guarantee of loans in exchange for a small fee. VOC conveyed partial budgetary independence on the state vocational education bureaucracies, making them less subject to political control.

CHARACTERISTICS OF THE PROGRAM

Exploitation of Ostensible Beneficiaries

The only program that was run in such a way as to leave the ostensible beneficiaries open to exploitation was the original HUD 235 program. In general, programs do aid their intended beneficiaries, if the beneficiary group is small and well defined, but an inefficient program will be expensive for the general public in comparison with the benefits provided.

Technically Difficult Task

Some jobs are more difficult than others; some are impossible. Although legislation is most apt to be impossible to implement when no one considers that problem in advance, even some laws that are carefully drawn can put the bureaucrats who administer them into technically difficult situations. The pesticides case illustrates both possibilities: The environmental aspects of pesticide control pose many exceedingly complex technical questions that have to be solved by government. On the other hand, the requirement that the agency certify effectiveness is a bright idea on which the agency just cannot deliver. Technical problems are also inherent in the control of the petroleum industry, providing low-cost housing in foreign countries, the fisheries management aspect of the fisheries program, and in the occupational planning functions assigned to vocational education. In general, however, the technical problems are not severe enough to explain the failures in these cases.

Jobs Exceed Competence of Personnel

Tasks are easy or difficult only in relation to the person who will perform them. The previous characteristic, however, referred to the nature of the entire activity assigned to the agency by Congress, whereas this one considers the way that activity is broken down into jobs for particular individuals. It is essential, therefore, to consider the general level of ability of the people employed by the agency even if the task is possible for someone.

Responses of the agencies to the knowledge that their personnel lacked the competence to carry out their jobs varied in the cases in which this was a problem. HUD ignored it, thereby producing the worst fiasco. The FEA recognized the limitations of its compliance force, so it never reassigned it to the more important and difficult job.

Decision Making in the Field

Programs differ in the locus and subtlety of decisions, but three required relatively subtle decisions to be made at the lowest levels of the hierarchy. These were HUD, AMS, and FEA. In the HUD program the decisions were made by appraisers in the field. The AMS inspectors at the plant level have to make the basic judgment on acceptable quality, but they can err in the direction of strict reporting because penalties are usually decided at a higher level. The FEA auditors in the refineries referred violations up through channels for a detailed review of the appropriate penalties, but with the auditors so overburdened, the important decision was which discrepancy or suspicion to pursue. It is significant that the decisions made in the field by AMS and FEA were relatively free from criticism. The bad decisions by the HUD appraisers might have been forestalled by tighter administration.

Structure of the Program is Conducive to Corruption

It should not be supposed that the conditions conducive to bribery and similar malfeasance are the same as those that leave decisions to the agent in the field. In the HUD case, there was overlap and bribery did occur. FEA employees were also vulnerable, but had a relatively good record. At ESAP it was the temporary employment relationship that caused problems.

Prospects for Outside Employment

The prospect of employment outside the agency is a two-edged sword. Whereas nearly every agency has some professionals whose performance is improved by their attempt to maintain professional standards, a problem arises when the prospect of outside employment influences the behavior of the bureaucrat. This may have been a factor in the overall performance of the FEA, including some of the problems of writing regulations. It was certainly a characteristic of ESAP and was also mentioned in connection with the inflated appraisals made by HUD personnel.

Complex Transactions

Complexity of transactions with organizations outside the federal government helps to create opportunities for corruption and favoritism. Again, this characterized ESAP and FEA in its writing of regulations.

Cooperation of Other Agencies

Each of the six agencies that required cooperation from, or coordination with, other government agencies suffered significant delays or more serious problems as a result. Some of the problems were relatively minor: for example, the delays encountered by ARA in processing grant proposals through various agencies. Others involved the failure of one agency to supply another with information, as, for example, the reluctance of AMS to report sanitary violations to FDA or of Customs to report pesticide shipments to EPA. When one agency relied on another to do the work, the slippage in control appeared to be immense: For example, the early use by FEA of IRS compliance officers seemed unsatisfactory and VOC claimed that it had limited powers over state and local agencies. When NARS tried to give suggestions to other agencies it was ignored.

CHARACTERISTICS OF THE AGENCY

The characteristics discussed in the two preceding sections result either from defects in the design of the legislation or from some problems inherent in the program. Errors made within the agency, or special characteristics of the agency to which the program is consigned, may also lead to failure.

Deference to Clients

One explanation for the reluctance of Customs to cooperate with EPA was the desire to expedite imports. More cogently, the AMS objected to subjecting its paying customers to a greater chance of criminal prosecution than other firms risked at the hands of the FDA. Similarly NARS had to maintain good relations with its paying customers. The client relationship of VOC is complex and political, since the federal bureaucracy relies on state and local agencies to generate political support for its programs and budgets. Similarly, APW had to be sensitive to the political power of various localities aided. All regulatory agencies are somewhat dependent on the regulated parties for information and personnel, and one expects government agencies to treat the citizens with deference, hence the judgment that a program suffered because of excessive deference must always remain subjective.

Misunderstanding or Incompatibility of Task

Misunderstanding of the objectives or their incompatibility with other functions of the agency was a problem in all eight of the cases in which the agency was required to change its professional role or approach to achieve success. HUD, which had approached the inspection process with the views of the lender, was moved to a position where the view of the borrower was more appropriate. ARA was supposed to change its approach from concern with long-run economic growth to immediate increases in employment. AMS, which had as its primary role technical assistance to the industry and encouragement of better processing, was supposed to report violations to the Food and Drug Administration for more heavy-handed regulatory action including possible criminal action. NARS was supposed to shift from a seller of consulting services to a policeman. Pesticides had just been moved from the Department of Agriculture, where the primary concerns were effectiveness of the products against pests and the safety of the users, to the Environmental Protection Agency with its orientation toward long-term effects on the environment. FEA was not required to change its general viewpoint, but was supposed to undertake a far more complex and technical task. The National Marine Fisheries Service found the task of fisheries management less congenial than its traditional role of assisting individual fishermen and increasing the use of fish. LEAA was trapped between orientation toward research and toward action. The administrators of the pilot-cities program never really decided which they wanted.

Intraagency Opposition

Opposition can be based on resistance to change, ideology, self-interest, or differences in professional judgment. Three of the programs themselves aroused strong opposition within the agency: Many HUD personnel disliked the original subsidy program and considered the repair program to be a nuisance and an insult. FEA compliance suffered from widespread ideological and practical opposition to controls at the higher levels of agency leadership. The AID housing program was considered impossible or useless by many within the agency, especially at its inception. In NARS, FISH, APW, and VOC, the general purposes of the program were well accepted by the agency, but unpopular aspects were ignored or sabotaged.

Administrative Deficiencies

Six of the 11 cases showed evidence of lapses in standard administrative techniques or bureaucratic procedures, often in defiance of the standard operating procedures of the agencies concerned. The clearest examples included the failure of many of the HUD field offices to follow routine contracting procedures and the general ignorance at HUD headquarters of what was happening in the field. The pesticides program, too, was bedeviled by lapses in record-keeping, which reflected some laxness in administration as much as difficulties with computer programming to handle the masses of information. Similarly, ESAP departed from standard procedures in permitting consultants to exercise line administrative authority and failing to keep records of meetings and decisions.

The LEAA was unable to set down in writing the regulations that it wished the pilot cities to follow because the agency could not decide on policy. At the FEA, the most serious administrative lapse was failing to establish the detailed rules for pricing and allocation. In a rather different category are the failures of VOC. This agency did not promulgate certain rules, keep certain records, or require states to submit meaningful follow-up data. One gathers the impression, however, that these specific failures were intentional, reflecting the fact that the administrators did not want to comply with certain aspects of the law. Thus the category of *poor administration* covers a wide variety of situations.

Personnel Problems:
Poor Staffing and Rapid Turnover

Poor staffing and rapid turnover are more likely to be symptoms of problems than independent sources of trouble. One expects such problems when government wages are too low relative to those paid by other employers for the same occupations. Turnover can be particularly serious when special features of the program drive good people away. In the LEAA and FEA cases, such features included vacillation and reversals of policy. The FEA also suffered from the uncertainty regarding its future, which made it difficult to recruit and retain good people.

Inordinate Delays in Regulations, Decisions,
or Action

Inordinate delay in the publication of regulations is such a common form of poor administration that it deserves special attention. It can reflect difficulty in establishing policy because of disagreement about goals (LEAA), the difficulty of resolving technical questions in a complex situation (FEA), problems of coordinating action with another agency (Pesticides and Customs), resistance by bureaucrats to parts of the legislation (VOC), or simple confusion (HUD). Sometimes the explanation is not obvious at all: For example, the National Marine Fisheries Service gives the appearance of administering its programs well, but the designation of particular fisheries as conditional has been painfully slow.

Regional Variations in Policy

Four of the 11 programs were subject to additional confusion at the regional office level. It would be difficult to characterize regional offices as a cause of failure, independent of poor administration and delay in writing regulations, but they do appear to add an additional layer of confusion and delay and to raise the overall level of managerial skill required for success. The four programs where regional offices were the focus of some troubles included HUD, Pesticides, FEA, and LEAA. The inherent difficulty with regional control is that the details of programs are ordinarily worked out between field offices and Washington so that action in the field can be made consistent both with reality and with policy. If this discussion must be relayed through a regional office that is not in tune with either policy or reality, the discussion is delayed and its quality deteriorates. To the extent that regional officials exercise some initiative, policies will differ in various parts of the country, which seems basically unfair and may result in attacks on the agency. The worst effect, however, is to further insulate the Washington headquarters from contact with reality. If someone from Washington visits field offices regularly, bits of gossip about program performance will circulate through informal channels, but even that source of information is eliminated by interposing regional administration.

Excessive Workload

An agency may be so overwhelmed with work that a particular task is left undone for lack of manpower. Distinguishing between insufficiency of resources and poor use of resources is, in practice, very difficult. Various HUD field offices had long delays in processing 518(b) claims, but whether this resulted from poor management or inadequate staffing is hard to say. As a somewhat different example, the FEA did not have nearly enough manpower assigned to the refinery audits, but it is not obvious that this resulted from inadequate staffing rather than poor personnel planning and deployment. In the pesticides case, the new law imposed a huge burden on an agency that was in a state of administrative chaos to begin with.

Failure to Attempt to Expand

The most puzzling feature of all the cases was the lack of an aggressive effort to expand the pesticides budget to match the new responsibilities. Bureaucratic theory, as well as popular wisdom, suggests that the agency would seize on the obvious burdens imposed by the new law as a lever to argue for vastly increased resources. But it did not.

Displacement of Goals

Displacement of goals is a very general term that includes a variety of situations in which the agency shifts its focus toward objectives different from those specified in the legislation. At least 7 of the 11 cases were characterized by displacement of goals. FISH, APW, FEA, and AID drifted into programs that they could do well, but which neglected some of the legislated task. AMS maintained the quality of products labeled with its shield, but ignored the adulterated food that entered distribution channels. Pesticides followed a legalistic approach to sampling that was so inefficient that it never accomplished the task. Finally, VOC measured planning in terms of documents, rather than activity.

CHARACTERISTICS OF THE ENVIRONMENT

Government agencies work in a political setting. The bureaucrats answer to the President and his staff and to Congress and its committees. The politicians, in turn, are subject to public pressure, including that from groups actively interested in the programs. As might be expected, particular features of the political environment did have some influence on the programs studied.

Haste to Spend

Five of the programs were characterized by intense pressure either to act quickly or to exhaust the budget quickly. It would seem, on the basis of this limited observation, that the perverse financial pressure exerted by an excessive budget is a significant cause of failure! In a sense, of course, the excessive financing is merely a symptom of the intense desire of the President or Congress to show some action in the face of a publicized problem, such as the oil embargo or a wave of rioting. In most instances, as well, it is the rate of increase in spending, not the absolute amount, that causes the problem. In the particular cases under consideration the time was not available to increase spending in an orderly way. For HUD, LEAA, and ESAP the reasons for the pressure to act quickly were basically political—the problems of housing the poor, reducing crime, and helping communities accept integration of schools will persist for a long time, but political leaders, having made the decision to attack one of these, must have the appearance of action before the next election.

In other cases, however, the explanation for the time pressure is technical. If we are to rely on government action to reduce cyclical unemployment, as in APW, the government must respond more quickly than the business cycle. Similarly, if controls by the FEA were to be relied upon during the embargo, they had to be instituted almost instantaneously. In the face of such strong pressures to act quickly, the goal of cost minimization is of little importance. But more serious than mere waste of resources is the fact that in all of these cases (except possibly ESAP) the rush to spend or act actually hindered the accomplishment of the explicit goals of the program. Administrators became so caught up in the details of spending rapidly that the policies and regulations that would have guided the spending into useful channels were never established, or were established only after years of wrangling. Thus, action was sacrificed to the appearance of action.

Spreading the Benefits

It is natural for a politician to try to shape a program in such a way that it confers benefits on his constituents. In programs that are initially intended to focus on a few geographic areas, this leads to a tendency to spread the available funds over an increasing number of recipients until there is not enough to do much anywhere. APW was a classic example of this. FISH spread benefits by limiting individual loans to such a small size that they could not be used to achieve the technical upgrading required by the law. It is equally significant, however, that the LEAA case showed no signs of pressure to spread the program.

Threat of Termination

The FEA control program was instituted by Congress over presidential opposition and maintained a precarious existence in the face of philosophical opposition from the top levels of the administration. In this setting, it was difficult both to create a sense of urgency about completing regulations and to recruit qualified people to enforce them. The threat of termination also induced the agency to devote effort to justifying its continued existence.

Excessive Expectations

At least 2 of the 11 programs operated in an atmosphere in which the public expected much more than the agency could deliver. The AMS was essentially certifying that the consumer would not be surprised by the contents of the can, rather than safety and freedom from nonobvious contaminants. The pesticides program was not able to certify safety and effectiveness and only the most flagrant environmental costs can be detected by its crude techniques.

These appear to exhaust the common features of the programs. HUD, Pesticides, and FEA were characterized by a vast number of different problems whereas NARS was not as seriously flawed. What is missing here is any way of appraising whether the program might have worked with only minor tinkering, or whether in fact many programs that do succeed have more serious structural problems. It is evident, however, that most of the difficulties that plagued implementation were either ostensibly managerial or were of the sort that should have been evident when the legislation was being considered. On the other hand, a good many of the problems that seemed so serious in Part I of this study do not appear to have had much impact on this particular selection of cases. A reexamination of the theory developed in Part I in the light of the cases forms the subject matter of the chapter after the next. But first a brief sketch of case studies by other scholars is in order.

CHAPTER **18**

Other Empirical Studies

The cases presented in Part II are notable not only for their common characteristics, but also for the absence of a number of features that the theoretical literature, summarized in Part I, might have led one to expect. In particular, the problem of nonmeasurable output did not seem important, but this will be reexamined in Chapter 19. It is notable, also, that only the HUD and the ESAP cases evidenced corrupt behavior, despite the expected bias in the selection of cases.

These unexpected results make it important to search other studies of government programs for additional themes. This search concentrates on case studies of particular agencies, programs, or episodes. Reflections on problems of top administration also contain useful insights about implementation but are ignored here because of their orientation toward political problems of presidents and cabinet officials.

The communal farm studied by Banfield got off to a bad start because the routine delays and changes in direction at the beginning were especially difficult for the poor farmers at whom the project was aimed.[1] After overcoming these troubles, the project collapsed completely just as it was beginning to appear financially successful, largely because the

[1]Edward C. Banfield, *Government Project* (Glencoe, Illinois:The Free Press, 1951).

government officials in charge of it never did understand the farmers, as discussed on page 103. In a sense, then, one can say that this was an experiment to see whether the agency had the technical knowledge (about people, as well as agriculture) to set up a communal farm. The answer was "No!"; the project ended, so the experiment taught us something.

In another sense, however, some more general elements were involved: The rapid changes in personnel and the rigid preconceptions about the aspirations and behavior of the farmers kept higher levels of administration ignorant of what was happening in the field. Because of the subtlety of the human interactions within the farm community, the misconceptions of the government officials were not dispelled by brief visits. Moreover, the shifting priorities of the agency robbed this one project of the attention that might have permitted it to succeed. The program was atypical in one respect, however. Once the farmers abandoned the project, failure was so obvious that the program was terminated. If the intended recipients of a program's benefits cannot be so readily identified, the program may persist even after the benefits have ceased.

Bardach studied the *implementation game,* in general, by focusing on the Lanterman–Petris–Short Act (L–P–S) in California.[2] L–P–S attempted to reform the treatment of the mentally ill by restricting involuntary commitments and moving toward community care of the mentally ill as a partial substitute for confinement in state hospitals. Bardach analyzed the maneuvering by various groups for control of new resources and to avoid any loss in old positions. The extended case study provides a background into which Bardach weaves most of the recent discussions of implementation, as well as an analytic framework in the form of descriptions of the games that people play to improve their own positions as implementation proceeds. This approach is inherently pessimistic for both analysis and implementation. For it suggests that not only must the analysis be carried out memo by memo, but, more significantly, successful implementation requires either planning in excrutiating detail or the continuing attention of a "fixer" who is committed to making the program work.

The New Towns In-Town program that Martha Derthick analyzed was a brainstorm of President Johnson.[3] The aim was to make large areas of surplus federal land available within cities to enable the cities to

[2]Eugene Bardach, *The Implementation Game:What happens after a Bill Becomes a Law,* (Cambridge, Massachusetts: M.I.T. Press, 1977).

[3]Martha A. Derthick, *New Towns In-Town:Why a Federal Program Failed* (Washington: The Urban Institute, 1972).

build new housing and related facilities. Eventually seven sites were selected, but after several years of maneuvering, all seven projects were total fiascoes.[4] Derthick recounts the agonies of the program touchingly. She is inclined to lay most of the blame upon the federal structure of government in the United States, which gives the national government little leverage in influencing states and cities. If one agency had been able to coerce all others to follow the plan, many difficulties would have been avoided, but the independence of state and local governments is not specifically to blame, since the cooperation of numerous federal agencies was also necessary.

If the program had a single fatal characteristic, it was the concentration of highly visible costs on such groups as the immediate neighbors of approved projects, as well as the lack of spokesmen for the unknown potential beneficiaries. The private cost–benefit calculations of interested groups thus provided only opposition. Because of the complexity of the federal–state–local approval process through which the projects had to wend, the opponents had ample opportunity to prevent action. This program failed at the political level. It is not clear that any changes in personnel or bureaucratic procedures could, or should, have saved it.

The situation that Ely Devons discussed was quite different.[5] He was involved in the British program to manufacture aircraft during World War II. There could be no doubt that all major groups and individual participants wanted the program to succeed, although such general commitment to goals does not eliminate squabbling over who will bear the costs or receive the credit for success. Although some of the problems Devons dealt with are peculiar to the conditions of forced draft production during wartime, of more general relevance was the difficulty of obtaining accurate information, since so many incentives existed for distorting actual data to conform with plans and aspirations.

Bela Gold analyzed a different set of World War II experiences in *Wartime Economic Planning in Agriculture.*[6] Despite the eloquent statements of political leaders, the commitment of various groups in the United States to alleviating shortages of food abroad was limited. The

[4]The Washington, D.C., project was the most monumental fiasco of all. Jane Rippeteau described the tangible results in "$7 Million School—No Pupils" (*Washington Post*, 18 January 1975, p. 1). In some other cases, the projects gradually degenerated into ordinary public housing projects—giving up the grander vision associated with the "New Towns In-Town" name.

[5]Ely Devons, *Planning in Practice* (Cambridge, England: The University Press, 1950); also see his *Papers on Planning and Economic Management*, ed. Sir Alec Cairncross (Manchester, England:Manchester University Press, 1970).

[6]Bela Gold, *Wartime Economic Planning in Agriculture:A Study in the Allocation of Resources* (New York:Columbia University Press, 1949).

costs of increasing the production and export of food would have been borne at home, but since the government would not inflict sacrifices on any domestic interests, the aspirations to help the world's hungry were not met. Gold recounts the struggles between Congress and the executive branch, between agencies, and within agencies, as well as among the various pressure groups. The basic problem was political: Who would pay for the benefits to be conferred on foreigners? But, in the absence of a firm decision from the top as to how these costs would be shared, the political questions pervaded all levels of the planning process, and vitiated it entirely:

> It is of particular significance for national planning, moreover, that the penetration of agricultural mobilization efforts by considerations of political expediency was not limited to the point of interaction among technical, personal and political pressures at the apex of the organization, but became pervasive. Through the operation of the personal motivations which were seen earlier to engender subservience to the managerial hierarchy, the consistently heavy emphasis on political expediency patently reflected in top-level decisions led in turn to an intensified preoccupation with such considerations at successively lower levels in these agencies. Herein lay one of the most direct causes of shortcomings in agricultural mobilization. In time, competent technicians appeared increasingly to be qualifying their expert, objective findings with allowances for political feasibility which were unverifiable and which they were clearly not competent to estimate. Resultant technical proposals were much more susceptible of ready compromise with political pressures but largely because of the prior inhibition and distortion of the technician's prior responsibilities. [7]

Gold suggested that although programs could fail because of physical, economic, or administrative infeasibility, in the case of wartime agricultural planning it was the less objective characteristic of political infeasibility that was primarily responsible. This judgment suggests that strong political leadership could have prevented failure.

Novick, Anshen, and Truppner analyzed the production controls attempted by the United States in World War II. [8] In contrast to agriculture, where the political problems were paramount, the most significant failures of industrial production controls originated during implementation. The authors discuss a variety of separate problems, but the three key issues were the following: failure to think through the full implications of the regulations being issued; the lack of authority over the military; and failure to confront directly the necessity of allocating resources.

Since no one had thought through the implementation process, the

---

[7]*Ibid.*, p. 542.

[8]David Novick, Melvin Anshen, and W. C. Truppner, *Wartime Production Controls* (New York:Columbia University Press, 1949).

regulations were both costly and unenforceable. In particular, the War Production Board was physically overwhelmed by a mountain of paper from which it could not extract the data necessary for planning. While this first problem would appear to be one that could be solved within agencies during peacetime, it appears from the FEA case (Chapter 11) that it is an experience repeated anew during each crisis. The second problem has a familiar ring: The War Production Board had no control over nonessential military uses of scarce materials. It was, therefore, forced to plead and negotiate with the army and navy. The Board was, thus, in the same weak position as so many other implementing agencies; that is, it required something from another agency without being able to offer much in return. Furthermore, the successful business executives in charge of the program, who were accustomed to having their orders carried out, could not adapt to the bureaucratic context where conducting negotiations and building incentives to obtain cooperation (both within the agency and with other government agencies) constituted the most important managerial tasks.

The final problem really combined these two: Since military contracts had top priority, but no system was devised to account for the inputs of scarce materials required for the contracts, firms had more orders of top priority than they could fill. When the top levels of the hierarchy fail to make the difficult allocation decisions they are made by someone else—perhaps some clerk who receives a friendly smile or a small gift.

The Pressman and Wildavsky study deals with the failure of an Economic Development Administration project in Oakland, California.[9] The authors place particular stress on the complex process requiring the cooperation or acquiescence in 70 decisions by various agencies. Even routine delays could accumulate sufficiently to destroy the value of a project. A program that attracts strong opposition is extremely vulnerable when so many separate approvals are required. The delays were made particularly maddening by the pressure to spend money quickly, which originated in the prediction that otherwise Oakland would erupt in riots. (The prediction, fortunately, failed.)

The authors examined the possibility of establishing some non-bureaucratic entity to carry out particularly urgent functions.[10] This was actually attempted in Oakland, and apparently the freedom from procedural and personnel restrictions was accompanied by a burst of enthusiastic effort by the participants. The special treatment also aroused

[9]Jeffrey L. Pressman and Aaron Wildavsky, *Implementation*.
[10]*Ibid.*, pp. 128–133.

opposition from people in other agencies who felt that their work was at least as important.

At a more fundamental level, the delays, in many cases, reflected genuine differences among the objectives of various agencies. An agency concerned with environmental quality had to delay a plan to fill in part of the bay until it could ascertain that damage would not be excessive. Similarly, an agency concerned with the safety of an airfield had to call for redesign of facilities that would obstruct flight paths. These types of problems are real. They cannot be sidestepped by changing the internal procedures of the agency in charge. Delays are caused not just by snags in the routine flow of paperwork, but also by purposive maneuvering for control of the program and sincere concern for the public welfare.

A general lack of power to force cooperation seems to be a common problem in programs that fail completely, or in the aspects that fail of programs that are generally successful. Programs differ greatly in the extent to which they rely on favors from other agencies. At one extreme, one can think of an agency like a fire department that hires and purchases most of its inputs in ordinary markets and provides services directly to residents of the community. At the opposite extreme was New-Towns-In-Town, where the office of new communities had to identify and obtain land (from agencies that were not eager to part with it) for purposes that met a variety of forms of resistance. The procedures themselves were complex, requiring a number of clearances and approvals, as well as planning at the local level. Under the circumstances, it is not very surprising that the agency did not succeed in establishing balanced new communities within major cities.

Intraagency differences may have to be resolved by the tedious and expensive process of bilateral negotiation just as interagency differences generally are. The question of where the line is drawn between cooperation and hard bargaining depends partly on the size of the organization and partly on the quality of administration. Within those subcomponents of the organization where firm hierarchical control persists, the employee can take a view as broad as that subcomponent, at least on the major issues. For the meaning of hierarchical control is that the administrator knows what is going on and rewards subordinates for acting in the interests of the entire organization under his control. At higher levels of aggregation, beyond the point where hierarchical control has broken down, the individual has no reward for trying to understand the purposes of the larger organization, let alone sacrificing the interests of his subcomponent to aid some other subcomponent of the larger organization.

Traditionally, economists have considered the negotiations of bilateral monopoly as influencing only the distribution of income, rather than the technical efficiency of production. This would reflect a very partial and limited view of the costs of negotiation, however. In particular, it ignores the heavy costs attendant on the time required to negotiate agreements, as compared with either market or hierarchical (dictated) solutions. Since negotiations are time consuming, programs are delayed. In some cases they are delayed sufficiently so that the crises they were expected to meet disappear. Efforts by the legislature to react quickly to a crisis by appropriating excessive funds for the new program simply raise the rewards that other agencies can obtain by hard negotiations, and thus increase the likelihood of long delays. Long delays in launching a program may be fatal when the coalition that tried to bring it into existence crumbles and those agencies originally willing to go along with the program decide to use their resources elsewhere.[11] Finally, even if the delays are overcome and the program put into effect, the effort undeniably absorbs vast amounts of managerial effort. Bargaining has been described as the unseen hand in government,[12] but club foot might be a more appropriate metaphor.

The costs of coordination were crushingly heavy in the Derthick and Pressman–Wildavsky studies. They were also serious in the cases studied by Bardach, Devons, and Novick. Difficulties in coordination were more commonly reflected in long delays than in outright conflict, but examples of both can be found. Delay, however, may be an independent source of difficulties, even when no coordination problems are evident. This seemed to be the situation in the Banfield study, where the normal bureaucratic processes were not quick enough to keep pace with the interpersonal dynamics of a small community. The delays in that case worsened as the particular project was relegated to lower and lower priority within the agency.

In addition to coordination problems, a few other themes are found in the case studies of failure. Foremost among these is the collection of difficulties that can be loosely grouped under the heading of information problems. Sheer ignorance in the central office of the facts as they were in the field contributed to the failure that Banfield described. Even there, however, the technical difficulty of accumulating, transmitting, and processing information was not so much the issue as was the ideology prevalent in the agency that blinded the observers to the implications of

---

[11]Bardach, *The Implementation Game*, deals with these issues.

[12]Roland N. McKean, "The Unseen Hand in Government," *American Economic Review* 55 (June 1965): 496–506.

the behavior that surrounded them. Devons and Gold noted the closely related phenomenon of information developed at lower levels in the organization being distorted to correspond with the expectations of the political leaders.

A final set of problems is associated with the pressure to achieve results, or at least to spend money, quickly. These pressures were particularly evident in the Novick, Devons, and Pressman–Wildavsky studies. The result in the former was the failure to think through the implications of all the paperwork that was initiated. In the Devons study, where the urgency was evident to all, the lower ranking specialists made necessary decisions at the appropriate times, but thereby usurped the authority of political leaders. In the Pressman–Wildavsky study the forecasts of disaster spurred attempts to shortcut the normal procedures.

A comparison of the generalizations from the cases of Part II with those from the cases summarized in this chapter indicates some differences in emphasis, most of which are readily attributable to the differences in the processes by which the two sets of cases were selected. The cases in this chapter, for example, did not include any instances of corruption, although one could remedy that deficiency quite readily by searching the backfiles of any good newspaper. The greater emphasis in the GAO cases on technical difficulty and on the creation of incentives for the private sector to act inefficiently probably stems from the stress placed by the GAO on meeting the objectives of the legislation, rather than the quality of the bureaucratic process, which more detailed analyses of agency behavior are likely to emphasize. It should also be noted that the development of cases in Part II included an opportunity for the agency to rebut charges of inefficiency or ineptitude, which they generally did by stressing the difficulty of the task.

Although a few of the minor themes found in the GAO cases cannot be discerned in the scholarly studies, all but one of the problems that the latter group includes are found also in the GAO studies. The one exception is the discrepancy between political and technical lead time noted by Devons, but that is closely related to the floundering of low-level bureaucrats in the cases where top-level decisions were delayed.

More noteworthy than the differences in the two sets of observations are the great similarities. In particular, the coordination problem dominates both sets of cases. This lends some support to the implication of the theoretical analysis that controlling resources in the absence of organized markets is an extremely cumbersome process. The other major common themes include the cumulation of delays (especially where coordination or numerous clearances are required), the difficulty of transmitting information upward through the hierarchy, and the asymmetry in the force with which narrowly defined special interests are represented relative to the more diffused interests of taxpayers and consumers in general. The substantial areas of overlap in the problems found in the two sets of cases lend support to the belief that the cases studied, although not a random sample in the statistical sense, are not a bizarre collection either. The difficulties encountered are broadly representative of the sorts of problems that can be expected in the implementation of public programs.

CHAPTER 19

Failure in Theory and in Practice

The hypotheses collected in Part I of this volume were derived from a variety of sources—theoretical, speculative, anecdotal, and empirical. They can certainly not be tested in any formal way by the use of the cases in Part II and especially not with the other studies mentioned in Chapter 18, since those studies inspired a number of the hypotheses. Nevertheless, it seems useful to compare the hypotheses of Part I with the generalizations from the case studies to see whether both are pointing in the same direction and have roughly similar coverage of potential problems.

Even a cursory examination of the hypotheses, however, is enough to show that many are too subtle to be examined at all in the condensed cases in this study. Even an informal examination, to say nothing of a formal test, of some would require the use of sophisticated psychological and sociological instruments in controlled settings. It remains generally true, however, that the hypotheses do not conflict with the generalizations from the cases. That observation is encouraging, but it should not lead to much smugness on the part of the many developers of the theory because even the mutually contradictory hypotheses seem to have some support from the cases. The implication, of course, is not that logic has been overturned, but rather that many of the hypotheses should be restated to limit their intended applicability to a narrower range of circumstances. The numerous forms of failure have a variety of causes.

Producing some order from the bewildering array of special situations is a worthy objective toward which only the most rudimentary beginnings can be made here.

The hypotheses were listed in Part I as they evolved from the review of the literature with the inevitable overlaps, duplication, and unevenness of coverage. This chapter, by contrast, discusses the major themes that ran through the analysis of circumstances that might be expected to lead to bureaucratic failure. Each major theme is accompanied by the numbers of the hypotheses that bear upon it, which provide a guide to the relevant discussion in Part I.

INFORMATION TRANSMISSION
(HYPOTHESES 2, 9, 19, 20, 21, 22, 23, 24, 25, 26, AND 31)

Information problems range from static in radio signals to the inability of a reader to understand what the writer of particular words wanted him to understand. The cases reviewed here did not provide any indication that the problems addressed by communications engineering were a serious difficulty. Except for extraordinary circumstances (such as natural disasters or wars), it appears that the technical problems of transmitting an adequate quantity and quality of information have been solved. This does not mean that the other aspects of communication (those that involve people) have been solved. Several characteristics of cases, discussed in Chapter 17, involve difficulties in communication, although these particular words were not used as a heading. For example, the characteristic of "ambiguous goals" means that disagreement exists on what the agency is trying to do. This could easily be described as an information problem in the broad sense. Similarly, the roots of the failures that involve "incompatibility of task" with a particular agency may very well lie in the difficulties of communicating unfamiliar kinds of information. The failures brought on by "regional variations" in administration are certainly related to communication. It thus appears that the theoretical focus on the transmission of information is appropriate, as long as the concern is with the broader aspects of the topic, rather than the engineering of adequate channel capacity.

MEASUREMENT OF OUTPUT
(HYPOTHESES 7, 11, 16, AND 27)

Although theory implies that difficulties in measuring output predispose the production of public goods to inefficiency, the evidence from the cases does not provide much direct support for this proposition. This superficial observation, however, is subject to three qualifications. In the first place, it is possible that numerous administrative problems could be remedied quite easily if final output could be measured. Thus what shows up as an "administrative deficiency" or "regional variation" or (especially) "displacement of goals" could actually be attributed to the inability of top management to measure output directly. It may also be that the GAO and other investigators have not detected the departures from legislative intent in the instances where output is difficult to measure. At the very least, inefficiency in the production of unmeasurable output requires more detailed study to identify than does a general breakdown of bureaucratic routine. Finally, if the head of the bureau wants to maintain control of its activities, he will propose new activities that are easy to implement. Since measurement of public goods tends to be difficult, the activities of the agency will drift away from provision of public goods to the activities that can be measured and controlled more easily. This incremental drift away from publicness did occur in the fisheries case.

TECHNICAL DIFFICULTY
(HYPOTHESES 5, 33, 39, 40, AND 63)

Measurability of output is one feature determining the degree of technical difficulty of the activity, but, of course, there are many others. Both theory and observation agree that technical difficulty of the task is often associated with failure. Programs that require planning far ahead seem to create special difficulties in the public sector, although the difficulties are worse in the political sphere than in the bureaucratic. Organization theory suggests that the combination of uncertainty in the environment with complexity of the task would also create particular difficulties. FEA and LEAA provide examples of this. Another type of technical difficulty was presented by the HUD case, where low-level employees had to make numerous unique decisions.

COORDINATION
(HYPOTHESES 28, 32, 35, 36, AND 61)

Theory and practice also agree on the difficulty of effectuating coordination of related activities. The cases certainly provide ample evidence of the problems of coordinating related government activities. It is particularly ironic that government intervention in the economy is often sought for the purpose of coordination and planning, which are among the tasks at which the government is least effective.

EXTERNALITIES (HYPOTHESIS 65)

Externalities could be subsumed under the coordination heading, but the emphasis here is on the agency's disregard of costs imposed on other agencies or individuals. This problem has received less attention in connection with the public sector than it has with regard to the private sector. The cases reviewed here did not provide any direct evidence of one agency imposing external costs on others, largely because agencies refused to comply with costly requests from other agencies. Either legal or technical compulsion is necessary before one agency can inflict costs on another.

POLITICAL PROBLEMS (HYPOTHESES 14, 43, 44, 46, 47, 49, 50, 53, 59, 60, AND 64)

Theory suggests that problems occurring in the political environment of a program may result in difficulties for program administration, including utter failure. The cases provide illustrations of the adverse effects of the political pressure to spend or to create the appearance of action, pressure to spread benefits widely among congressional districts, the threat that the program will be terminated, and the inability of political leaders to agree about the objectives of the program. The picture of the political difficulties that emerges from the cases is not much different from that sketched in the theory, although the cases place more emphasis on vacillation, indecision, and frantic haste to make up for lost time, whereas the theory stresses conflict among unified and decisive pressure groups. The two are not necessarily contradictory, since politicians, as well as bureaucrats, may avoid making decisions until the relative strengths of the pressure groups are apparent. Nevertheless, the cases probably capture more realistically the groping and confusion than does the notion of monolithic pressure groups who comprehend the costs and benefits to them from every policy proposal.

The hypotheses suggested that programs are more likely to succeed if they receive the direct attention of either the public or the top-level political leadership. A second theme is that failure is more likely when the agency confronts serious disagreements among interest groups or the political leadership. If the dissidents can exit from the government service (Hypothesis 60), these disagreements are not as serious as they are when the service is compulsory. This is a special case of Hypothesis 49, that the imposition of heavy costs on an identifiable group is likely to lead to failure. When the group bearing the costs consists of the inhabitants of a particular geographic area (Hypothesis 64) its objections have particular force in the political system of the United States. Hypothesis 59, that failure is more likely when costs are widely diffused, appears to contradict Hypothesis 49. The two can be reconciled, however, by noting that the small group that bears heavy costs may try to block a program by exerting political pressure to prevent the agency from carrying out the program. On the other hand, when the costs of failure by the agency are widely diffused, the failure may not stir up any public outcry. Finally, Hypothesis 47 notes that leaving policy decisions to the agency may be conducive to failure. Delegation of policy making may reflect either inattention or disagreement by politicians. The agency will be inclined to vacillate and evade issues, rather than stirring up a direct confrontation.

RAPID CHANGE IN ENVIRONMENT OR TASK
(HYPOTHESES 8, 18, AND 34)

If the conditions that an agency faces change rapidly, it will find success more difficult to attain. Although this proposition from the theory seems unassailable, the only example among the cases is the FEA, where the embargo ended before the enforcement machinery was in place. The cases provide ample confirmation of the popular wisdom regarding the long delays in implementing or changing bureaucratic action that are the basis for the difficulty in dealing with change.

INTERNAL CONTROLS OF BUREAUCRATS
(HYPOTHESES 3, 4, 10, 12, 48, 66, 67, 68, 69, 70, AND 75)

Several hypotheses touch on the central problem of the conflicting loyalties of the bureaucrat: He may follow the orders of his superior; he may do what seems to him to be in the interests of his agency or of the public; or he may conform to the standards of his profession. The extent to which these objectives can be made consistent with achieving the purposes of the legislation is the central question in designing efficient organizations. Several of the cases provided illustrations of this problem, especially in connection with programs that required changes in the professional roles of employees. In the summary of characteristics, this is listed as "incompatibility of task." The more dramatic instances of conflict between hierarchical orders and morality or patriotism were not present in these cases.

QUALITY OF PERSONNEL
(HYPOTHESES 28, 29, 71, AND 72)

Incompetence of personnel relative to the task was a problem in several cases. The hypotheses, however, included a more elaborate structure of propositions about hiring standards, professionalism, and turnover that could not be examined. One question is why the quality of personnel might be expected to vary among agencies for positions of the same pay level. The other basic theme is the deleterious effect of ambition on the functioning of bureaucracy, which implies that the agencies that attract the ambitious will be most likely to fail. This may have been a contributing element to the vacillation and confusion at the very top levels of the agencies that attracted presidential attention.

INDEPENDENCE OF AGENCY
(HYPOTHESES 1, 45, AND 52)

An agency may be financially or organizationally independent. Financial independence includes two separate aspects: (a) generation of revenues through sales of products or services and (b) exemption from audit by the legislature and its agencies. At the federal level in the United States, the latter is rare or nonexistent. Three of the cases, however, involved a significant degree of financing of agency activities from revenues generated by sale of services. In addition, the Vocational Education case, as an example of revenue sharing, involved very similar problems in that the state bureaucrats were supported by the federal government but were accountable to the state legislatures. The cases did not include examples of extreme organizational independence (e.g., independent commissions or self-governing public universities) that is designed to limit hierarchical control.

MISCELLANEOUS AGENCY CHARACTERISTICS
(HYPOTHESES 6, 13, 15, 17, 30, 37, 41, 73, AND 74)

A number of hypotheses related failure to such characteristics of the agency as age, rate of growth, size, complexity of organization, and diversity of tasks. The cases did not provide an opportunity to test any of these. This is particularly unfortunate because organizational structure is the easiest variable to change, but the theoretical and empirical justification for reorganization is woefully thin.

ORIGIN OF PROGRAM (HYPOTHESES 42 AND 51)

The basic hypotheses regarding the origin of the program held that failure was more likely in programs initiated late in the legislative process or high in the administrative hierarchy. The former would hold because of the poor quality of hasty legislation, whereas the latter was premised on the inattention to implementation problems in programs designed primarily for political impact. Several of the cases (notably including HUD, Fisheries, AID, and LEAA) fell into these categories. The characteristics that are most closely related to such unfortunate origins are oversimplification of the law and haste to spend in order to create the appearance of progress.

CORRUPTING STRUCTURE
(HYPOTHESES 54, 55, 56, 57, AND 58)

Both the hypotheses and the cases agree that some programs are structured in such a way as to be conducive to corruption. This may be a matter of the details of the arrangements (e.g., whether valuable privileges are given away or auctioned off) or it may be inherent in the activity (e.g., inspection of private facilities for violations that are expensive to correct).

ERRONEOUS ANALYSIS AND IGNORANCE
(HYPOTHESIS 62)

Although the mechanism by which erroneous analysis and ignorance could be expected to lead to failure is obvious, the sources of such error are less so. The development of the hypotheses suggested that error and ignorance, in excess of the state prevailing among educated people generally, are most likely where political and ideological considerations interfere with observation and analysis. The egregious problems of error and ignorance appear to characterize the political level of government, rather than the bureaucratic.

Although most of the hypotheses found some reflection in the cases, it is also worth asking whether they provided an adequate explanation of the problems encountered, and especially, whether they could be used to forecast failure at the moment the law is passed. The discrepancies between the hypotheses and the cases involved some differences in emphasis, as well as some specific items that, although not inconsistent with the theoretical exposition, were also not given any prominence by it. The poor quality of the underlying legislation is the most significant difference in emphasis. Whereas the hypotheses did suggest that laws could be poorly written, the hasty, careless, and irresponsible lawmaking exemplified by HUD, FEA, and AID remains startling to the politically naive. Similarly, the lapses in routine bureaucratic skills, such as keeping records and moving papers on time, were more consistent with the anecdotal view of bureaucracy than the theoretical. The specific items that should be included in a check list of problems include the increased difficulty in coordination and administration introduced by regional offices and the reactions of bureaucrats to the threat of termination. The implications of this somewhat lugubrious collection of problems for the role of government must be examined in the next chapter.

CHAPTER 20

Bureaucratic Failure, Market Failure, and the Role of Government

The preceding chapters have stressed the failures of government, but the call for government action results from dissatisfaction with the results of the market process. Sometimes the dissatisfaction is poorly founded, reflecting frustration with the inevitable toils and troubles visited on mankind, but at other times it is grounded in a correct perception of the imperfections from which markets may suffer. A balanced view of the situation, however, requires not just a recital of the departures of governments or markets from theoretical perfection, but rather an analysis of the situations where (allowing for the imperfections of both governments and markets) either more or less government action would improve human welfare. That task is too large to complete here, but this chapter will provide a start.

THE ROLE OF GOVERNMENT IN A MARKET ECONOMY

Microeconomic theory has two basic purposes: First, to show that under conditions of perfect competition markets allocate resources with perfect efficiency; and, second, to show that when the conditions of perfect competition are not met one can imagine a more efficient allocation of resources than that provided by the market. Since the first task has been so well done for such a long time, it is not surprising that the efforts of theorists have been devoted primarily to analyzing the imperfections. The past decade has seen increasing concern with another task; that is, devising institutional arrangements that would actually move the economy closer to the perfect efficiency that one can imagine. Most of the theoretical work has been limited to rather abstract remarks about using taxes and subsidies to correct market prices, however.

What is required now is some form of cost–benefit analysis of government intervention. In the absence of a well-developed understanding of government behavior, however, it is not possible to carry out that cost–benefit analysis in advance of trying the intervention. Since the failed experiments of government are rarely discontinued, studies of failure are of little use unless they include generalizations for contemplated programs. Such generalizations are, implicitly or explicitly, based on a theory of government behavior, which is not available in a widely accepted form. Policy analysis, thus, provides us with (a) studies of particular cases, (b) controversial attempts to predict the results of future programs on the basis of partially relevant experience, and (c) a series of assertions, fairly plausible at the extremes but becoming intensely controversial in the middle range, about the appropriate functions and interventions of government. For example, the externalities inflicted by my choice of a necktie are too trivial to become a concern of government, whereas the quantity and quality of effluent that your plant dumps in the river are matters of legitimate public concern. But what about the quality of the medicine that your plant manufactures (currently regulated) or the frequency with which I scrape peeling paint from my house (regulated in the suburb in which I live) or the adequacy of my financial provision for sickness (which it is proposed that the federal government regulate)? One can analyze the ways in which the market fails to allocate resources perfectly in all these areas, but in the absence of detailed knowledge of government behavior the argument about whether government regulation is an improvement rests more on political philosophy, prejudice, and cliches than on anything very convincing to the uncommitted.

Accordingly, although this section draws together the analyses of market failure to come up with some indication of the types of activities in which one can imagine a better solution than that provided by the market, these must be combined with the far less complete and rigorous analysis of political failure, as well as the insights about bureaucratic failure collected earlier, to see whether the failures of markets can be corrected by governments.

The economic theory of public expenditure incorporates several of the cases of market failure.[1] The basic question asked by the theory is as follows: Is there some set of goods such that, although the individual consumer values them as he values private goods, the private market will not supply them, or will supply an inadequate quantity? Inadequate quantity has a specific meaning; that is, marginal social benefit exceeds marginal social cost, so the welfare of society as a whole could be improved by diverting resources from other uses to supply more of the good in question. Social benefit and social cost are typically defined as the (weighted) sums of individual benefits and costs. If a set of goods can be found that is not provided adequately by private markets, then government may have a role to play even in an economy that is devoted solely to satisfying individual preferences. To summarize the results of a long and convoluted theoretical discussion, it does turn out that the market will supply inadequate quantities of certain types of goods. If such public goods are to be supplied in sufficient quantity, they must be supplied collectively, and this usually is taken to mean by a *government*, that is, an organization with the power to tax all occupants of a particular area in order to obtain resources to supply collective goods.[2]

Public goods are defined by economic theory; the term is not a description of what governments do. Some public goods are not provided by government and some of the goods that governments provide are not public. For the moment, however, the discussion will be restricted to public goods provided by government. It is possible to identify a few special characteristics of goods that put them in the public category. The first of these is *jointness of supply*. At the extreme, this means that if a good is available to one person, exactly the same units of that good can be entirely available to another person at no additional cost. The traditional examples are national defense and navigation aids; the army defends a certain territory, but the addition of another citizen to that same territory does not increase the difficulty of the army's task, nor does it reduce the quality of service offered to others. Similarly, the

[1]The early public goods literature was reviewed by Richard A. Musgrave in *The Theory of Public Finance: A Study in Political Economy* (New York: McGraw-Hill, 1959), pp. 61–89. Musgrave was largely responsible for introducing these concepts into the American literature. A good start on the mass of more recent literature is John G. Head, *Public Goods and Public Welfare* (Durham, North Carolina: Duke University Press, 1974).

[2]Mancur Olson, *The Logic of Collective Action: Public Goods and the Theory of Groups* (Cambridge: Harvard University Press, 1965), discusses provision of collective goods by private groups.

lighthouse that shines for your ship can guide my ship at no additional cost. It has been widely recognized that the category of pure public goods in this (Samuelsonian) sense is extremely limited. As additional consumers of a service are added, costs may go up or quality may deteriorate. The essential point turns out to be a rather more traditional one from economic theory; that is, the cost of providing a constant level of service to an additional consumer is less than the average cost per consumer.

Several aspects of this require emphasis. The first is that the definition refers only to the cost of additional consumers, whereas average and marginal costs are ordinarily defined in terms of levels of output. The second is that the territory involved is assumed to remain constant. Finally, the quality of service is assumed to be maintained at a constant level. Thus it may cost more to defend a larger territory or to improve the quality and quantity of defense (quantity and quality are often difficult to distinguish). It remains true, however, that additional people can be born, or move, into a country without necessitating more expenditures to maintain the same quantity and quality of defense. Frequently governments provide goods that do not meet the stringent criterion of having the cost of serving another person equal to zero. Parks and highways may become crowded so that quality deteriorates, or costs or service go up. If quality can be kept constant at a cost per additional person lower than the average cost per person (as may be true in a great research library, for example), then the good still qualifies as a public good under this definition.

A completely separate aspect of publicness is that exclusion of nonpayers is too expensive to be considered feasible. If a person refuses to pay for a movie ticket, he is excluded from the theater. If he refuses to pay for the fireworks display, he can probably still see it. Exclusion of nonpayers is significant not only for fairness, but to generate information about which goods people prefer and in what quantity. If the nonpayer can be excluded from consuming the good, he reveals his true preference when he chooses to go without rather than pay. If someone cannot be excluded from enjoying the good, he may be tempted not to pay. (In very small or cohesive groups various social pressures may prevent such behavior. They do not work well in anonymous national markets.) The nonexclusion (or free rider) characteristic applies to national defense, just as the jointness-of-supply characteristic does. The lighthouse, however, could probably be equipped with a device to turn off the light for ships that refused to pay a share of the cost. Such a device would be easier to build now than it would have been century ago—before the development of modern communications techniques. Thus feasibility of exclusion depends on technology and on economics. Although one could contrive to turn off the beacon for the nonpaying ship, it would not be efficient because the cost of leaving the light on all the time is negligible. It would, however, be efficient to charge tolls on city streets, if it could be done cheaply and without disrupting traffic (by some metering device built into the car, for example), because each additional car on a city street at rush hour imposes an appreciable delay on all other cars, which sums to a very heavy cost. It has been traditional to regard the exclusion of nonpayers from city streets as economically infeasible, but that may well cease to be true as technology develops.

Although jointness and nonexcludability are usually cited as the basic characteristics of public goods, compulsion has been mentioned as a third possible criterion.[3] The distinction can be made between goods that a free rider can enjoy if he so chooses and goods that everyone is compelled to consume—like them or not. National defense has both those characteristics; city streets are available to every motorist, but no one is compelled to drive on them; the sound of the fireworks display is compulsory, people can avert their eyes but not their ears. The distinction between a compulsory good and a negative externality depends on whether you like what you are forced to take. Generally, economics assumes free disposal of excess quantities. Even if perfume is free, one need not open the bottle (or accept another free sample) when one tires of the scent. If one lives in Hershey, Pennsylvania, however, even the good smell of chocolate can cloy; it becomes a negative externality because the individual is compelled to consume more than he would choose at a price of zero. When goods are compulsory because of technology, the public often demands government action. Governments often legislate compulsion when it is not imposed by technology, however, which is an entirely separate matter.

With the introduction of compulsory goods, the definitions become less clear. Governments have taken on a wide range of functions that fit only uneasily within the public-goods framework. These include attempting to stabilize the economy by monetary, fiscal, or incomes policy; redistributing income by taxes and transfers of money or goods; establishing the framework of laws and courts to permit private transactions; maintaining competition in the private sector; and regulating

[3]John G. Head, "Public Goods: The Polar Case," chapter 1 of *Modern Fiscal Issues. Essays in Honor of Carl S. Shoup*, ed. Richard M. Bird and John G. Head. (Toronto: University of Toronto Press, 1972).

transactions in the private sector. These functions require some government expenditure, but their basic importance lies in their impact on the private sector. The impact on the government budget does not measure the cost. In addition to the government spending and the private spending to comply, an important component of the total cost of a compulsory activity is the direct reduction in the welfare of those citizens who do not like it.

A great many goods that are sold in the market would decrease the utility of many people if consumption were compulsory, but since people can ordinarily choose what they wish to consume, that is rarely a problem. The music that I dislike does not bother me when it is available free in the radio frequency spectrum, but it does bother me when it is highly amplified sound that I cannot control. Differing appraisals of the identical commodity are common and do create problems whenever consumption is compulsory. The scent of flowers is visited on the flower lover and the hay-fevered, alike.

It is often assumed that some of the costs of an ignorant electorate and some of the benefits of a literate labor force are imposed on all other citizens and consumers. The technical compulsion provides part of the justification for the legal compulsion to consume education. This could take the form of compelling the attendance of all children in the public school system, but in the United States it does not. The device of permitting private firms and groups to compete with the tax-supported public service has been used for schools, as well as recreational facilities, libraries, and the employment service.

Permitting people to substitute private for public services allows greater satisfaction of diverse preferences as well as lower public spending. If everyone is compelled to consume the tax-supported service (and it is not a pure Samuelsonian public good in the sense that the marginal cost of another client equals zero) the total public cost of that level of service will be higher than it would be if some people chose a private substitute. In the long run, however, public support via the tax mechanism provides less generously for a service than does private support.[4] A mixed system may end up with a higher tax cost and higher level of services if the well-supported private sector sets a standard to which the public activities must measure up. Compulsory service also inflicts a cost on the bureaucrats supplying that service. Hirschman analyzed the responses of unhappy customers: one possibility is to exit

[4]See James M. Buchanan's illuminating analysis of the British experience, "The Inconsistencies of the National Health Service," chapter 3 of *Theory of Public Choice: Political Applications of Economics*, ed. Buchanan and Robert D. Tollison (Ann Arbor: The University of Michigan Press, 1972).

from the firm; that is, to switch to a different supplier. Another possibility is to voice protest in various ways.[5] If the customer is forbidden to exit to a private supplier, he must voice his protest about the quality of the government service through the political mechanism. This can cause much more difficulty for the bureaucrat than the quiet departure of some of his clientele, particularly if those who voice their protest are articulate and skillful in the use of political channels.

The school system in the United States is set up in such a way as to weaken protest. Those who feel very strongly about the quality of schooling and can afford private schools exit from the public system. The more affluent tend to be the ones with the time and contacts to make themselves heard. Thus the most effective protest is drained off. If public schools were compulsory, they would be subject to more severe criticism. If, on the other hand, the U.S. were to switch to a voucher system, the cost of exit would be reduced enough to mute all criticism. The public schools, if they continued to exist, would react to the direct pressure of loss of massive numbers of students in order to survive, but it seems likely that voucher payments as a proportion of total tuition would gradually decrease. Bureaucratic failure is most likely to be observed where easy exit has drained off the potential opposition of the articulate and energetic.

Governments are often urged to take on a variety of other functions where the issue is not jointness, excludability, or compulsion, but rather the quantity and quality of information available to the individual. Yet the remedies generally do not stop at providing more information (e.g., each drug label might be required to provide space for the remarks of the Food and Drug Administration, which, however, would not have the power to prevent sales or use). Instead, the agency is given the power actually to make decisions that involve balancing a number of risks, costs, and pleasures. Such decisions cannot be made *scientifically* since the *correct* decision depends on the preferences of the individual consumer. The agency with the responsibility for weighing such intangible factors might sometimes allow political considerations, or even the welfare of individuals within the agency, to influence its decisions.

Even if one assumes the benevolence of the bureaucrats, however, it is still necessary to ask whether large organizations can deal well with large amounts of information and whether agencies can administer complex programs. The first question was considered on a theoretical level by Arrow, with conclusions similar to those of Tullock; that is, as

[5]Albert O. Hirschman, *Exit, Voice, and Loyalty: Responses to Decline in Firms, Organizations, and States* (Cambridge: Harvard University Press, 1970), esp. pp. 44–45.

the volume of information collected at the lower ranks is transmitted upward, the qualitative aspects tend to be lost and the excessive quantity is filtered by accepting only what agrees with the perceptions held by those at higher levels.[6] This agrees with Gold's analysis of the modification of technical appraisals by considerations of political feasibility (p. 256).

Another broad area in which the appropriateness of market decisions has been questioned is the choice between consumption and investment.[7] Several questions can be raised: (a) Do people on average save enough to give future generations an adequate stock of capital? (b) How many individuals fail to save enough for their own old age? (c) Can governments increase the overall rate of capital accumulation? (d) Can governments improve the choice of particular investments to be undertaken? The first question has been refined and reexamined so often that little comment is necessary here. Individuals may save in order to be reasonably sure of a comfortable old age, despite uncertainty about the length of life and the costs they will encounter. They may also accumulate capital in order to make their own descendants or favorite charities better off. In addition, they may want to hold capital until death simply for the power that it affords. Whether these varied motives induce individuals to save enough for future generations depends on what is meant by "enough." As long as per capita real income is rising, theory offers no standard, whatsoever, concerning this.[8] If many individuals are improvident, despite a sufficient general rate of saving, the appropriate policy would appear to be the compulsory purchase of annuities, which is one aspect of the U.S. Social Security program.

The question of whether governments can increase the rate of savings is an empirical one. The answer is no. The federal government in the United States has rarely consumed less than its income in recent years. The fact that the national debt increases more rapidly than productive investments of the government shows this. State and local governments save in some years, but they are more profligate than the citizens from whom taxes are extracted.

This leaves the question of whether the government can improve the allocation of investment. This is the point to which economists have

---

[6]Kenneth J. Arrow, *The Limits of Organization*, The Fels Lectures in Public Policy Analysis (New York: W. W. Norton, 1974), esp. pp. 54, 75.

[7]The literature on this topic is vast, permeating much of the writing on economic development and on cost–benefit analysis. For an introduction see William J. Baumol, "On the Discount Rate For Public Projects," Chapter 6 of *Public Expenditures and Policy Analysis,* ed. Robert H. Haveman and Julius Margolis (Chicago: Rand McNally, 2nd edition, 1977).

[8]Even if income per capita is declining, standard theory cannot tell us that we are saving too little. Benevolent sentiments suggest that we should leave our descendants better off than we now are; but do we feel obliged to make them *much* richer?

devoted the most attention in analyzing rates of return to various investments, as well as the rules and decision processes for these investments. Particular investment decisions by the federal government have been made quite poorly. Low rates of return have often been accepted, even when better projects were available. Benefits have been exaggerated.[9] In effect, investments have been used as expensive devices for changing the income distribution in ways that conform with political imperatives, rather than ethical standards.[10] If politicians are trying to benefit particular groups, only by chance will returns for society as a whole be positive.[11] Nor are these results surprising, in view of (a) the short time-horizons of key decision makers; (b) the fact that most investments provide particular benefits to certain groups and areas, which makes them inherently politically charged and hence less amenable to analysis; and (c) the fact that key analysts and decision makers in the public sector owe their positions to bureaucratic skills and reward structures, which are not related to maximizing the returns from investments.[12] It thus seems highly unlikely that government is capable of increasing the aggregate amount of investment, or improving its allocation among uses. The technique of leaving resources in the hands of individuals to invest as they see fit will certainly provide better for future generations, which was the central message of Adam Smith two centuries ago.

UTILITY-REDUCING ACTIVITIES
OF GOVERNMENT

Legal or technical compulsion to consume a good may result in a direct reduction of individual welfare, but the extent of utility-reducing

[9]Robert H. Haveman, *The Economic Performance of Public Investments: An Ex Post Evaluation of Water Resource Investments* (Baltimore: The Johns Hopkins Press for Resources for the Future, 1972).

[10]For empirical studies of income redistribution by means of expenditure programs, see Burton A. Weisbrod, "Income Redistribution Effects and Benefit–Cost Analysis," pp. 177–222, and James T. Bonnen, "The Distribution of Benefits from Cotton Price Supports," pp. 223–254 of *Problems in Public Expenditure Analysis*, ed. Samuel B. Chase, Jr. (Washington: Brookings, 1968), Papers presented at a conference of experts held 15–16 Sept. 1966, and published in the *Studies of Government Finance* Series.

[11]D. L. Shapiro, "Can Public Investment Have a Positive Rate of Return?" *Journal of Political Economy*, (March–April 1973): 401.

[12]See, e.g., Graham T. Allison and Morton H. Halperin, "Bureaucratic Politics: A Paradigm and Some Policy Implications," pp. 40–79 in *Theory and Policy in International Relations*, ed. Raymond Tanter and Richard H. Ullman (Princeton: Princeton University Press, 1972); Richard N. Goodwin, *The American Condition* (Garden City, N.Y.: Doubleday, 1974), p. 255; Charles L. Schultze, *The Politics and Economics of Public Spending* (Washington: Brookings, 1968), pp. 85–86; and William A. Niskanen, Jr., *Bureaucracy and Representative Government* (Chicago: Aldine-Atherton, 1971), ch. 12.

activities of government is very difficult to estimate. Detailed analysis of programs is required to make the estimate because many activities that sound attractive have utility-reducing aspects. Any program supported from general tax revenue inflicts compulsory costs on taxpayers as a whole in order to benefit those who receive the services of the program. Traditional cost–benefit analysis tries to weigh the aggregate costs against the aggregate benefits, but encounters (among others) the difficulty that the program may be designed to benefit a particular group at the expense of the general public and, hence, that the benefits and costs are not supposed to be commensurable. Rather than trying to determine whether gross benefits exceed gross costs, therefore, the objective here will be the narrower one of trying to assess whether the gross benefits of the program were in fact positive. Even this limited objective involves highly subjective estimates and weighing of the gains of some people against the losses of others.

Despite these problems, I will venture an appraisal of the cases studied. The HUD 235 program, had it been well-administered, would have helped some poor people at the expense of general taxpayers. As it was actually administered, however, it is apparent that many of the recipients of service suffered a net reduction of welfare as a result of the program. Some ended up in worse housing and contracted large debts for overpriced and decrepit structures. If the group of intended recipients of benefits is drawn more widely to include the slum owners who sold decayed property at excessive prices, the program may have produced benefits for recipients. In that case, however, most citizens would probably consider the program a disservice to humanity, even apart from tax cost. The subsidy for repairs was a successful, albeit expensive, transfer program.

The fisheries program benefited those fishermen who received the loans at low interest rates. In the overcrowded fisheries, however, the benefit was offset by a cost to other fishermen in the form of reductions in the average catch. Even in those fisheries where the total catch did not decline, each person retained in the industry decreased the profits of others. The gross benefit was thus negative. The innovative activity that the agency was supposed to support was ignored in the loan program.

The pesticides program could have provided some benefits by alleviating the external costs of pesticides, if it had been well administered. Such regulation inevitably delays innovation, however, and the costs of that delay combined with the false assurance of safety and effectiveness make it seem doubtful that the agency produced any benefits during the period covered by this study.

The Agricultural Marketing Service is an interesting case because it provides an example of a form of government action often recommended by economists; namely, the noncoercive provision of information that will presumably assist individuals in making rational decisions. The evidence suggests, however, that consumers ignore the grade labels on fruits and vegetables. Packers often do not bother to print the grade information they are entitled to use. Furthermore, it seems doubtful that most consumers have any understanding of the qualities actually being graded. Although the grading system does have its uses within the channels of trade—uses for which firms are willing to pay—it is not clear that the consumer obtains any better information than he does from a brand name. In any event, the agency did not impose negative benefits on the public and by pushing the industry to improve quality it may have provided unmeasurable positive benefits.

An evaluation of Accelerated Public Works must be made on other bases, since the ostensible purpose of the program was to transfer funds to locations suffering from high unemployment. To the extent that the transfers were directed toward areas where unemployment was no worse than average, the whole point of the transfer mechanism was defeated. Many of the transfers, of course, did go to needy communities, but the study indicated the force of the contrary political and bureaucratic pressures.

The pilot cities program of LEAA requires a similar appraisal because the research component was lost in the confusion, leaving transfers to particular cities as the only useful function. Since the pilot cities were not selected on the basis of need, however, it is not clear that the program had any benefits for taxpayers in general. The localities did benefit from some of the projects that were funded, and perhaps even from the development of local expertise, but in view of the staff time wasted by the high-level confusion, this was an expensive transfer program.

The program by NARS to simplify paperwork is the easiest to evaluate. It imposed no costs aside from the budgetary ones and produced no benefits whatsoever. The FEA retail compliance effort also delivered no output during most of its existence, but the costs of regulation were very high, indeed, during the brief period when the retail ceilings were binding. At the producer and refinery level the ceilings did constrain some selling prices for years after their imposition, with obvious damage to the economy. Although the major problems have been political, rather than bureaucratic, the chaotic administration of the controls imposed additional costs by absorbing the time of industry executives. The controls on crude-oil prices illustrated one of the ironies of regulation: If enforcement had been better, damage to the economy would have been greater, but laxity of administration that aided the economy also served the thoroughly immoral purpose of rewarding those who broke the law.

The corrupt OE program may have delivered something. Those seeking grants received some funds, even after the kickback. Whether their research produced anything for their communities cannot be answered from the evidence at hand. Although it is tempting to consider the corruption of the contracting process as a completely separate issue from the effectiveness of the contracted research, the two may not be independent. If government funds go to those who are willing to participate in illegal or unethical activities, the resulting research may well be meretricious.

Analysis of the vocational education case is also complex. Many students undoubtedly benefit from vocational education, but the argument that a strong national interest justifies the special funding seems quite strained. By insulating the vocational schools from local control, the funding method undoubtedly decreases the public accountability of the schools, as well as increasing administrative expenses. The funding mechanism also makes coordination of facilities and planning essentially impossible.

The AID program is a pure public good, from the viewpoint of the U.S. citizen. When AID housing funds subsidized mortgages for the relatively rich in foreign countries, my welfare suffered. If this reaction were general, the program could be said to have inflicted negative benefits. This aspect of the program was not a bureaucratic failure, however, since it was not contrary to the legislation. As the program has evolved, with the prodding of the bureaucracy, it has also become less distasteful. Whether it actually produces any positive benefits for U.S. taxpayers is a question that requires a far subtler analysis.

This brief survey suggests a few tentative generalizations about utility-reducing activities:

1. Such activities are most common when the government is dealing with complex issues having numerous interrelationships that are not obvious to the average voter or politician. The baneful effects of rent control and rationing, for example, are still not widely understood. Interventions in certain complex areas of social welfare and foreign affairs are also probably counterproductive.
2. Regulatory activities are more likely to be utility reducing than are either the directly exhaustive uses of resources by the government or transfers. The reason for this is that regulation generally involves some manipulation of parts of complex processes, whereas

other government activities are more strictly limited to the readily visible impacts.

3. Some government activities produce no outputs, either positive or negative. Their existence may raise the costs of other agencies, but basically they just absorb resources. This is most likely where there is no contact with the public, so no one has the incentive to complain.

4. Regulatory agencies tend to drift toward ineffectuality; that is, toward producing no changes in the behavior of the regulated. By being ineffectual, the agency avoids reducing the utility of anyone who might complain.

5. When benefits are conveyed to small groups by any method other than transfer, they are likely to be utility reducing. It is cheaper to give someone $100,000 than to have him build an unnecessary building in order to earn a profit of $100,000. It is even worse for the public as a whole to give him some monopoly privilege that permits him to extract an extra $100,000 via the marketplace.

6. Programs that are justified as redistributive may be captured by the wrong group and hence become utility reducing.

7. A very common utility-reducing activity of government is providing false assurance to the public that quality and safety are being controlled by the government agency.

THE DESIGN OF INCENTIVE SYSTEMS

Whereas some of the utility-reducing activities of government are required by the legislation, others are products of bureaucratic implementation and, hence, could presumably be eliminated by the careful design of incentive systems. Incentive systems in small organizations can be constructed by those at the top of the hierarchy, but in an organization as large as the federal government the authority to construct the incentive systems must be delegated to lower levels of the hierarchy.

This raises a number of problems.[13] Suppose that someone as intelligent and perceptive as you or I were to be assigned the task of constructing a proper incentive system (with associated measures of

---

[13]Charles L. Schultze discusses the role of incentives, but mainly from the view of the benevolent and omniscient social planner arranging rewards so the greedy will do good by doing well. See "The Role of Incentives, Penalties, and Rewards in Attaining Effective Policy," chapter 6 of *Public Expenditures and Policy Analysis*, ed. by Robert H. Haveman and Julius Margolis (Chicago: Markham Publ. Co., first ed., 1970).

output) for the Employment Service. That analyst would be confronted immediately with some broad policy questions that should have been (but never will be) resolved at the political level, including whether the ultimate goal is to speed economic growth by helping firms to locate suitable employees, to help the unemployed obtain the best possible jobs, to administer the unemployment compensation system, to give special assistance to the most disadvantaged members of the labor force or to specified minority groups, or some combination of these and others. Even if the broad goals could be agreed on, the analyst would still face a variety of questions that are mainly technical, but too complex to answer with the knowledge we now have.

Is it, for example, more useful to offer a large-scale service to place disadvantaged individuals on short-term job assignments, or would those resources be better spent in teaching people how labor markets work so that they can find temporary jobs on their own? Is it more productive to spend a lot of time with an applicant who has a poor chance of success, or a smaller amount of time with each of a larger number of more promising job seekers? Is an hour spent on job development more productive than an hour spent on placement? Some of the questions at this level will eventually yield to sufficiently imaginative and painstaking analyses, but decisions often cannot wait for the analysis. Answering these questions is just the first step toward devising the incentive schemes for employees to follow.

Another problem is measuring performance in particular tasks: One can assign a certain number of points for each job developed, or alternatively require each employee to devote a certain amount of time to the task, but one cannot be certain that time will be well spent, nor can one be sure that the numbers are not simply made up or otherwise doctored to comply with regulations or the incentive structure. Furthermore, some important aspects of the quality or quantity of performance will defy measurement entirely. Thus the incentive system will suck effort into the measurable activities, very likely leaving nonmeasured aspects performed worse than they would have been in the absence of any attempt to provide incentives.

These are the easy problems, however. The less tractable ones relate to finding the wise and perceptive analyst (assuming that you and I are unavailable), and the incentives for anyone to comply with the recommendations. In other words, the large organization must delegate to its lower ranks even the setting of goals and the rewarding of compliance. Even in those activities where measurement is possible, therefore, the behavior may not agree with the preferences of the top ranks of the hierarchy. Once a government has grown so large that the legislature can no longer specify in detail the structure of output measurements and incentives, it is no longer possible to have output-oriented rules and procedures even in those parts of the organization in which they seem appropriate. If such rules cannot be imposed from the top of the hierarchy, they do not serve the purpose of permitting the top level to control the output of the bottom without worrying about details of administration. If the knowledge to devise the measures and incentives reposes only at relatively low levels in the hierarchy, then control has already broken down.

The basic fallacy of conventional efforts to improve management in government, including cost–benefit analysis, program planning and budgeting, management by objective, and zero base budgeting, is the assumption that at each level in the hierarchy the superior (or his staff of analysts) has the knowledge and desire to train his subordinates to jump through the socially correct hoops. If that assumption were correct at each level, there would be no need for the managerial reforms being proposed. Even when the primary objectives of the agency are easy to understand and communicate, the interrelationships with other agencies and objectives are not. A particular agency may be charged with aiding the rehabilitation of urban housing, but that leaves unanswered myriads of questions regarding its decisions that influence the fiscal strength of central cities compared with suburbs, the racial mix of neighborhoods, and the rate at which people consume energy. Likewise, the postman knows what kind of speedy, accurate, and courteous service postal patrons prefer, but should he also offer information to the F.B.I.?

Olson suggested that experiments be conducted in selling government output, since even nonmeasurable services can be evaluated by individuals in free markets, as long as exclusion of nonpayers is possible.[14] Although such experiments would be useful in obtaining information about the demand for government activities, they would encounter exactly the sorts of difficulties discussed above. It is difficult to see how the incentives to conduct such studies correctly could be delegated to the low ranks in the hierarchy where the work would have to be done. The experiments would probably have to be conducted by someone outside the agency, whereas only the agency would be in a position to generate the cost data that would also be necessary. The cost data could, in most cases, be generated only at a very low level in the hierarchy because of

[14]Mancur Olson, "Evaluating Performance in the Public Sector," pp. 355–409 in *The Measurement of Economic and Social Performance*, ed. by Milton Moss (New York: Distributed by Columbia University Press for the National Bureau of Economic Research, 1973), NBER Studies in Income and Wealth No. 38.

the intermingling of various functions and the problems of quality variation.

All this suggests that it is only in activities in which the federal government actually competes in the market place that output-oriented measures can be of much use. This is not a very broad range of functions, nor does it include the traditional sorts of public goods. The actual situation, moreover, is still bleaker than this cursory appraisal would suggest. For even when the government is in direct competition with a private firm, the terms of the competition are generally such that no judgment of superior efficiency can be derived by observing that the government agency persists, while its rivals expire or struggle. It is possible to imagine some cases in which the federal agency received no subsidies, special privileges, or captive customers. In this case, the comparison would be fair, but the enterprise could hardly be producing a public good.

THE SOCIAL EQUIVALENT OF BANKRUPTCY

Several of these themes can now be summarized by noting the importance of bankruptcy in the private sector, and the infrequency of the equivalent phenomenon in the public sector.[15] The probability that a new private firm will succeed and prosper is very small. The vast majority are closed or discontinued voluntarily or involuntarily. It is often noted that old bureaus rarely die. This observation is usually combined with the suggestion that many have outlived their usefulness. The task has been accomplished or the problem has disappeared, but the once relevant organization still potters on. This view may be correct, but the difference between *new* firms and *new* bureaus is far more significant. The new firm that embodies a new idea or product probably embodies an incomplete, partially ineffectual, or otherwise unacceptable idea. The literature on innovation is filled with false starts, failures, near misses, desperate revisions, and changes of management—as well as bankruptcy—before the consumers are convinced that the new idea is worth its cost.[16] During the period when bankruptcy threatens, the entrepreneur will frequently work inhumanly long hours to make the innovation satisfactory to the public. This is the stage—that of refinement and reworking of halfbaked ideas under the harsh spur of

[15]Herbert Kaufman, *Are Government Organizations Immortal?* (Washington: Brookings, 1976.

[16]See, e.g., the case studies in John Jewkes, David Sawers, and Richard Stillerman, *The Sources of Invention* (New York: Norton, 2nd ed., 1969).

bankruptcy—that is totally lacking in the public sector. It seems likely that most government activities are failures at the moment they are launched—just as most private ones are. But whereas the private failures are nipped in the bud or drastically reshaped, the public ones continue.

PUBLICNESS AND FAILURE

As the size and composition of the group of benefit recipients narrows, the chances of bureaucratic failure diminish and the chances of political failure increase. Most programs with benefits accruing to small geographic areas or other narrow groups are inappropriate activities for the federal government. Yet such programs are closely watched by their clients and hence offer the bureaucracy less discretion than do programs with widely diffused benefits. It is with regard to programs providing narrowly focused benefits that the argument of the pressure group theorists rings true: If the bureaucracy does not follow the law, it is because Congress wrote the law incorrectly, since both are responding to the same pressures. Since widely diffused interests are generally not represented in pressure groups, this implies that the programs that are carried out best by the bureaucracy are the ones that should not have been attempted at all.

SIZE AND FAILURE

As the size of government increases, the probability and extent of failure also increases for a variety of reasons. *Size of government* is an elusive concept. Among other things, it can refer to the number of issues currently being debated in Congress, the number of established agencies or functions, the number of employees, or the size of the budget. Since size is such an ambiguous concept it will be useful to explore the mechanisms by which increases in the size of various measures can worsen performance.

Size Defined as the Number of Issues Currently Debated

As the current political agenda becomes increasingly crowded, the quality of the legislation suffers and the likelihood that the legislation reflects the preferences of the general public decreases. The overloading of the administration and Congress results in sloppy legislation in a technical sense; that is, poorly written bills and hurried compromises that contain inconsistencies. A more serious problem is the lack of time for Congress to reflect on the full implications of particular bits of legislation. As the agenda becomes more crowded, the legislation comes to reflect the specialized interests of particular agencies within the administration and particular committees of Congress.

Public participation in the legislative process also suffers as the number of issues increases. Patriotic participation in affairs of state is always locked in uneasy combat with self interest: No citizen receives enough of the benefit or cost to make it worthwhile for him to spend time on legislation that affects the people in general. The limited time that people will devote for patriotic reasons is exhausted on a handful of issues. Even with unlimited good intentions, moreover, as the number of issues increases, the proportion to which the public *can* devote any attention grows smaller. The two basic mechanisms for public participation are *voting on the issues* and *pressure of public opinion* in response to detailed coverage in the news media. The voting mechanism at the national level is always confused by the multiplicity of issues. The media can raise issues to the attention of the public between elections; but only a few issues can share the headlines at one time.

Size Defined as the Number of Functions in Existence

The problems associated with adding new activities rapidly are distinct from those related to having many ongoing activities. From the viewpoint of hierarchical control by the President, we can say that addition of another activity or expansion of an existing activity will have as one of its costs the deterioration in the performance of other functions of the organization. Thus, since size itself creates problems, increases in size impose external costs. It might appear at first sight that once the federal government became so large that good hierarchical control broke down, further additions to size did not contribute additional problems. This does not necessarily follow because degree of control is a continuous concept, rather than being two discrete states and because control can break down at any level. The consequences are severe even if control has already broken down at higher levels to have the level of breakdown pushed still lower. Also, the formal mechanisms permit control to be exercised during crises, but the question of what constitutes a crisis depends on the other activities occupying top levels of the hierarchy.

This becomes, essentially, a question of the domain within which *bureaucratic free enterprise,* with its heavy costs of coordination through bilateral negotiations, predominates, as compared with the domain within which an official can coordinate activity in the interests of the organization that he supervises. Whether this occurs at the level of the entire government, cabinet department, bureau, or smaller organizational unit obviously depends on the functions entrusted to government. As the number and complexity of functions increase and government employment increases to serve a larger population, the number and size of individual agencies increase until coordination at that level, too, breaks down, to be replaced by the time-consuming negotiating process with its uncertain distribution of benefits and heavy costs.

Coordination by the President or Congress is obviously impossible for most of the routine activities. Of the activities and events at a certain time, some will attract top-level attention. Spanier and Uslander suggest that bureaucratic power is greatest in those areas that are deemed routine or unimportant by the President, Congress, and the public. As the government becomes larger, however, events that would have merited presidential attention in a smaller government cease to.[17] The implication of rationing top-level attention for crisis periods and pet projects is that much policy just happens as a result of the myriad decisions farther down the line.

Congressional attention is limited just as presidential attention is. Whereas the President economizes on his scarce time by relying on his staff, itself a bureaucracy subject to the problems of control, Congress relies primarily on a division of tasks, which are allocated to specialized committees and subcommittees. Division of labor is a well-recognized technique for accomplishing large tasks, but specialization has its costs. In particular, as the number and complexity of functions requiring congressional scrutiny increase, Congress is faced with several unsatisfactory choices. It can subdivide still further (formally or informally), but as the size of the relevant reviewing committee for a particular function decreases, the system comes to resemble the justly denounced control by legislators, rather than control by the legislature. The specialist also tends to lose the balanced view of the whole government, which is the main reason for congressional decision making. Congress can avoid extreme specialization only by looking less closely at the activities of the agencies. In practice, Congress has reacted to the higher work loads in all those ways. Particular details of administration that directly concern constituents or narrow interest groups are selected for careful review,

---

[17]John W. Spanier and Eric M. Uslander, *How American Foreign Policy is Made* (New York: Praeger, 1974), pp. 21–22.

but agencies are generally scrutinized by only the handful of legislators knowledgeable in that area. The inescapable point is that the quality of legislative policymaking and control has to be inversely related to the number and complexity of activities.

Appleby lamented the tendency of the nation to allow private groups to take over a variety of governmental functions (for example, bankers control the Federal Reserve and scientists control the National Science Foundation). He suggested that, "These disintegrating tendencies are actually a political corruption of government of the same basic kind as the disproportionate influence on government of a gambling ring."[18] It seems plausible, however, that this results not from fear of government, as Appleby claimed, but rather from an overloading of the political channels. The citizen cannot hope to learn enough about all the activities of government to press individual agencies to act in the public interest, nor would he have much influence, so even the most public spirited has little incentive to try.

Size Defined as the Number of Employees

Number of employees is one of the most common measures of the size of an organization, and many of the problems of hierarchical control have traditionally been related to the difficulties raised by the sheer masses of people. Brecht cites the old joke: "A departmental headquarters that contains a thousand employees needs no outside world to be busy; they can keep busy all alone in intra-agency quarrels."[19] Tullock's model provides a more precise statement of this tendency.[20] The leader's job is to see that as much effort as possible is used to further the objectives of the organization, but as the organization under him grows in size, he has less knowledge of what is being done and what should be done by each person and fewer means to influence that behavior in the appropriate way. Furthermore, as the organization of which his unit is a component grows, the leader has less knowledge of what he is supposed to do to further the purposes of the larger organization and less incentive to pursue those larger purposes as a means of improving his own position. Williamson's model of the firm makes explicit the relationship between size and loss of control, but he has abstracted from

[18]Paul Henson Appleby, *Morality and Administration in Democratic Government* (Baton Rouge: Louisiana State University Press, 1952), p. 211.

[19]Arnold Brecht, "How Bureaucracies Develop and Function," *The Annals of the American Academy of Political and Social Science* 292 (March 1954): 1–10; issue on "Bureaucracy and Representative Government," p. 7.

[20]Gordon Tullock, *The Politics of Bureaucracy* (Washington: Public Affairs Press, 1965), pp. 142–164.

many of the difficulties encountered in the public sector.[21] In particular, the quantity and quality of output are so difficult to measure, and the revenues of the bureau are so far removed from any market test, that one cannot be certain that the output of the marginal employee is even positive, let alone equal to his marginal cost. Even Niskanen's argument that the bureau must convince the sponsor that output has increased in order to justify a higher budget is not conclusive.[22] Convincing the sponsor may not be equivalent to increasing output; more important, the sponsor, too, takes a partial view in that the subcommittee concerned with a particular activity will not consider the costs resulting from the looser control of all other activities that attends the expansion of the particular one.

Employment is imperfect as a measure of size. The problems of controlling equal numbers of typists, infantrymen, welders, school teachers, and antitrust lawyers are quite different. Furthermore, in recent years the federal government has controlled growth in the number of bureaucrats by contracting for a variety of services and emphasizing grants to state and local governments. These techniques result in more difficult problems of coordination and control than would spending the same budget on federal employment. Some of the inflexibility of administrative and personnel procedures can be overcome by these devices, but (as noted earlier) the inflexibility is the symptom of lack of control over output, rather than the source of the major problems of administration.[23]

Not only do control problems increase with the growth in the number of government employees, of at least equal importance is the deterioration in the quality of the bureaucrats to be controlled. It is standard to assume that the supply curve for labor slopes upward. In practice, most government positions are characterized by a relatively narrow range of possible wage rates at a moment of time. Yet someone can be found who is willing to fill almost any position at almost any wage rate. The variable that permits this is quality. If quality actually is an objective measure of expected productivity on the job, the analysis is perfectly straightforward. With every increase in government employment, productivity will decline because of the steady deterioration in quality of personnel. Those highly productive people who enjoyed government would be hired first. As government expanded, less qualified people would be hired.

---

[21]Oliver E. Williamson, "Hierarchical Control and Optimum Firm Size," *Journal of Political Economy* 75, No. 2 (April 1967): 123–138.

[22]Niskanen, *Bureaucracy and Representative Government*, pp. 24–30.

[23]Bruce L. R. Smith and D. C. Hague, *The Dilemma of Accountability in Modern Government; Independence versus Control* (London: MacMillan, 1971), pp. 3–69.

The actual situation is a good deal more complex because of the nu-numerous dimensions of quality, some of which are not measures of productivity on any job (e.g., race or sex), whereas others may be measures of productivity on particular jobs, but not necessarily the one under consideration (e.g., I.Q. or strength). One cannot state with certainty, therefore, than an expansion of employment will *necessitate* the hiring of less-productive employees, but if the hiring criteria are at all related to productivity, an increase in employment will be accompanied by a decrease in average productivity.

The nature of the problem is most clearly apparent at the very highest ranks, where most surveys show the federal government to lag seriously behind the private sector in monetary compensation.[24] The peculiar circumstances of government employment offer nonmonetary rewards (*psychic income*) to some people. It would seem easier to find 1000 able people adequately compensated by current levels of monetary and psychic income than 10,000, particularly since the psychic income of being a top official must vary inversely with the number of such positions. It would also seem that such positions would be more attractive to people who are motivated to accomplish good things for the public if the chances of accomplishing something are greater. Yet the expansion of government, and consequently of bureaucratic free enterprise, has increased the difficulty of doing anything for the country and has made it easier to use the government position to further personal ends. This makes the positions less attractive to the patriotic and more attractive to the corrupt.

The other question is whether the ablest people will actually be selected from those available. In Tullock's model, those who arrive at the higher levels are both able enough to perceive which decision will lead to promotion and amoral enough to make that decision, regardless of ethical or ideological considerations. In a less cynical way, one might argue that the bureaucratic skills rewarded are not necessarily correlated with the ability to forecast correctly events in the outside world, to analyze the consequences of government decisions, to manage large organizations, or to allocate resources wisely. In either case, one must inquire about the influence of size on the promotion process. As the

---

[24]The traditional approach to examining the adequacy of government salaries compares positions, e.g., a B.S. civil engineering position in government and the private sector. See U.S. General Accounting Office, "Federal White-Collar Pay Systems Need Fundamental Changes", Report FPCD–76–9, 30 Oct. 1975. If one looks at the characteristics of individual people, it appears that the federal government pays its employees more than they would earn elsewhere. See Sharon P. Smith, *Equal Pay in the Public Sector: Fact or Fantasy* (Princeton: Industrial Relations Section of Princeton University, 1977).

organization grows, each person at a given hierarchical rank deals with a smaller fraction of the organization's activities; hence his superior performance in that job offers less assurance of ability to perform in a more comprehensive role. Of course, one can argue that the position to which he is promoted will also be restricted. At some level, however, he will be appointed to the rank that actually makes most policy for the agency, which will occur at a lower level the larger the government is. Hence policy will be made by more narrowly skilled people the larger is the organization. Furthermore, as the organization grows, a greater proportion of people will be engaged in purely inward-looking activities such as coordination and negotiation with other government agencies. Proficiency in such activities will undoubtedly be helpful in obtaining promotions, but it may not be related to productivity in carrying out the mission of the agency. Promotion, to the extent that it is based on ability, therefore, is not likely to be based on the *relevant* ability.

Once hierarchical coordination has broken down, it must be replaced by bargaining where the interests of two agencies diverge significantly, but for a large class of issues the interests of the agencies do not seem to be sufficiently divergent to necessitate much haggling. In the presence of moderate amounts of good will, agencies can trade favors or exchange information on an informal and cooperative basis.[25] Much coordination occurs through casual contacts, old friendships, and other informal channels. How is the functioning of the informal network of friendships and contacts influenced by the size of the organization? If one assumes that each employee has the same number of informal contacts regardless of the size of the organization, then the probability that his circle will include the appropriate specialist from elsewhere in the organization obviously decreases as the total size of the organization increases. The fact that he may find the appropriate person through a mutual friend does not improve the situation, because that relationship, too, has not grown with the size of the organization.

Size Defined as Expenditure

With the increasing tendency for the federal government to become a conduit through which funds are transferred to the private sector or to state and local governments, measuring the size of the federal government by expenditure, rather than employment, is superficially attractive. Indeed, budgetary measures of the impact of government (usually

[25]R. E. Goodin "The Logic of Bureaucratic Backscratching," *Public Choice* 21 (Spring 1975): 53–67.

expenditures as a fraction of GNP) are standard in the public finance literature. The difficulty with this approach is that for any activity with a regulatory component, the budgetary costs do not give any indication of total costs, which must include the resources expended by the private sector in discovering, interpreting, complying, with and attempting to change the regulations. Thus, any cost–benefit analysis of the SEC would have to learn the costs imposed on the private sector by the agency. This is entirely distinct from the equally difficult problem of measuring the benefits.[26] Other agencies, such as the ICC, have inflicted heavy, but not easily measurable, costs on the private sector, as well as necessitating substantial direct outlays for compliance.[27]

More generally, regulatory activities have more impact on the economy than do exhaustive activities, whereas transfers to individuals or governments have the least impact per dollar and also create the fewest problems for control of other government activities. But only the transfers are easily separated from other spending in the standard accounts. More significantly, most transfers and exhaustive uses of resources also have some regulatory components. Furthermore, all government activities provoke private attempts to secure special favors (rent seeking) or to avoid burdens (rent avoidance).[28]

Budgetary measures of government size tend to be relative; that is, to express expenditures as a percentage of GNP. This slides over a difficult conceptual and empirical problem. All the models of hierarchical control suggest that a basic problem is directing the activities of large numbers of people. If this is correct, then the United States, with one-third of gross domestic product absorbed by government, faces greater difficulties of control than the Netherlands, with half of gross domestic product absorbed by a smaller government. This, too, is an oversimplification because differences in the controllability and burden of different activities should be considered in any serious analysis of size of government.

Conclusions about Size and Failure

The preceding section suggested that adding to the number of federal employees or adding new activities exerts some negative effects on all existing activities of government. If the new program is relatively inde-

[26]Stigler found no benefits for the investor in new issues. See "Public Regulation of the Securities Market", chapter 6 of George J. Stigler, *The Citizen and the State* (Chicago: University of Chicago Press, 1975).

[27]See, e.g., Thomas Gale Moore, *Freight Transportation Regulation: Surface Freight and the Interstate Commerce Commission* (Washington: American Enterprise Institute for Public Policy Research, 1972), AEI Evaluative Studies #3.

[28]Gordon Tullock, "Rent Seeking" (Blacksburg: Virginia Polytechnic Institute and State University, Center for Study of Public Choice, 1978), Working Paper No. CE 78-2-8.

pendent of existing activities, the external costs borne by other programs are widely diffused and rather small for any one activity. They result mainly from the declining quality of labor and the scarcity of time and energy for control by all participants including the President, Congress, bureaucrats and the electorate. If the activity requires specific changes in existing activities—as does any generalized requirement that all agencies consider, for example, environmental impact, energy use, or income distribution—then the costs can be very heavy.

Costs in time cannot be directly translated into costs borne by the individual citizen, however. One may be tempted to estimate man-hours expended by bureaucrats, multiply by an average wage, and consider the result to be the cost to the taxpayers. The more fundamental measure, however, is the value of the goods and services forgone, which is more difficult to determine. The loss of final output may be quite small if, as suggested above, most input is consumed within the organization anyway. On the other hand, any attempt to maintain output at a constant level under those circumstances will require an immense increase in inputs. When the government output reduces the welfare of citizens as a whole, of course, any reduction in output should be considered a benefit, not a cost.

LIVING WITH FAILURE

The focus of the preceding chapters has been on failure, which lends an inherently pessimistic tone to the whole work. By looking at what has failed, one can make some surmises about what will fail, but one cannot say much about what might succeed. Government can and does accomplish many things. Only a handful of anarchists argue that we would be better off with no government at all. But many people argue that we would be better off with somewhat less government than we now have. In particular, if the activities that reduce welfare could be avoided, those that have failed could be eliminated, and those that are certain to fail could be nipped in the bud, welfare would certainly be improved. This raises the crucial question of the appropriate functions of government, where appropriateness includes the feasibility, as well as the desirability, of the functions.

When Humboldt wrote *The Limits of State Action* he was concerned with the harm that the state does to individuals when it attempts to look after their welfare.[29] Difficulties of administration entered into the ar-

---

[29]Wilhelm von Humboldt, *The Limits of State Action* (Cambridge, England: The University Press, 1969 [written c. 1791–1792]), chapter 3.

gument, but more because of the repressive measures that tended to accompany failure than because of the failure itself. Opposition to state intervention has rested on such ethical and ideological grounds since that time. At the other extreme, the Benthamite tradition has emphasized the benefits to individuals from specific government interventions. The most striking characteristic of Bentham's own prescriptions was his keen perception of the fallibility of man and importance of pursuit of pleasure as a motivation—combined with the assumption that the lawmakers and the administrative machinery were as perfect as Bentham, himself.[30] Much the same atmosphere has permeated the reform literature since that time. The conservatives have been dogmatic, whereas the interventionists have argued about particular undeniable problems—and assumed that government could improve upon the situation. The weak links include the following: (a) the design of the legislation by self-interested politicians, rather than philosopher kings or computers registering the preferences of voters; (b) the implementation of programs by bureaucrats who also pursue their own interests; and (c) the costs that any new program inflicts on the quality of existing programs.

In a very important sense this study is misleading because it analyzes programs that can be seen (for the most part) to have failed. Yet in practice, rarely is an explicit and unambiguous mistake made. The decisions seem correct bit by bit and piece by piece, but the outcome is bad. The worst part is that most of the problems are well known; for example, the agency is told to spend $500 million, so it does succeed in spending, but has insufficient time to control the use of the funds. The explicit rule leading to the problem—expiration of appropriations at year end—can be (and has been) eliminated, but still the problem remains in administrative procedure. Everyone knows of the problem, but is helpless to correct it within the rules of the game as it is played.

Perhaps Aristotle was right when he said, "To the size of states there is a limit, as there is to other things, plants, animals, implements." But if large nations will not break themselves up into city–states, they will find that large bureaucracies, having all the problems I have recounted, will be necessary to implement policy. One can argue that the nation should learn to live with imperfections rather than attempting governmental solutions, which will *necessarily and predictably* create additional problems. One could strive for enough knowledge to assess the benefits and costs (including externalities) of government action. At a much less interesting level, one might be able, case-by-case, to suggest minor

---

[30]Jeremy Bentham, *An Introduction to the Principles of Morals and Legislation* (New York: Hafner Press, 1948).

changes in arrangements that would decrease some of the problems involved. This is the public administration approach. It is good for consulting business because the changes suggested are always close enough to the mainstream to be implemented feasibly.

The scholarly analyses of bureaucracy mirror the contradictions of public opinion: general recognition of bureaucratic problems combined with constant cries for imposition of still more difficult tasks on government. "Almost all the classical works dealing with bureaucracy are preoccupied with one basic dilemma—namely, whether the bureaucracy is master or servant, an independent body or a tool—and if a tool, whose interests it can be made to serve."[31] That question, however, cannot be answered on the general level. The answer depends on the particular types of task imposed, the particular techniques required by the legislation, the extent to which the government is already overburdened—and any number of other matters as well. This is why the perceptive analyses of bureaucracy are accompanied by conclusions that seem weak and pedestrian in comparison.

Tullock comes closest to the correct approach when he suggests that much of modern bureaucracy is simply a mistake, because the tasks that have been assigned cannot be performed by bureaucracies.[32] The problems are so deepseated that ingenious tinkering will not solve them. The public sector has been burdened by too many functions, many of which individually could be accomplished, but which are jointly too much. Prior to 1929 the problem was kept under control by a prevailing mythology about the appropriate functions of government, just as the equivalent myth of the inflationary consequences of unbalanced budgets kept total spending—and inflation—under control. Just as budgets can be unbalanced with impunity during occasional depression years, so can inappropriate functions occasionally be undertaken by government without dire consequences. Still, the taboos protected society from itself as long as they were believed; once they were broken, nothing stood in the way of continuing expansion of federal activity and ever increasing deficits. The managerial reforms of the Taft and Harding administrations seemed to equip the federal government to take on more functions, but reform of management did not really extend the limits of congressional and presidential control.

In a sense, the United States has been living on its managerial capital, since the slow retirement of bureaucrats from the civil service and the still slower change in prevailing attitudes prevent the grosser effects of political overloading from being immediately manifest. Thus Tullock

---

[31] S. N. Eisenstadt, "Bureaucracy and Bureaucratization," *Current Sociology* 7 (1958): 100.
[32] Tullock, *The Politics of Bureaucracy*, p. 193.

may have overstated the prevalence of greedily ambitious bureaucrats in the civil service (although probably not among presidential appointees) simply because profession, tradition, and ideology may have protected many agencies. But with the conditions that lead to Tullock's mechanism holding sway, it is only a matter of time until each agency succumbs. Similarly, the United States has moved increasingly toward the conditions that Friedrich found to lead to corruption.[33] Yet manifestations of this so far appear to have been confined mainly to the higher political reaches.

Despite frequent reiteration, the assumption that the overloaded political agenda results inevitably from the increased complexity of modern life has rarely been subject to close scrutiny. Foreign and military problems have always posed threats to the survival of nations. If individuals are now more vulnerable to destruction, it might also be argued that our nation is less vulnerable to small military miscalculations than it was during its first century. Domestically, the vast improvements in transportation have destroyed local monopolies in most goods and services and have thus freed the consumer of the necessity of relying on the government for protection. Similarly, technological change has enlarged the range of choice of materials and products, so firms and consumers are far less vulnerable to natural calamities or man-made restrictions in supply. The growth in individual wealth has also given families some breathing space so they are not constantly scrambling to avoid disaster.

Governments have taken on additional functions, however, and the surrounding rhetoric has suggested that this was a matter of necessity. Policy analysis could at least indicate the full costs of such behavior, but a general scaling down of legislative and presidential aspirations would require either the reimposition of some constitutional rule or some restructuring of political incentives and rewards, the shape of which I cannot imagine. At a second level, one can establish a checklist of concerns for Congress in drafting legislation. The proposals for an implementation review of new bills fall in this category. Such a review could alleviate the most egregious problems, but would not resolve underlying difficulties and could not cope with the havoc wrought by last-minute legislative compromises. At a third level come the guidelines for administrators and regulation writers, but the federal bureaucracy includes such a wealth of technical expertise in these matters that the frequent lapses have political roots that will not yield to easy managerial remedies.

[33]Carl Joachim Friedrich, *The Pathology of Politics: Violence, Betrayal, Corruption, Secrecy, and Propaganda* (New York: Harper & Row, 1972), p. 155.

Selected References

ꜱ

This list excludes sources whose relevance is limited to only one case, but includes some items on bureaucratic implementation not cited in the text.

Aaron, Henry J. *Shelter and Subsidies.* Washington: Brookings, 1972.

Albrow, Martin, *Bureaucracy.* New York: Praeger, 1970.

Appleby, Paul Henson. *Morality and Administration in Democratic Government.* Baton Rouge: Louisiana State University Press, 1952.

Argyris, Chris. "Some Causes of Organizational Ineffectiveness within the Department of State." U.S. Department of State, Center for International Systems Research, *Occasional Papers,* Number 2, 1966.

Arkes, Hadley, *Bureaucracy, the Marshall Plan, and the National Interest.* Princeton: Princeton University Press, 1972.

Arrow, Kenneth J. *The Limits of Organization.* The Fels Lectures in Public Policy Analysis. New York: Norton, 1974.

Arrow, Kenneth J. *Social Choice and Individual Values.* New York: Wiley, 1963 (1st ed., 1951).

Bailey, Frederick George. *Strategems and Spoils: A Social Anthropology of Politics.* New York: Schocken, 1969.

Bailey, Stephen K. and Edith K. Mosher. *ESEA: The Office of Education Administers a Law.* Syracuse: Syracuse University Press, 1968.

Banfield, Edward C. *Government Project.* Glencoe, Illinois: Free Press, 1951.

Bardach, Eugene, *The Implementation Game: What Happens After a Bill Becomes a Law.* Cambridge: M.I.T. Press, 1977.

Barnard, Chester Irving. *The Functions of the Executive.* Cambridge: Harvard University Press, 1938.

Bauer, Raymond A. and Kenneth J. Gergen, eds. *The Study of Policy Formation.* New York: Macmillan, 1968.

Bauer, Raymond A., Ithiel de Sola Pool, and Lewis Anthony Dexter. *American Business & Public Policy: The Politics of Foreign Trade.* Chicago: Aldine-Atherton, 2nd ed., 1972 (1st ed. 1963).

Baum, Bernard Helmut. *Decentralization of Authority in a Bureaucracy.* Englewood Cliffs, N.J.: Prentice-Hall, 1961.

Bélanger, Gérard and Jean-Luc Migué. "Toward a General Theory of Managerial Discretion." *Public Choice,* Spring 1974: 27–47.

Bentham, Jeremy. *An Introduction to the Principles of Morals and Legislation.* New York: Hafner Press, 1948.

Bernstein, Marver H. *The Job of the Federal Executive.* Washington: Brookings, 1958.

Bernstein, Marver H. *Regulating Business by Independent Commission.* Princeton: Princeton University Press, 1955.

Beveridge, Sir William Henry. *The Public Service in War & in Peace.* London: Constable, 1920.

Bird, Richard M. and John G. Head, eds. *Modern Fiscal Issues. Essays in Honor of Carl S. Shoup.* Toronto: University of Toronto Press, 1972.

Blau, Peter M. *The Dynamics of Bureaucracy: A Study of Interpersonal Relations in Two Government Agencies.* Chicago: University of Chicago Press, rev. ed., 1966 (1st ed. 1955).

Blau, Peter M. and W. Richard Scott. *Formal Organizations: A Comparative Approach.* San Francisco: Chandler, 1962.

Blaustein, Arthur I. and Geoffrey Faux. *The Star Spangled Hustle.* Garden City, N.Y.: Anchor, 1972.

Borcherding, Thomas E., ed. *Budgets and Bureaucrats: The Sources of Government Growth.* Durham, North Carolina: Duke University Press, 1977.

Boyer, William W. *Bureaucracy on Trial: Policy Making by Government Agencies.* New York: Bobbs-Merrill, 1964.

Brecht, Arnold. "Bureaucratic Sabotage." *The Annals of the American Academy of Political and Social Science* 189, Jan. 1937: 48–57.

Breton, Albert. *The Economic Theory of Representative Government.* Chicago: Aldine, 1974.

Brown, Richard E. *The GAO, Untapped Source of Congressional Power.* Knoxville: University of Tennessee Press, 1970.

Buchanan, James M. *Public Finance in Democratic Process: Fiscal Institutions and Individual Choice.* Chapel Hill: University of North Carolina Press, 1967.

Buchanan, James M. and Robert D. Tollison, eds. *Theory of Public Choice: Political Applications of Economics.* Ann Arbor: University of Michigan Press, 1972.

Bureaucracy and Democratic Government. In *The Annals of the American Academy of Political and Social Science,* 292, March 1954.

Burnham, James. *The Managerial Revolution.* New York: John Day, 1941.

Campbell, D. T. "Systematic Error on the Part of Human Links in Communication Systems." *Information & Control,* 1958: 334–369.

Carroll, Stephen J., Jr. and Henry L. Tosi, Jr. *Management by Objectives: Applications and Research.* New York: Macmillan, 1973.

Carson, Robert B., Jerry Ingles, and Douglas McLaud, eds. *Government in the American Economy. Conventional and Radical Studies on the Growth of State Economic Power.* Lexington, Massachusetts: Heath, 1973.

Chambliss, William J. "Vice, Corruption, Bureaucracy, and Power." *Wisconsin Law Review,* 1971: 1150–1173.

Chase, Samuel B., Jr., ed. *Problems in Public Expenditure Analysis.* Washington: Brookings, 1968.

Cohen, Harry. *The Demonics of Bureaucracy: Problems of Change in a Government Agency.* Ames: Iowa State University Press, 1965.

Corazzini, Arthur J. "Equality of Employment Opportunity in the Federal White-Collar Civil Service." *Journal of Human Resources,* Fall 1972: 424–445.

Crossman, Richard Howard Stafford. *The Diaries of a Cabinet Minister.* 2 vols. New York: Holt, Rinehart and Winston, 1975, 1976.

Crozier, M. *The Bureaucratic Phenomenon.* Chicago: University of Chicago Press, 1964.

Dahl, Robert A. and Charles E. Lindblom. *Politics, Economics, and Welfare: Planning and Politico-Economic Systems Resolved into Basic Social Processes.* New York: Harper, 1953.

Dale, H. E. *The Higher Civil Service of Great Britain.* Oxford: Oxford University Press, 1941.

Davis, David Howard. *How the Bureaucracy Makes Foreign Policy.* Lexington, Massachusetts: Heath, 1972.

Davis, Otto, M. A. H. Dempster & Aaron Wildavsky. "A Theory of the Budgetary Process." *American Political Science Review,* Sept. 1966: 529–547.

DeAlessi, Louis. "Implications of Property Rights for Government Investment Choices." *American Economic Review,* March 1969: 13–24.

Derthick, Martha A. *New Towns In-Town, Why a Federal Program Failed.* Washington: Urban Institute, 1972.

Devons, Ely. *Papers on Planning and Economic Management.* Sir Alec Cairncross, ed. Manchester, England: Manchester University Press, 1970.

Devons, Ely. *Planning in Practice.* Cambridge, England: The University Press, 1950.

Dillon, Conley Hall. *The Area Redevelopment Administration. New Patterns in Developmental Administration.* College Park: Bureau of Governmental Research of the University of Maryland, 1964.

Dimock, Marshall E. and Gladys Ogden Dimock. *Public Administration.* New York: Rinehart, 1953.

Downs, Anthony. *Inside Bureaucracy.* Boston: Little, Brown, 1967.

Downs, Anthony. "The Successes and Failures of Federal Housing Policy." *The Public Interest,* Winter 1974: 124–145.

Drucker, Peter F. "The Sickness of Government." *The Public Interest,* Winter 1969: 3–23.

Edelman, Murray. "Governmental Organization and Public Policy." *Public Administration Review,* Autumn 1952: 276–283.

Edelman, Murray and R. W. Fleming. *The Politics of Wage–Price Decisions: A Four-Country Analysis.* Urbana: University of Illinois Press, 1965.

Eisenstadt, S. N. "Bureaucracy and Bureaucratization" (a trend report and bibliography). *Current Sociology,* 1958: 97–164.

Etzioni, Amitai. *A Comparative Analysis of Complex Organizations: On Power, Involvement, and Their Correlates.* New York: Free Press, 1961.

Etzioni, Amitai. *A Sociological Reader on Complex Organizations.* New York: Holt, Rinehart and Winston, 2nd ed., 1969.

Feller, Irwin. "Managerial Response to Technological Innovation in Public Sector Organizations." *Management Science,* Oct. 1980: 1021–1030.

Feller, Irwin and Donald C. Menzel with Lee Ann Kozak. *Diffusion of Innovations in Municipal Governments.* University Park: Pennsylvania State University Institute for Research on Human Resources, Center for the Study of Science Policy, 1976.

Fesler, James W. "Administrative Literature and the Second Hoover Commission Reports." *American Political Science Review,* LI, No. 1, March 1957: 135–157.

Follett, Mary Parker. *Dynamic Administration: The Collected Papers of Mary Parker Follett,* Henry C. Metcalf and L. Urwick, eds. New York: Harper, 1941.

Fox, John Ronald. *Arming America: How the U.S. Buys Weapons.* Boston: Division of Research, Graduate School of Business Administration, Harvard University, 1974.

Francis, Roy G. and Robert C. Stone. *Service and Procedure in Bureaucracy: A Case Study.* Minneapolis: University of Minnesota Press, 1956.

Friedrich, Carl Joachim. *The Pathology of Politics: Violence, Betrayal, Corruption, Secrecy, and Propaganda.* New York: Harper & Row, 1972.

Galper, Harvey. "The Federal Government Expenditure Process: A Case Study." *Yale Economic Essays* 7, Spring 1967: 214–269.

Gardiner, John A. *The Politics of Corruption: Organized Crime in an American City.* New York: Russell Sage Foundation, 1970.

Gardiner, John A. *Traffic and the Police: Variations in Law-Enforcement Policy.* Cambridge: Harvard University Press, 1969.

Gaus, John M. *Reflections on Public Administration.* University: University of Alabama Press, 1947.

Gaus, John M., Leonard D. White, and Marshall E. Dimock. *The Frontiers of Public Administration.* New York: Russell & Russell, 1967 (1st publ. 1936).

Gaus, John M. and L. P. Wolcott. *Public Administration and the United States Department of Agriculture.* Chicago: Public Administration Service, 1940.

Gellhorn, Ernest. *Administrative Law and Process in a Nutshell.* St. Paul, Minnesota: West, 1972.

Ginzberg, Eli and Robert M. Solow. "Some Lessons of the 1960's." *The Public Interest,* No. 34, Winter 1974: 211–220.

Gold, Bela. *Wartime Economic Planning in Agriculture: A Study in the Allocation of Resources.* New York: Columbia University Press, 1949.

Goodin, Robert E. "The Logic of Bureaucratic Back Scratching." *Public Choice* 21, Spring 1975: 53–67.

Gore, W. J. and F. S. Silander. "A Bibliographical Essay on Decision Making." *Administrative Science Quarterly,* 1959; 97–121.

The Government as Regulator. Vol. 400 of *The Annals of The American Academy of Political and Social Science,* Marver H. Bernstein, ed. March 1972.

Gross, Neal, Joseph B. Giacquinta, and Marilyn Bernstein. *Implementing Organizational Innovations: A Sociological Analysis of Planned Educational Change.* New York: Basic Books, 1971.

Gulick, Luther and L. Urwick, eds. *Papers on the Science of Administration.* New York: Institute of Public Administration, Columbia University, 1937.

Guttman, Daniel and Barry Willner. *The Shadow Government . . .* New York: Pantheon, 1976.

Halberstam, David. *The Best and the Brightest.* New York: Random House, 1969.

Halperin, Morton H. *Bureaucratic Politics and Foreign Policy.* Washington: Brookings, 1973.

Handler, Joel F. and Ellen Jane Hollingsworth. *The "Deserving Poor": A Study of Welfare Administration.* Institute for Research on Poverty (University of Wisconsin) Monograph Series. Chicago: Markham, 1971.

Hargrove, Erwin C. "The Study of Implementation." Urban Institute Working Paper 0797-01. Washington: 12 March 1975.

Harris, Joseph Pratt. *Congressional Control of Administration.* Washington: Brookings, 1964.

Haveman, Robert H. *The Economic Performance of Public Investments: An Ex Post Evaluation of Water Resource Investments.* Baltimore: The Johns Hopkins Press for Resources for the Future, 1972.

Haveman, Robert H. and Julius Margolis, eds. *Public Expenditures and Policy Analysis.* Chicago: Markham, 1970.

Hayek, Friederich A. *Individualism and the Economic Order.* Chicago: Henry Regnery, 1972 (1st ed. 1948).

Herring, E. Pendleton. *Public Administration and the Public Interest.* New York: McGraw-Hill, 1936.

Heydebrand, Wolf V., ed. *Comparative Organizations: the Results of Empirical Research*. Englewood Cliffs, N.J.: Prentice-Hall, 1973.

Hill, Michael J. *The Sociology of Public Administration*. London: World University, Weidenfeld and Nicolson, 1972.

Hirsch, Werner Z. *Urban Economic Analysis*. New York: McGraw-Hill, 1973.

Hirschman, Albert O. *Exit, Voice, and Loyalty: Responses to Decline in Firms, Organizations, and States*. Cambridge: Harvard University Press, 1970.

Hirschman, Albert O. and Charles E. Lindblom. "Economic Development, Research and Development, Policy Making: Some Converging Views." *Behavioral Science* 7, 1962: 211–222.

Holden, Matthew, Jr. "'Imperialism' in Bureaucracy." *American Political Science Review* 60, No. 4, Dec. 1966: 943–951.

Hook, Sidney, ed. *Human Values and Economic Policy*. New York: New York University Press, 1967.

Humboldt, Wilhelm von. *The Limits of State Action*. Cambridge, England: The University Press, 1969.

Hutchins, John G. B. *The American Maritime Industries and Public Policy*. Cambridge: Harvard University Press, 1941.

Hyneman, Charles S. *Bureaucracy in a Democracy*. New York: Harper, 1950.

Jacob, Charles E. *Policy and Bureaucracy*. Princeton, N.J.: Van Nostrand, 1966.

Jevons, W. S. *Methods of Social Reform*. New York: Augustus Kelley, 1965.

Jewkes, John. *The New Ordeal by Planning: The Experience of the Forties and the Sixties*. New York: St. Martin's Press, 1968.

Johnson, Miriam. *Counter Point, The Changing Employment Service*. Salt Lake City: Olympus Publishing, 1973.

Kaufman, Herbert. *Are Government Organizations Immortal?* Washington, D.C.: Brookings, 1976.

Kaufman, Herbert. "Emerging Conflicts in the Doctrines of Public Administration." *American Political Science Review* 50, 1956: 1057–1074.

Kaufman, Herbert. *The Forest Ranger, A Study in Administrative Behavior*. Baltimore: Johns Hopkins Press for Resources for the Future, 1960.

Kaufman, Herbert with Michael Couzens. *Administrative Feedback: Monitoring Subordinates' Behavior*. Washington: Brookings, 1973.

Keith-Lucas, Alan. *Decisions about People in Need: A Study of Administrative Responsiveness in Public Assistance*. Chapel Hill: University of North Carolina Press, 1957.

Kingsley, John Donald. *Representative Bureaucracy: An Interpretation of the British Civil Service*. Yellow Springs, Ohio: The Antioch Press, 1944.

Knorr, Klaus. "Failures in National Intelligence Estimates." *World Politics* 16, No. 3, April 1964: 455–467.

Landsberger, Henry A. "The Horizontal Dimension in Bureaucracy." *Administrative Science Quarterly* 6, No. 3, Dec. 1961: 299–332.

Lane, Frederick C. *Ships for Victory, A History of Shipbuilding under the U.S. Maritime Commission in World War II*. Baltimore: Johns Hopkins Press, 1951.

Lange, Oskar, and Fred M. Taylor. *On the Economic Theory of Socialism*. New York: McGraw-Hill, 1964.

Leff, Arthur Allen. "Economic Analysis of Law: Some Realism about Nominalism." *Virginia Law Review* 60, No. 3, 1974: 476.

Leiserson, Avery. *Administrative Regulation: A Study in Representation of Interests*. Chicago: University of Chicago Press, 1942.

Levitan, Sar A. *Federal Aid to Depressed Areas: An Evaluation of the Area Redevelopment Administration*. Baltimore: Johns Hopkins Press, 1964.

Lindblom, Charles E. "Bargaining: The Hidden Hand in Government." Santa Monica, California: The Rand Corporation, 22 February 1955, RM–1434–RC.

Lindblom, Charles E. "The Science of 'Muddling Through.'" *Public Administration Review* XIX, No. 2, Spring 1959: 79–88.

Long, Norton E. *The Polity*. Chicago: Rand McNally, 1962.

Lowi, Theodore J. "American Business, Public Policy, Case Studies and Political Theory." *World Politics* XVI, July 1964: 677–715.

Lyden, Fremont J., George A. Shipman, and Morton Kroll, eds. *Policies, Decisions, and Organization*. New York: Appleton-Century-Crofts, 1969.

Lynn, Laurence E., Jr., and John M. Seidl. "Policy Analysis at HEW: The Story of the Mega-Proposal." *Policy Analysis* 1, No. 2, Spring 1975: 248.

Maass, Arthur. *Muddy Waters: The Army Engineers and the Nation's Rivers*. Cambridge: Harvard University Press, 1951.

MacAvoy, Paul W. and John W. Snow. *Regulation of Entry and Pricing in Truck Transportation. Ford Administration Papers on Regulatory Reform*. Washington: American Enterprise Institute, 1977.

MacGregor, David Hutchison. *Public Aspects of Finance*. Oxford: Clarendon Press, 1939.

Mancke, Richard B. *Squeaking By: U.S. Energy Policy since the Embargo*. New York: Columbia University Press, 1976.

Mansfield, Harvey C. *The Comptroller General*. New Haven: Yale University Press, 1939.

Mansfield, Harvey C. "Reorganizing the Federal Executive Branch: The Limits of Institutionalization." *Law and Contemporary Problems* 35, No. 3, Summer 1970: 461–495.

March, James G., ed. *Handbook of Organizations*. Chicago: Rand McNally, 1965.

Marris, Peter and Martin Rein. *Dilemmas of Social Reform: Poverty and Community Action in the United States*. Chicago: Aldine, 2nd ed., 1973.

Martin, Roscoe Coleman, ed. *Public Administration and Democracy: Essays in Honor of Paul H. Appleby*. Syracuse, N.Y.: Syracuse University Press, 1965.

McGregor, Douglas. *The Human Side of Enterprise*. New York: McGraw-Hill, 1960.

McKean, Roland N. "Divergencies between Individual and Total Costs within Government." *American Economic Review*, May 1964: 243–9.

McKean, Roland N. "The Unseen Hand in Government." *American Economic Review* 55 June 1965: 496–506.

Merton, Robert K., Ailsa P. Gray, Barbara Hockey, and Hanan C. Selvin. *Reader in Bureaucracy*. Glencoe, Illinois: Free Press, 1952.

Meyer, Marshall W. *Bureaucratic Structure and Authority, Coordination and Control in 254 Government Agencies*. New York: Harper & Row, 1972.

Michels, Robert. *Political Parties: A Sociological Study of the Oligarchical Tendencies of Modern Democracy*. New York: Hearst's International Library Co., 1915.

Miles, Rufus E., Jr. "Considerations for a President Bent on Reorganization." *Public Administration Review* 37, No. 2, March–April 1977: 155–162.

Milkman, Raymond H., Christopher Bladen, Beverly Lyford, and Howard L. Walton. *Alleviating Economic Distress: Evaluating a Federal Effort*. Lexington, Massachusetts: Heath, 1972.

Millett, John D. *Organization for the Public Service*. Princeton: Van Nostrand, 1966.

Mises, Ludwig von. *Bureaucracy*. New Haven: Yale University Press, 1944.

Moore, Thomas Gale. *Freight Transportation Regulation: Surface Freight and the Interstate Commerce Commission*. Washington: American Enterprise Institute, 1972, Evaluative Studies, Number 3.

Morgenthau, Hans Joachim. *The Purpose of American Politics*. New York: Knopf, 1960.

Moss, Milton, ed. *The Measurement of Economic and Social Performance. Studies in Income and*

Wealth, No. 38. New York: National Bureau of Economic Research, Distrib. by Columbia University Press, 1973.

Mouzelis, Nicos P. *Organization and Bureaucracy: An Analysis of Modern Theories.* Chicago, Aldine, 1968.

Mueller, Dennis C. "Public Choice: A Survey." *Journal of Economic Literature* XVI, No. 2, June 1976.

Musgrave, Richard A. *The Theory of Public Finance: A Study in Public Economy.* New York: McGraw-Hill, 1959.

Musgrave, Richard A. "The Voluntary Exchange Theory of Public Economy." *Quarterly Journal of Economics* 53, No. 2, Feb. 1938: 213–237.

Musgrave, Richard A. and Alan T. Peacock, eds. *Classics in the Theory of Public Finance.* London: International Economic Association and Macmillan, 1958.

Nelson, James C. *Railroad Transportation and Public Policy.* Washington: Brookings, 1959.

Neustadt, Richard E. *Presidential Power: The Politics of Leadership.* New York: Wiley, 1960.

Niskanen, William A., Jr. *Bureaucracy and Representative Government.* Chicago: Aldine-Atherton, 1971.

Niskanen, William A. *Structural Reform of the Federal Budget Process.* Domestic Affairs Study No. 12. Washington: American Enterprise Institute, 1973.

Noll, Roger G. *Reforming Regulation: An Evaluation of the Ash Council Proposals.* Washington: Brookings, 1971.

Normanton, E. L. *Accountability and Audit of Governments: A Comparative Study.* New York: Praeger, 1966.

Norris, Donald F. *Police-Community Relations. A Program that Failed.* Lexington, Massachusetts: Heath, 1973.

Novick, David, Melvin Anshen, and W. C. Truppner. *Wartime Production Controls.* New York: Columbia University Press, 1949.

Olson, Mancur. *The Logic of Collective Action.* Cambridge: Harvard University Press, 1965.

Olson, Mancur. "The Principle of 'Fiscal Equivalence': The Division of Responsibilities among Different Levels of Government." *American Economic Review,* May 1969: 479–487.

Ostrom, Vincent. *The Intellectual Crisis in American Public Administration.* University: University of Alabama Press, 1973.

Parkinson, C. Northcote. *Parkinson's Law and Other Studies in Administration.* Boston: Houghton Mifflin, 1957.

Perrow, Charles. "The Analysis of Goals in Complex Organizations." *American Sociological Review* 26, December 1961: 854–866.

Peter, Laurence J. and Raymond Hull. *The Peter Principle.* New York: William Morrow, 1969.

Plott, Charles R. "Some Organizational Influences on Urban Renewal Decisions." *American Economic Review,* May 1968: 306–321.

Polanyi, Michael. *The Logic of Liberty: Reflections and Rejoinders.* Chicago: The University of Chicago Press, 1965 (1st publ. 1951).

Pressman, Jeffrey L. and Aaron Wildavsky. *Implementation...* Berkeley: University of California Press, 1973.

Price, James L. *Organizational Effectiveness: An Inventory of Propositions.* Homewood, Illinois: Irwin, 1968.

Pryke, Richard. *Public Enterprise in Practice.* New York: St. Martin's Press, 1972.

Pryor, Frederic L. "Elements of a Positive Theory of Public Expenditures." *Finanzarchiv* 26, No. 3, Dec. 1967: 403–430.

Redford, Emmette S. *Democracy in the Administrative State*. New York: Oxford University Press, 1969.

Redford, Emmette S. ed. *Public Administration and Policy Formation: Studies in Oil, Gas, Banking, River Development, and Corporate Investigations*. New York: Greenwood Press, 1969 (1st publ. 1956).

Riggs, Fred Warren, *Administrative Reform and Political Responsiveness: A Theory of Dynamic Balancing*. Beverly Hills, California: Sage, 1970.

Robbins, Lionel. *The Economic Problem in Peace and War: Some Reflections on Objectives and Mechanisms*. London: Macmillan, 1947.

Samuelson, Paul A. "The Pure Theory of Public Expenditure." *Review of Economics and Statistics* 36, No. 4, November 1954: 387–389.

Schlesinger, James R. *Defense Planning and Budgeting: The Issue of Centralized Control*. Washington: Industrial College of the Armed Forces, National Security Management Monograph Series, 1968.

Schubert, Glendon A., Jr. *The Public Interest*. Glencoe, Illinois: Free Press, 1960.

Schultze, Charles L. *The Politics and Economics of Public Spending*. Washington: Brookings, 1968.

Scott, Anthony. *National Resources: The Economics of Conservation*. Toronto: McClelland and Stewart, 1973 (1st ed. 1955).

Selznick, Philip. *TVA and the Grass Roots: A Study in the Sociology of Formal Organization*. Berkeley: University of California Press, 1949.

Shackleton, J. R. "Corruption: An Essay in Economic Analysis." *The Political Quarterly* 49, No. 1, Jan–March 1978: 25–37.

Shannon, Claude E. and Warren Weaver. *The Mathematical Theory of Communication*. Urbana: University of Illinois Press, 1959.

Shapiro, D. L. "Can Public Investment Have a Positive Rate of Return?" *Journal of Political Economy*, March–April 1973: 401.

Sharkansky, Ira. *Public Administration: Policy-Making in Government Agencies*. Chicago: Markham, 1970.

Silverman, David. *The Theory of Organizations: A Sociological Framework*. New York: Basic Books, 1971.

Simon, Herbert A., Donald W. Smithburg, and Victor A. Thompson. *Public Administration*. New York: Knopf, 1950.

Sindler, Allan P., ed. *Policy and Politics in America: Six Case Studies*. Boston: Little, Brown, 1973.

Slesinger, Jonathan A. "A Model for the Comparative Study of Public Bureaucracies." *Papers in Public Administration*, No. 23. Ann Arbor: University of Michigan, Bureau of Government, Institute of Public Administration, 1957.

Smith, Bruce L. R. and D. C. Hague. *The Dilemma of Accountability in Modern Government: Independence versus Control*. London: Macmillan, 1971.

Smith, Sharon P. *Equal Pay in the Public Sector: Fact or Fantasy*. Princeton: Industrial Relations Section of Princeton University, 1977.

Somers, H. M. *Presidential Agency: The Office of War Mobilization and Reconversion*. Cambridge: Harvard University Press, 1950.

Spanier, John W. and Eric M. Uslander. *How American Foreign Policy Is Made*. New York: Praeger, 1974.

Stigler, George J. *The Citizen and the State: Essays on Regulation*. Chicago: University of Chicago Press, 1975.

Tanter, Raymond and Richard H. Ullman, eds. *Theory and Policy in International Relations*. Princeton: Princeton University Press, 1972.

Thompson, Victor Alexander. *Bureaucracy and Innovation*. University: University of Alabama Press, 1969.

Tillman, Robert O. "Emergence of Black-Market Bureaucracy: Administration, Development, and Corruption in the New States." *Public Administration Review* 28, No. 5, Sept.–Oct. 1968: 437–444.

Tribe, Laurence H. "Policy Science: Analysis or Ideology?" *Benefit-Cost and Policy Analysis 1972*. Chicago: Aldine, 1973.

Truman, David B. *The Governmental Process*. New York: Knopf, 2nd ed., 1971.

Tullock, Gordon. "The General Irrelevance of the General Impossibility Theorem." *Quarterly Journal of Economics* 81, No. 2, May 1967: 256–270.

Tullock, Gordon. *The Politics of Bureaucracy*. Washington: Public Affairs Press, 1965.

Tullock, Gordon. *Private Wants, Public Means: An Economic Analysis of the Desirable Scope of Government*. New York: Basic Books, 1970.

U.S. Bureau of the Budget. "Progress in Measuring Work." *Management Bulletin*, August 1962.

U.S. Bureau of the Budget. "Measuring Productivity of Federal Government Organizations." Sept. 1964.

U.S. Congress. Joint Economic Committee. Joint Committee Print. "Measuring and Enhancing Productivity in the Federal Sector." A study prepared by representatives of the Civil Service Commission, General Accounting Office, and Office of Management and Budget. 92nd Congress, 2nd Session, 4 August 1972.

U.S. Department of Agriculture Graduate School. *What We Learned in Public Administration during the War*. 1949.

Vogely, William A. "A Case Study in the Measurement of Government Output." Santa Monica, California: Rand Corporation, RM–1934–RC, 9 July 1957.

Wagner, Richard E. *The Public Economy*. Chicago: Markham, 1973.

Warner, W. Keith and A. Eugene Havens. "Goal Displacement and the Intangibility of Organizational Goals." *Administrative Science Quarterly* 12, 1968: 539–555.

Warwick, Donald P., with Marvin Meade and Theodore Reed. *A Theory of Public Bureaucracy: Politics, Personality, and Organization in the State Department*. Cambridge: Harvard University Press, 1975.

Wasserman, P. *Measurement and Evaluation of Organizational Performance: An Annotated Bibliography*. Ithaca, N.Y.: Cornell University, Graduate School of Business and Public Administration, 1959.

Webb, Adrian. "Social Service Administration: A Typology for Research." *Public Administration* (London) 49, Autumn 1971: 321–339.

Weidenbaum, Murray. *The Modern Public Sector: New Ways of Doing the Government's Business*. New York: Basic Books, 1969.

Wildavsky, Aaron. *Dixon-Yates: A Study of Power Politics*. New Haven: Yale University Press, 1962.

Williamson, Oliver E. "Hierarchical Control and Optimum Firm Size." *Journal of Political Economy* 75, No. 2, April 1967: 123–138.

Willrich, Mason, with Philip M. Marston, David G. Norrell, and Jane K. Wilcox. *Administration of Energy Shortages*. Cambridge, Massachusetts: Ballinger, 1976.

Wilson, James Q. "The Bureaucracy Problem." *The Public Interest*, No. 6, Winter 1967: 3–9.

Wilson, James Q. *Political Organizations*. New York: Basic Books, 1973.

Wittfogel, Karl A. *Oriental Despotism: A Comparative Study of Total Power*. New Haven: Yale University Press, 1957.

Woll, Peter. *American Bureaucracy*. New York: Norton, 1963.

Index

QUANTITATIVE STUDIES IN SOCIAL RELATIONS

Consulting Editor: Peter H. Rossi

UNIVERSITY OF MASSACHUSETTS
AMHERST, MASSACHUSETTS